IMAGES
of Aviation

MONTGOMERY AVIATION

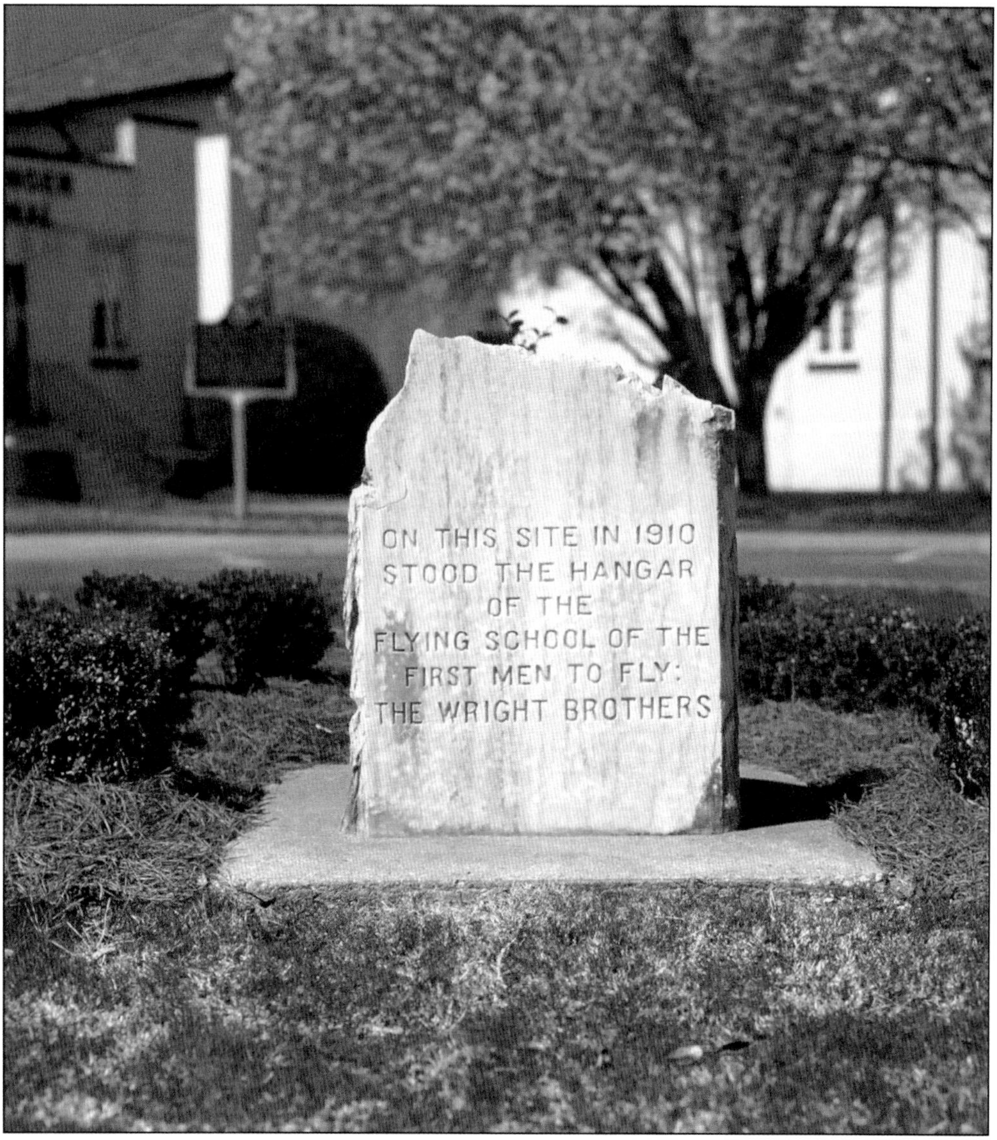

This modest stone marker, located on the grounds of Maxwell Air Force Base, is the sole reminder of a 100-acre cotton field that was once the site of the nation's first civilian flying school and Alabama's first airfield. The marker's simple inscription reads, "On This Site In 1910 Stood the Hangar of the Flying School of the First Men to Fly: The Wright Brothers." (Author's collection.)

ON THE COVER: Student aviators Walter Brookins (left) and Archibald Hoxsey are pictured at the Wright brothers' flying school in Montgomery. The region's short winters, mild climate, and abundance of flat farmland made Montgomery an ideal site for flight training. In less than 10 years, these same factors would bring military flight training to Montgomery. (Special Collections and Archives, Wright State University.)

IMAGES
of Aviation

MONTGOMERY AVIATION

Billy J. Singleton

ARCADIA
PUBLISHING

ISBN 978-0-7385-5259-0

Published by Arcadia Publishing
Charleston, South Carolina

Printed in the United States of America

Library of Congress Catalog Card Number: 2007927917

For all general information contact Arcadia Publishing at:
Telephone 843-853-2070
Fax 843-853-0044
E-mail sales@arcadiapublishing.com
For customer service and orders:
Toll-Free 1-888-313-2665

Visit us on the Internet at www.arcadiapublishing.com

For my wife, Sylvia, and daughters Lacey, Sarah, and Sally, who patiently endured summer vacations in search of aviation history in Alabama.

Contents

ACKNOWLEDGMENTS

The author gratefully acknowledges the support and encouragement of the following individuals and organizations in making this book possible: Jerome Ennels; Wesley Phillips Newton; Office of Public Affairs, Maxwell Air Force Base, Alabama; Maj. Paul Griggs, 187th Fighter Wing, Alabama Air National Guard; Mark Pace; Bill Hudgens, Montgomery Aviation; Marie Force, Delta Air Transport Heritage Museum; Meredith McLemore, Alabama Department of Archives and History; Phil Perry, executive director, Montgomery Alabama Regional Airport Authority; Toni Jeske, archivist, Special Collections and Archives, Wright State University; Norman F. McGowin Jr.; Dr. James Griffin, executive director, Southern Museum of Flight; Wayne Novy, Southern Museum of Flight; Susan Robertson, Civil Air Patrol; Hill Goodspeed, National Museum of Naval Aviation; Sylvester Jackson, United States Air Force Historical Research Agency, Maxwell Air Force Base; and Paul Robertson Photography.

The author is especially grateful and deeply indebted to director George Cully and Bonita Harris of the Air University Office of History, Maxwell Air Force Base, Alabama; the staff of the U.S. Air Force Historical Research Agency (USAFHRA), Maxwell Air Force Base, Alabama; and my editor, Kate Crawford. Their guidance, encouragement, and contributions helped to make this dream a reality.

The images of the Wright brothers' flying school included in Chapter One are provided courtesy of the Special Collections and Archives, Wright State University.

Introduction

Aircraft parked on the flight line of Maxwell Air Force Base are a testament to the sophistication and complexity of military aviation in the 21st century. Massive hangar structures, built to protect these multimillion dollar investments in the nation's arsenal of democracy, tower above the other buildings of this small city of more than 10,000 military and civilian personnel. Four stories above this vast complex, specialists in the air traffic control tower direct the movements of aircraft operating from a runway that extends more than a mile in length. Base Operations, the gateway for arriving and departing aircraft, is located near the convergence of the flight line and the parking apron. In the center of the small circular drive leading to the base operations and passenger terminal building, easily overlooked among the imposing structures nearby, is a modest stone marker. Chiseled into the marble face of the marker is a simple inscription: "On This Site In 1910 Stood the Hangar of the Flying School of the First Men to Fly: The Wright Brothers." This monument is the sole reminder of a 100-acre cotton field that was once the site of the nation's first civilian flying school and Alabama's first airfield.

The evolution of this Montgomery County cotton field into one of the nation's earliest flying fields began on the morning of February 15, 1910, as Wilbur Wright, eldest of the brothers credited with the first powered, controlled, and sustained flight in a heavier-than-air machine, arrived at Union Station in Montgomery. Wright's visit to the city was part of a tour of the southeastern states to search for a suitable site to establish a spring training camp for student aviators. Harsh weather conditions in their native Ohio prevented the brothers from utilizing their flying field at Huffman Prairie during the months of winter and early spring each year. Wright's requirements for the new site were simple: a region having short winters, a mild climate, and flat, unobstructed farmland; conditions the brothers considered suitable for the operation of their flying machine. Prior to his arrival in Montgomery, Wright had visited Augusta and Atlanta, Georgia, and Jacksonville, Florida, where he carefully examined local weather conditions and topography but had not been successful in finding a site suitable for their purposes.

In Montgomery, Wright first visited the Commercial Club, a predecessor to the city's chamber of commerce. Introduced to Fred S. Ball, an attorney who served as the organization's president, Wright explained the purpose of his visit. Recognizing the potential benefits of having an aviation enterprise in Montgomery, Ball formed a committee to determine how the city might support the proposed venture. That afternoon, Wright was escorted to several locations in the Montgomery area including the state fairgrounds, the city's country club, and Vandiver Park. By the end of his first day in the city, Wright was convinced that Montgomery had enough flat, treeless land to suit his needs. The following morning, local businessman Frank D. Kohn learned of the aviator's presence in the city. Kohn contacted Wright to offer him the use of a 100-acre tract of land located on the Washington Ferry Road 3 miles west of the city. Following an extensive inspection of the site, Wright determined the property was well suited for flying and was located far enough from the city to provide a degree of seclusion. Wright then visited the weather bureau, where he reviewed the city's meteorological records for the previous six-year period. He learned that Montgomery had only one half the recorded rainfall of other cities being considered, and the average wind velocity was just 7 miles per hour, conditions he considered very favorable for flying.

Wilbur Wright traveled to central Alabama seeking a genial climate and suitable grounds for the establishment of a training camp for student aviators. In Montgomery, Wright not only found the conditions he required, but equally important, the city was committed to the development of aviation. On March 26, 1910, just six weeks after his brother's visit, Orville Wright ascended above the cotton fields west of Montgomery in a derivative of their 1905 Wright Flyer design, the first flight of an airplane in Alabama. During their two-month tenure in Montgomery, Orville and his five student aviators accomplished a number of significant milestones, including one of the earliest night flights in aviation history. Although their time in Montgomery was brief, the Wright brothers and their flying machine captured the imagination of the public and created a fertile environment for the evolution of aviation in Alabama.

From this auspicious beginning, the citizens of Montgomery embraced the idea of the airplane and the concept of flight training, a relationship that has endured for more than 90 years. An essential part of this relationship has been the integration of the airplane into the inventory of the nation's armed forces. With the rapid expansion of military aviation during the First World War, the flat terrain and mild weather conditions of central Alabama again brought flight training to Montgomery, this time on a much larger scale. Taylor Field, located southeast of the city in the Pike Road Community, became one of 14 primary aviation training fields in the Aviation Section of the U.S. Signal Corps, the predecessor to the Army Air Service. Established in November 1917, the 800-acre facility included 16 large hangars, repair shops, sleeping quarters, a hospital, and a swimming pool. Before the end of the war, approximately 200 training aircraft were operating from the field. Closed at the end of the First World War, Taylor Field would again serve the needs of military flight training during the Second World War as an auxiliary landing field for the basic flight-training program at Gunter Field.

Originally constructed as an engine and repair depot to support the flight training operations at Taylor Field and five other aviation training sites in the Southeast during the First World War, Maxwell Air Force Base has been a dominant influence in the lives of Montgomery residents for more than a generation. Completed in July 1918, the field was designated an engine and repair depot, one of only three aviation depots in the inventory of the Army Air Service. Fittingly the base was constructed on the same parcel of land selected by Wilbur Wright as the site of the nation's first civilian flying school less than a decade earlier. On November 8, 1922, the post was named Maxwell Field in honor of 2nd Lt. William C. Maxwell of Atmore, Alabama. The field became Maxwell Air Force Base as a result of the September 1947 creation of the U.S. Air Force as a separate branch of service.

The relocation of the Army Air Corps Tactical School from Langley Field, Virginia, to Montgomery in 1929 provided the foundation for the evolution of Maxwell Field into a center of continuing education. Unique in its mission, the tactical school was created to provide officers of the Air Corps and other military services the opportunity to learn strategy, tactics, and techniques related to the employment of air power. During the Second World War, graduates of the tactical school assumed positions of leadership that directed American air power to achieve superiority over the Axis powers in Europe and Asia. In March 1946, the need for a coordinated and unified program of continuing education for career officers resulted in the establishment of Air University at Maxwell Field. The creation of Air University was unique in that it was the first time responsibility for education had been centralized in one headquarters without other diverting responsibilities for students. Initially, Air University consisted of three schools that served as the nucleus for the courses of instruction: the Air War College, Command and Staff School, and the Air Tactical School. Since its founding, Air University has become a vital part of the U.S. Air Force, providing a coordinated program of advanced courses of study necessary to prepare officers to assume increasingly important assignments in command and staff positions.

Although a military facility, Maxwell Field has, on many occasions, served a dual role to meet the civilian aviation needs of the city of Montgomery. During the formative years of air travel, the field provided the means to introduce Montgomery residents to the safety, efficiency, and capability of air transportation. This was especially true during the years following the end of the First World War and the August 1929 dedication of the city's new municipal airport on the Upper Wetumpka Road. An example of this relationship occurred on April 17, 1925, as the first official air mail for Montgomery arrived at Maxwell Field from New Orleans. The flight was conducted to determine the feasibility of connecting airmail service from the Gulf Coast to the transcontinental service at Chicago. First Lt. Robert D. Knapp of Maxwell Field piloted the first two segments of the route from New Orleans to Montgomery via Mobile. Although scheduled airmail service would not be inaugurated in the city until 1932, Maxwell Field served an important role in demonstrating the viability of this service within Alabama and the southern United States.

Perhaps the most notable event in the history of Maxwell Field's service to the community was the humanitarian relief effort that originated at the base during the March 1929 flooding of central Alabama. Excessive rains caused heavy flooding of communities in the central portion of the state, rendering highways and railroads in the affected area impassible. Thousands of people attempted to flee but became trapped in communities isolated by the floodwater. Unable to provide relief by road or rail, Gov. Bibb Graves called on Maj. Walter Weaver, commanding officer of Maxwell Field, to assist in the rescue effort. During the next six days, pilots from Maxwell flew 281 missions and dropped more than 50 tons of supplies to flood victims in what was considered to be the most significant relief mission in the history of the Army Air Corps.

By 1940, preparations for United States' intervention in the escalating crisis in Europe had begun. In a war Pres. Franklin Roosevelt believed would be won through the use of superior air power, the Army Air Corps began establishing the infrastructure to meet the requirements of a War Department directive to train 7,000 pilots on an annual basis. Designated Southeast Air Corps Training Center, Maxwell Field became one of only three regional training centers of the Army Air Corps, with jurisdiction over all aviation training facilities in the Southeast. Before the end of the war, more than 100,000 aviation cadets completed preflight, basic, or advanced training at Maxwell Field. So many pilots, navigators, and bombardiers transitioned through the base that "The road to Tokyo leads through Maxwell Field" became a common theme among cadets.

The rapid expansion of the Air Corps pilot training program resulted in an immediate need for additional flying fields. In August 1940, the Montgomery Municipal Airport was acquired through lease by the Army Air Corps and activated as a basic flying training school. Named in honor of Mayor William A. Gunter, who had been instrumental in the original development of the airport and its subsequent transition into a military facility, Gunter Field produced more than 12,000 American, British, and French cadets during the Second World War. With 400 aircraft based at the field, the skies over Gunter were described as having the densest air traffic in the world. Seven auxiliary landing fields, constructed to reduce congestion at Maxwell and Gunter, were located in the Montgomery area. Two of these, the Montgomery Regional Airport and the Wetumpka Municipal Airport, continue to operate more than six decades later as civilian facilities.

The conversion of the municipal airport into a military training field meant Montgomery no longer had the means to accommodate passenger and airmail service to the city. Initially Eastern Air Lines was allowed to continue using the former municipal airport to provide this service. However, increased training activity in 1941 caused air traffic to become too congested for continued airline operations. In another example of the cooperative relationship between the military and the city of Montgomery, Walter Weaver, commanding officer of Maxwell Field, agreed to let Eastern use some of its facilities until a new airport could be constructed. In March 1941, 508 acres of land located seven miles west of the city on the Selma Highway were selected to be the site of the new municipal airport. Dedicated on July 1, 1943, the field had three paved runways, a concrete parking apron, and the most modern boundary, runway, and beacon lighting available. The field was named in honor of Ens. Clarence Moore Dannelly, a Montgomery native who lost his life in an aircraft accident in December 1940 at the Pensacola Naval Air Station. Dannelly was the first Montgomery resident to lose his life in preparation for war.

The end of the Second World War brought to a close the most remarkable period in the history of aviation in Montgomery. The 100-acre cotton field that was once the site of the nation's first civilian flying school had evolved into a massive military aviation training school where more than 100,000 cadets were trained for combat in the skies over Europe and Asia. With the passing of only 30 years, the sound of a lone flying machine above the cotton fields west of the city had been replaced by the thunderous roar of hundreds of military aircraft over Montgomery.

In March 1910, the promise of short winters, a mild climate, and flat farmland brought the Wright brothers and the nation's first civilian flying school to Montgomery. Less than a decade later, the army constructed one of the earliest military aviation training fields near the city for the same reasons. At Montgomery, the Wright brothers and the military found an ideal environment for training young aviators to operate flying machines. More important than the climate or terrain, they discovered a city deeply committed in its support of aviation and the development of military airpower. More than any other factor, this level of commitment will ensure the legacy of aviation in Montgomery during the second century of powered flight.

One

The Wright Brothers

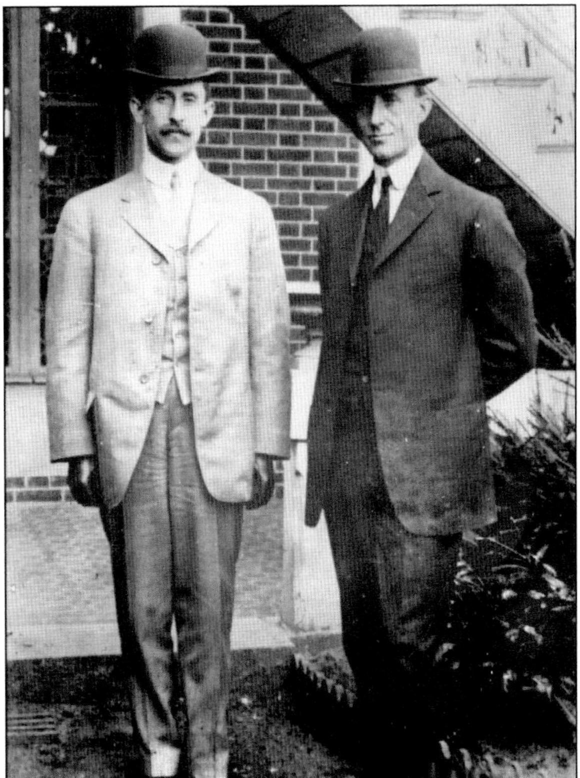

Credited with the first powered, controlled, and sustained flight in a heavier-than-air machine, Orville and Wilbur Wright established the nation's first civilian flying school to train pilots for their newly formed aerial exhibition company. After visiting several locations in Tennessee, Georgia, and Florida, Wilbur Wright choose Montgomery as the site of their school because of the region's short winters, mild climate, and abundance of flat farmland.

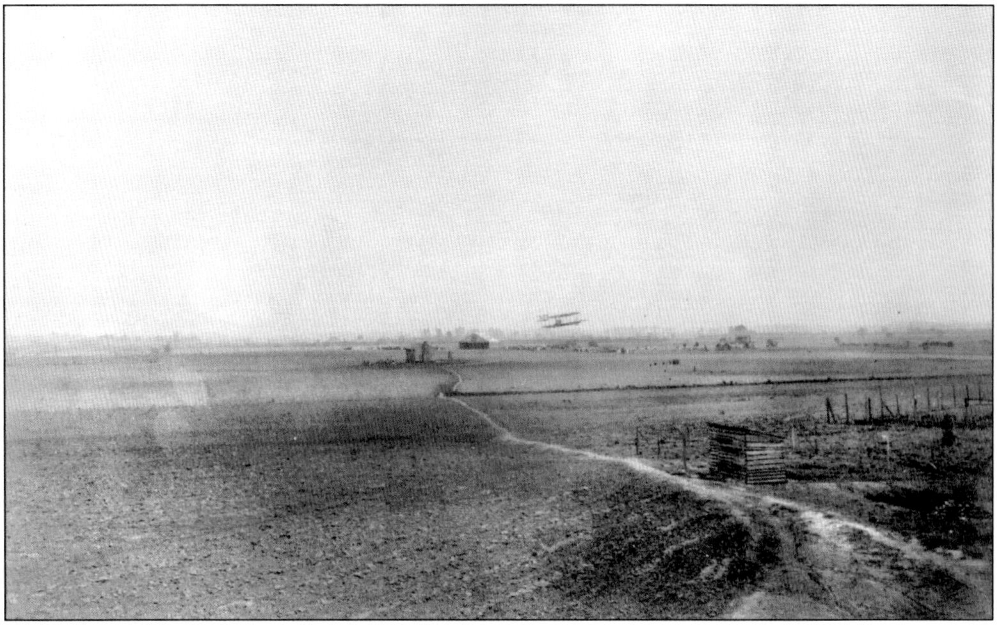

Local businessman Frank D. Kohn offered the Wrights a 100-acre parcel of property located three miles west of Montgomery on the Washington Ferry Road. After inspecting the site, Wilbur Wright determined the former cotton field was well suited for flying and provided a degree of seclusion with which to conduct their flying activities. Kohn allowed the Wrights free use of the property during their stay in Montgomery.

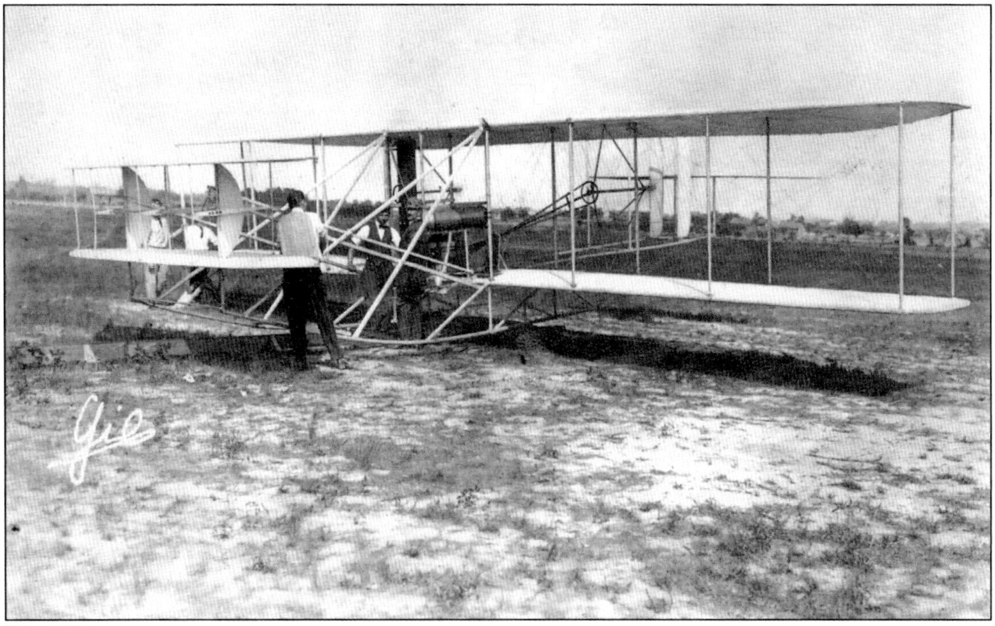

The Flyer was transported to Montgomery in seven large crates aboard the Louisville and Nashville Railroad. The Flyer weighed 900 pounds and was powered by a four-cylinder, water-cooled engine that developed approximately 35 horsepower. This machine had been flown by Wilbur Wright the previous year from Governor's Island to the Statue of Liberty and back during the Hudson-Fulton Centennial Celebration in New York City.

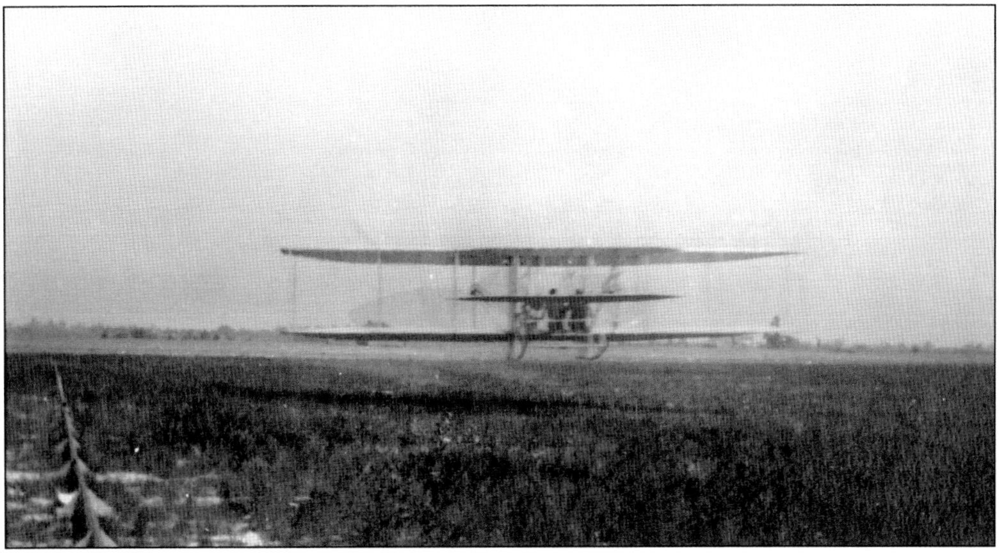

The undercarriage of the Flyer consisted of two landing skids. For takeoff, the machine would be placed on a monorail, 192 feet in length and built in 16-foot sections so that it could be easily repositioned into the prevailing wind. The weighted catapult system previously used to accelerate the machine down the launch rail was not utilized in Montgomery. The monorail system is visible in the lower left corner of the photograph.

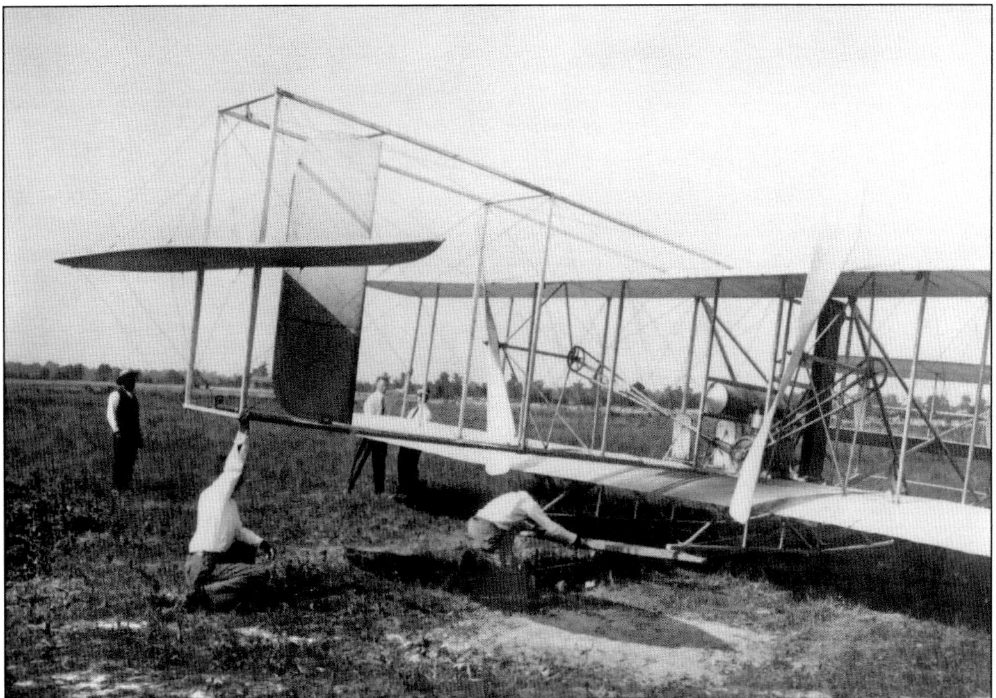

The Flyer was placed on a small platform equipped with tandem rollers before being positioned on the launch rail for takeoff. When the machine reached flying speed, the pilot would deflect the elevator and the machine would lift from the rail, leaving the launch platform behind. The Wrights did not add wheels to their aircraft designs until after leaving Montgomery.

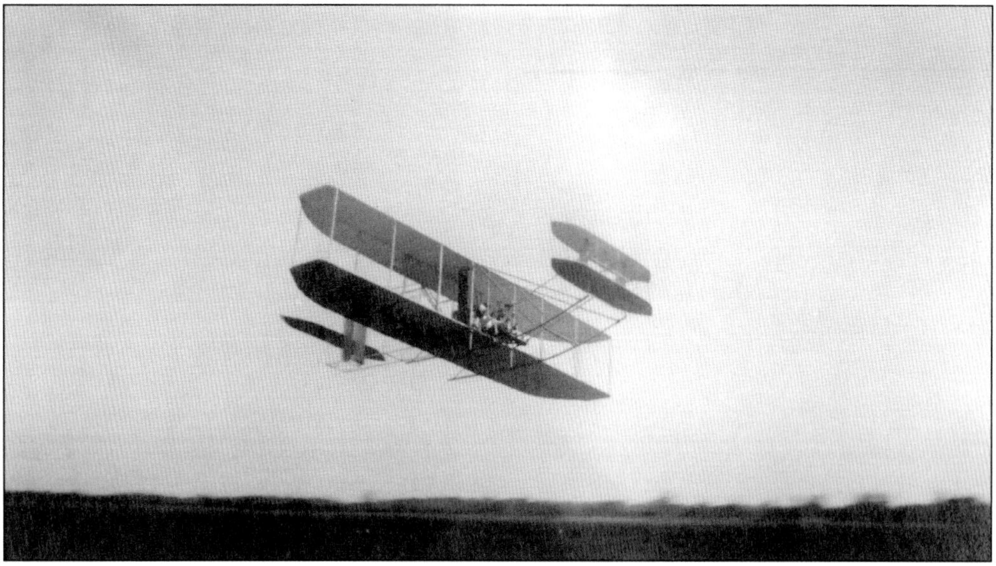

On March 26, 1910, Orville Wright ascended in the Flyer to a height of 50 feet and remained aloft for approximately five minutes, the first flight of an airplane in Alabama. Because flying activities were not scheduled to begin until the following week, few spectators were on hand to witness the historic event. This image depicts a subsequent flight with a passenger on board.

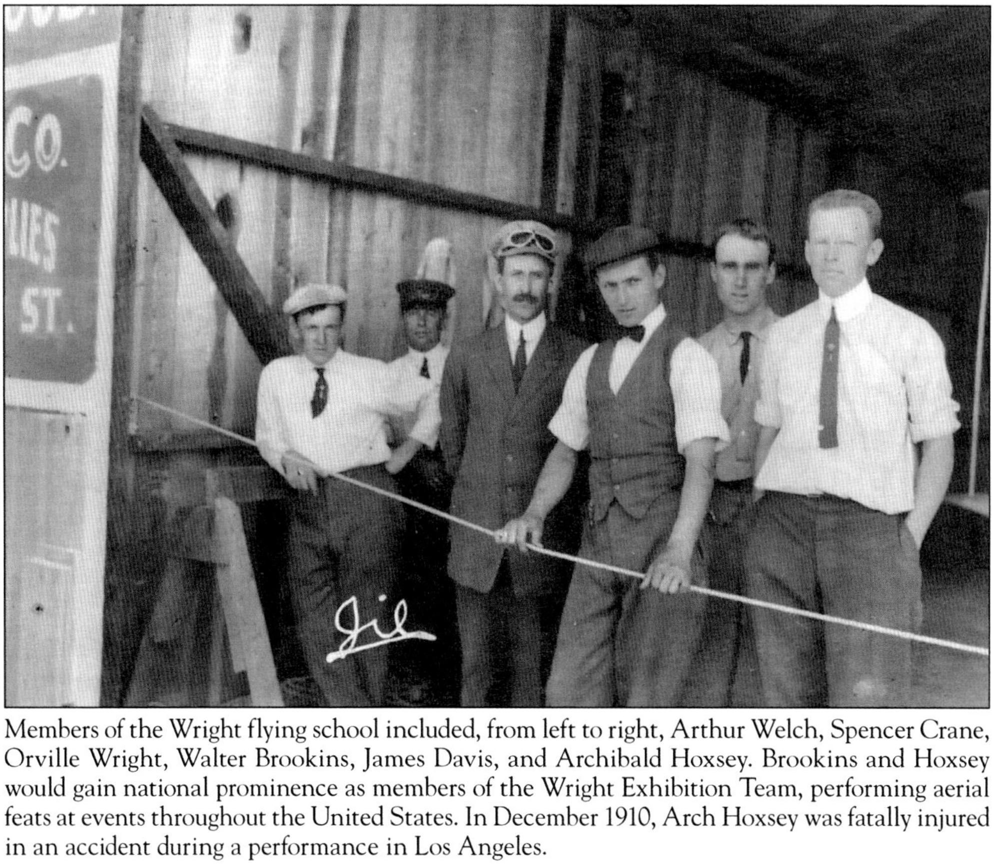

Members of the Wright flying school included, from left to right, Arthur Welch, Spencer Crane, Orville Wright, Walter Brookins, James Davis, and Archibald Hoxsey. Brookins and Hoxsey would gain national prominence as members of the Wright Exhibition Team, performing aerial feats at events throughout the United States. In December 1910, Arch Hoxsey was fatally injured in an accident during a performance in Los Angeles.

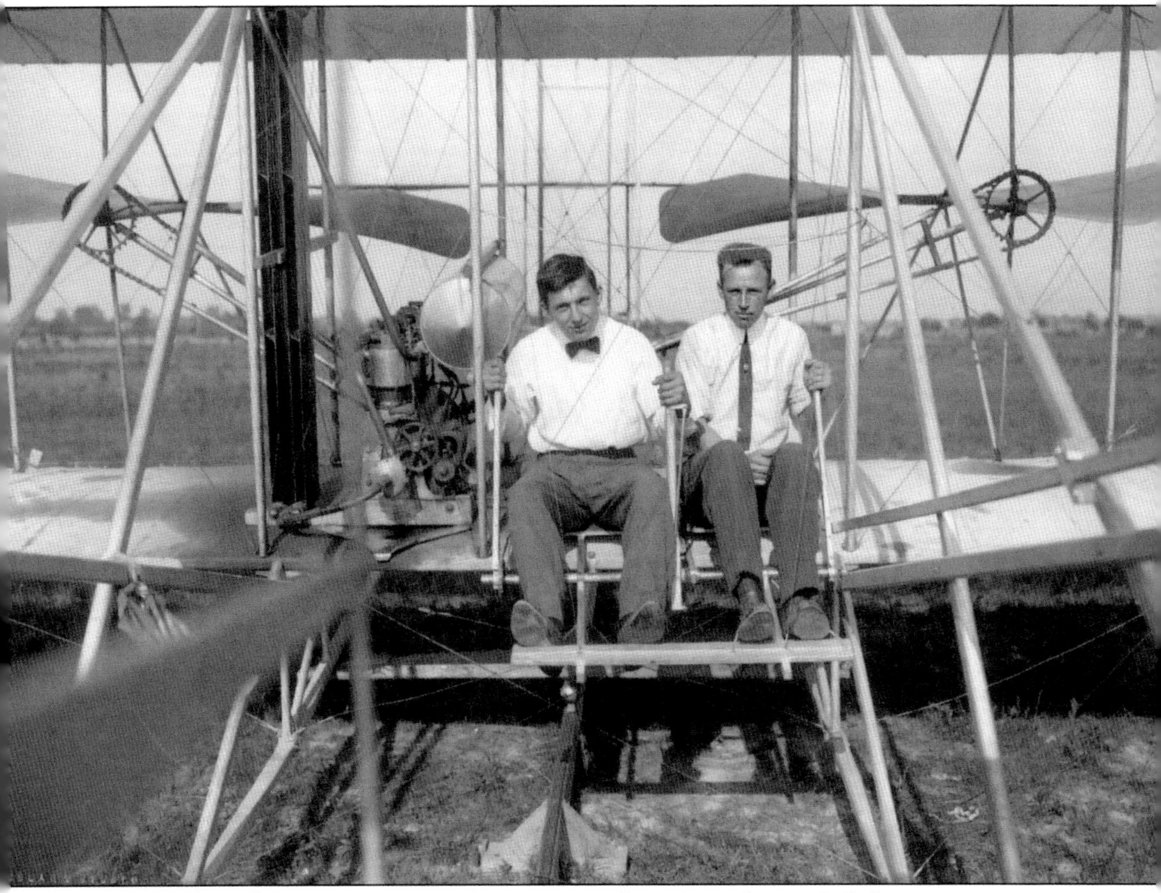

The aircraft used in Montgomery was a transitional machine that included improvements to earlier Wright designs. Dual seats were provided in an upright, side-by-side arrangement with a control lever for the rudder and wing warping system located between the seats. The elevator control lever, used to raise or lower the nose of the machine, was located outboard of each seat. This arrangement allowed student aviators to be trained to operate the Flyer. At Montgomery, student aviator Walter Brookins achieved a number of significant milestones. Brookins learned to operate the Flyer from the right-hand seat as an instructor, becoming the first civilian pilot to achieve this distinction. In May 1910, Brookins (left) and Hoxsey (right) completed one of the first night flights in aviation history from the Kohn property near Montgomery.

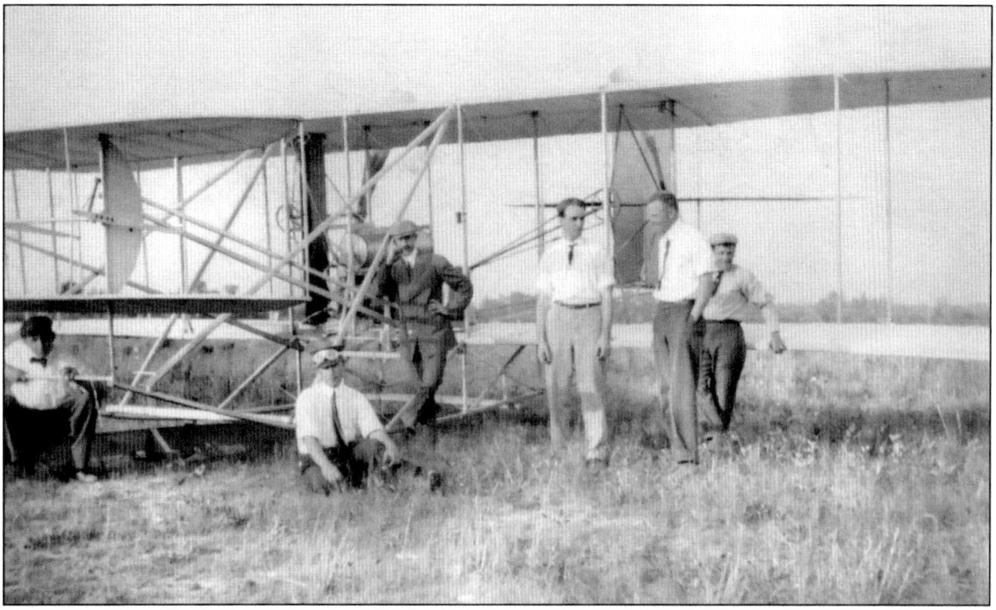

Many spectators thought Orville Wright (third from left) and his students appeared to be dressed for church rather than flying. Weather conditions permitting, the school operated daily except Sunday. Pilots of the Wright Exhibition Company were forbidden from drinking, gambling, and flying on Sunday.

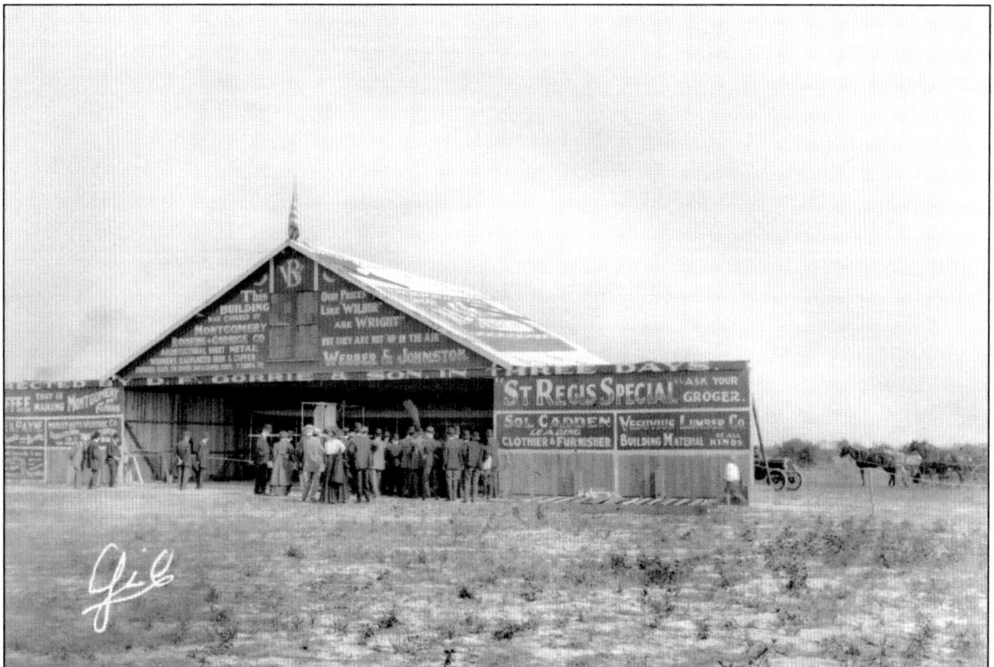

A shed to protect the machine was constructed by the D. F. Gorrie and Sons Lumber Company. The materials and labor were donated by local merchants in exchange for the right to place advertisements on the structure. The building, large enough to hold two flying machines, was constructed on a slight rise adjacent to the milepost No. 3 on the Washington Ferry Road.

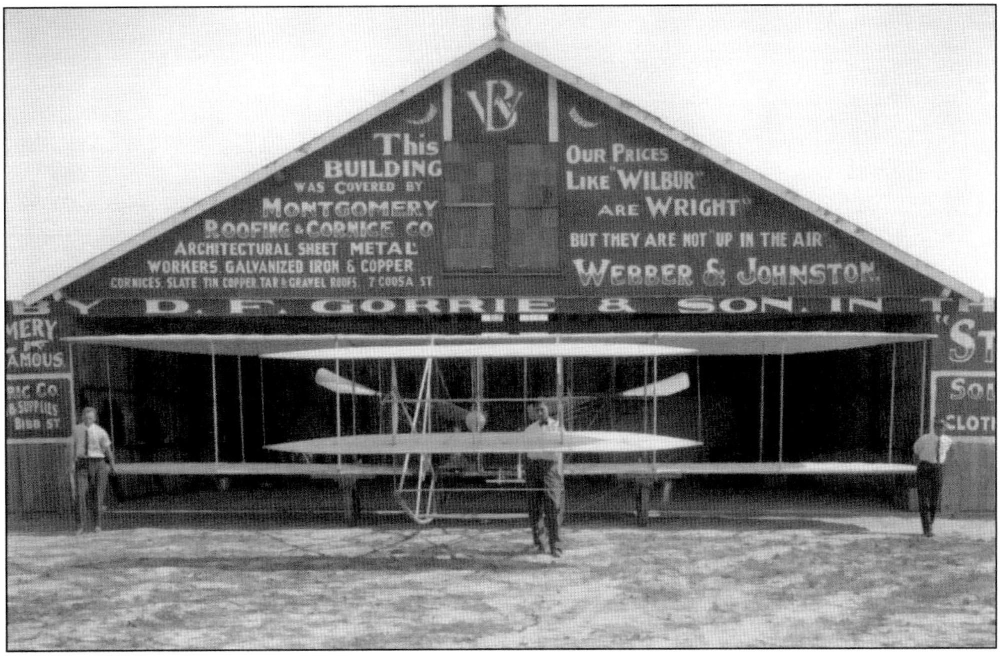

Student aviators Archibald Hoxsey (left), Walter Brookins (center), and Spencer Crane remove the Flyer from the shed. Advertisements of local merchants adorn the structure. Webber and Johnston, a local clothier, proudly proclaimed, "Our prices like Wilbur are Wright but they are not up in the air." The initials of the Wright brothers are interwoven into an emblem at the apex of the structure.

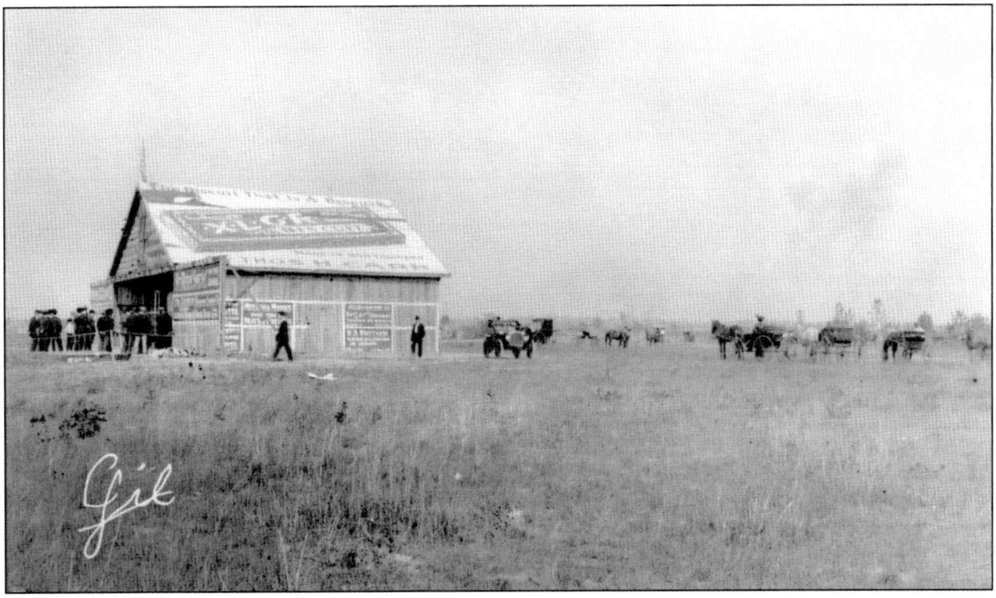

Local residents traveled by foot, horse-drawn carriage, and automobile to observe the flying activities. The Mobile and Ohio Railroad offered a shuttle service from Union Station to the field after Orville Wright authorized the release of the school's flying schedule to the public. The fare for a round trip was 25¢. This created the opportunity for hundreds of Montgomery residents to see a flying machine for the first time.

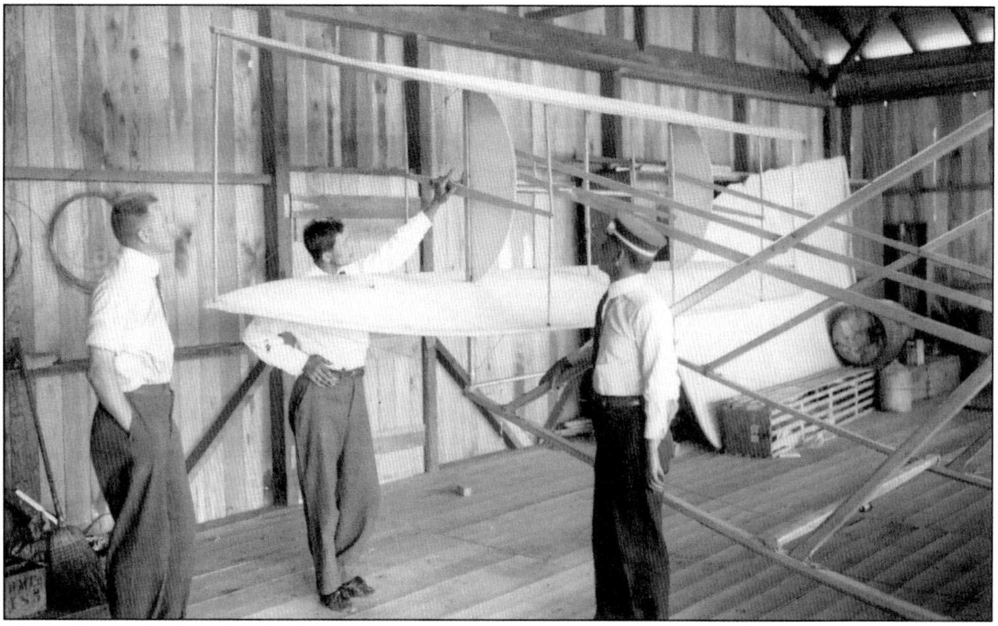

Students inspect the forward elevator assembly of the machine. The dual elevator surfaces were used to control the up-and-down movement of the Flyer. This arrangement would be eliminated in subsequent Wright designs in favor of a rear-mounted assembly. The vertical, semicircular planes located between the elevators were known as "blinkers." These vanes helped to stabilize the machine during turns by preventing the nose from dropping.

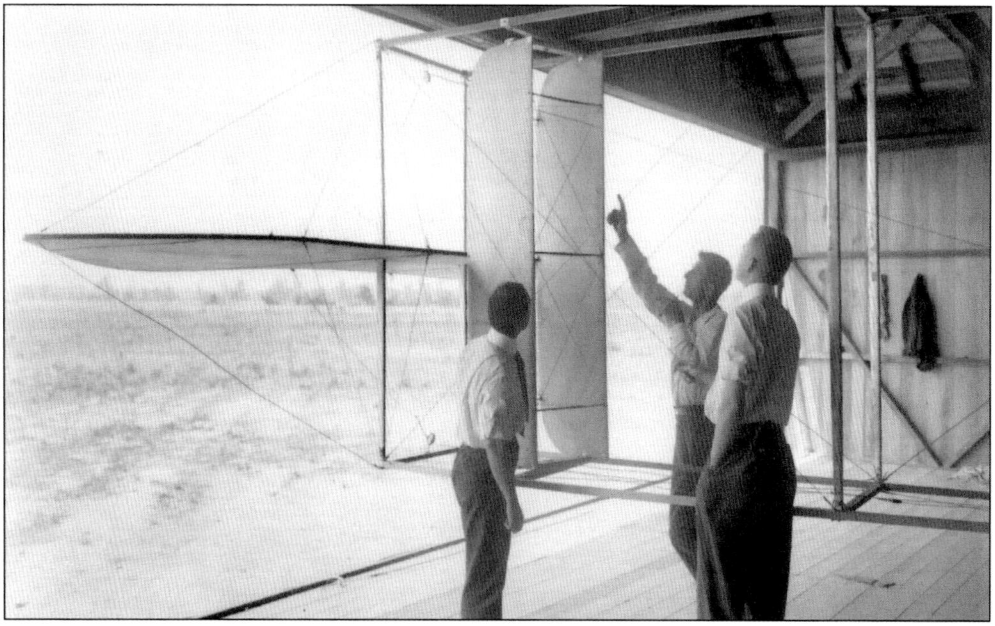

At Montgomery, Orville Wright made a significant modification to the Flyer by adding a horizontal plane directly behind the two upright planes located at the rear of the aircraft. The Wrights felt this modification would improve stability and simplify handling of the machine in the air. Orville Wright's initial flight at Montgomery was the first time this concept was tested on a Wright design.

Wright student Spencer Crane examines one of the two propellers that provided the thrust necessary to propel the machine through the air. The Wrights calculated that two propellers rotating slowly would produce more thrust than a single propeller spinning rapidly. Propellers measured 8.5 feet in length and were fabricated at the Wright shop in Dayton.

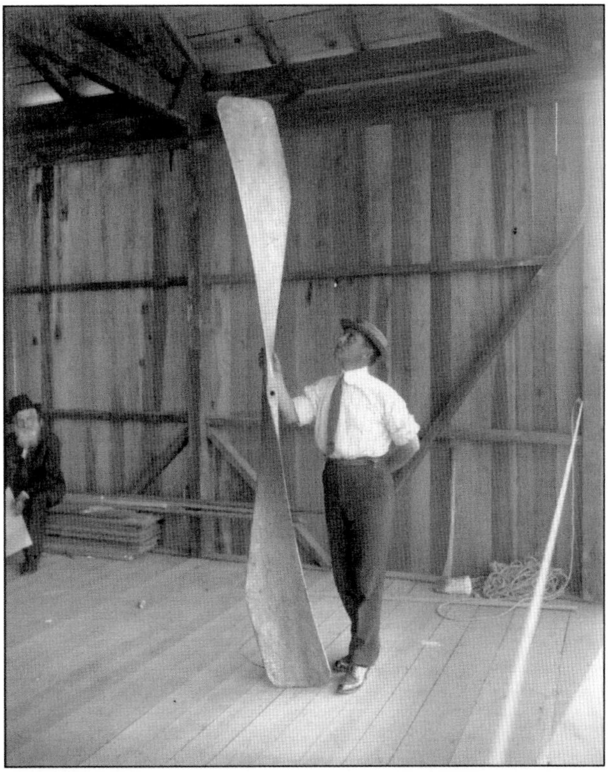

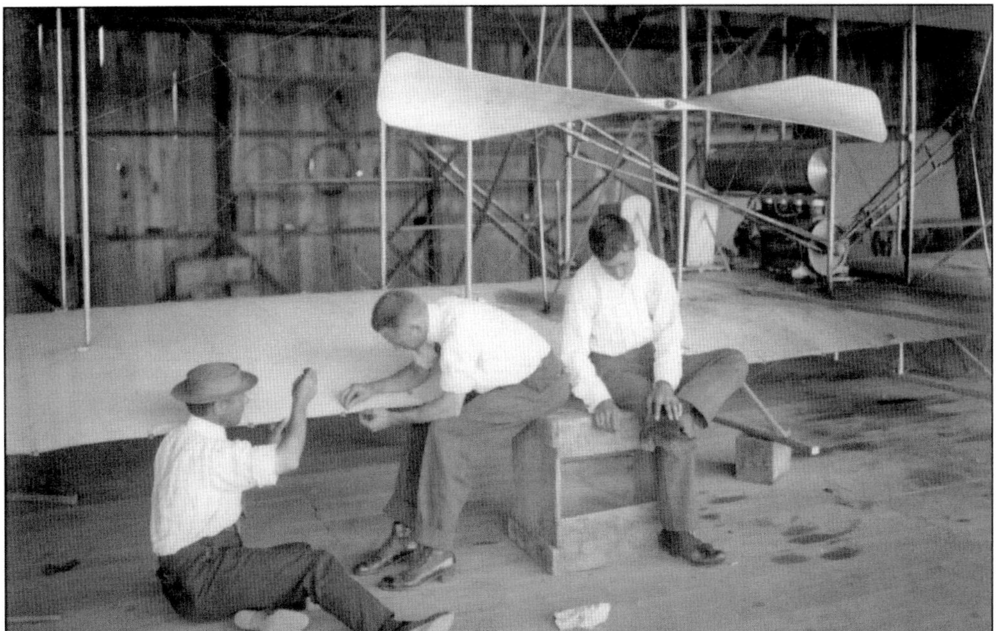

In addition to being trained to operate the Flyer, students at the Wright school learned to maintain and repair the machine. In this image, students repair a section of the muslin fabric that covered the wing structure.

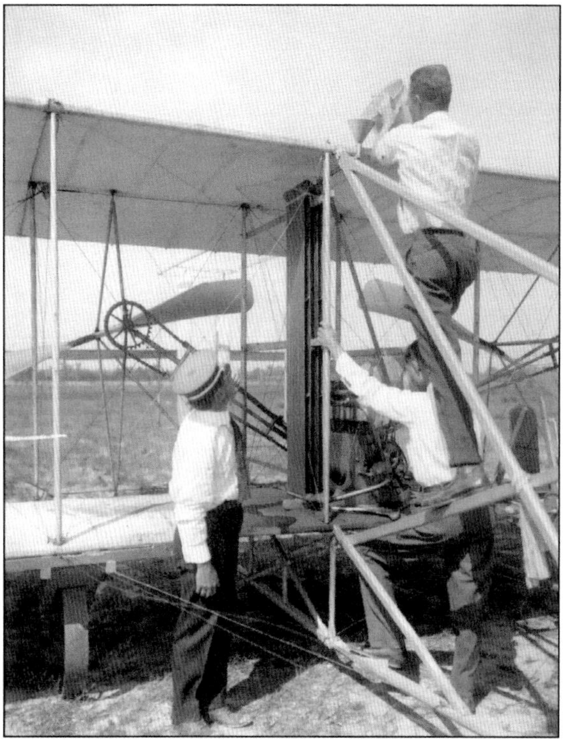

Using a bucket and funnel, Arch Hoxsey fills the radiator of the water-cooled engine before a flight. The wheel visible under the wing was part of a mechanism used to maneuver the machine on the ground.

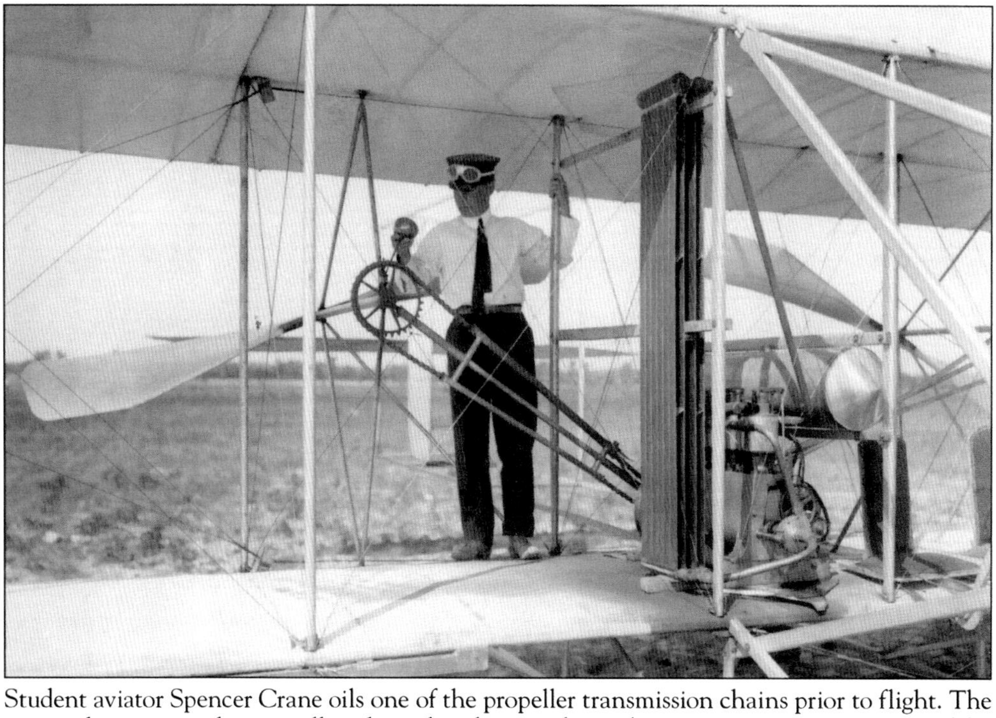

Student aviator Spencer Crane oils one of the propeller transmission chains prior to flight. The engine drove two pusher propellers through a chain-and-sprocket transmission system. One of the chains was crossed to produce a counter-rotation of the propellers to reduce the effects of torque. With no internal lubrication system, the chain drive required service at regular intervals.

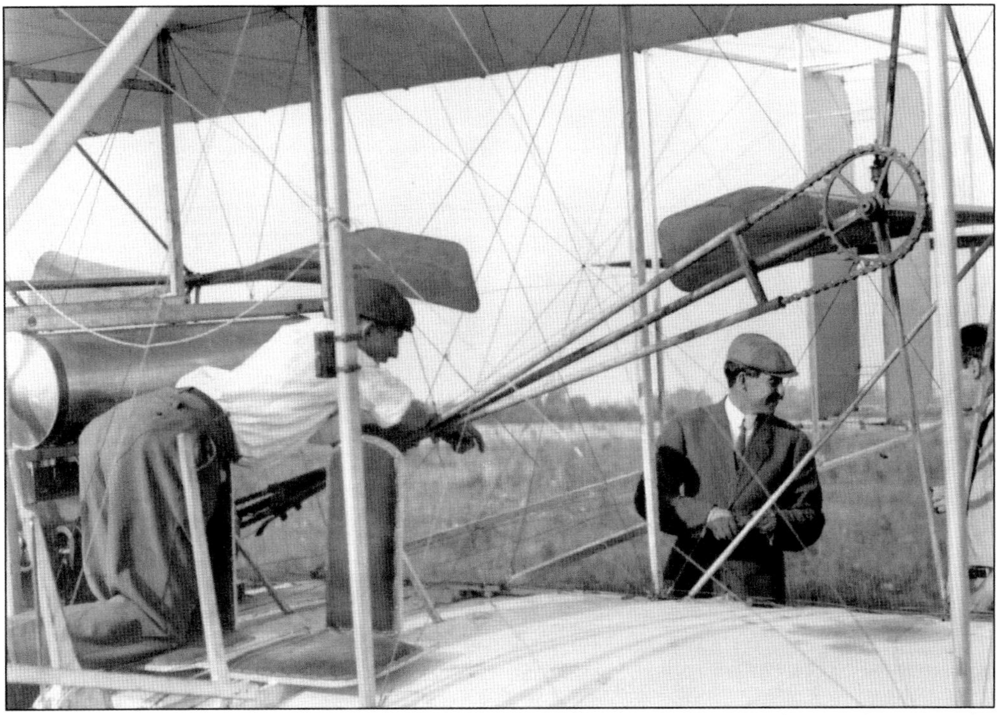

The extensive network of wooden struts and wire bracing used to strengthen and support the biplane arrangement of the wings is evident in this view of the Flyer. The airframe of the Flyer was constructed primarily of spruce. The wire bracing formed a strong yet flexible truss between the two wings.

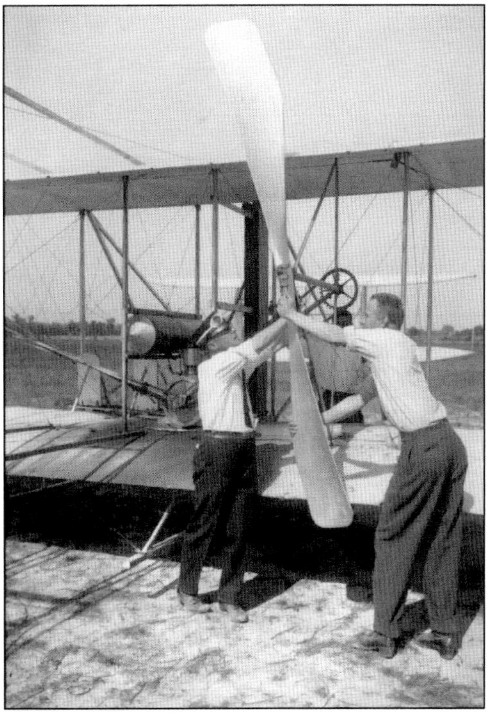

Students Spencer Crane (left) and Arch Hoxsey prepare to start the Flyer. Starting the engine required a rapid pull on the propellers, a sometimes difficult and laborious task. During engine start, dry batteries and a coil were used for ignition. Once the engine was operating, a high-tension magneto provided power for ignition.

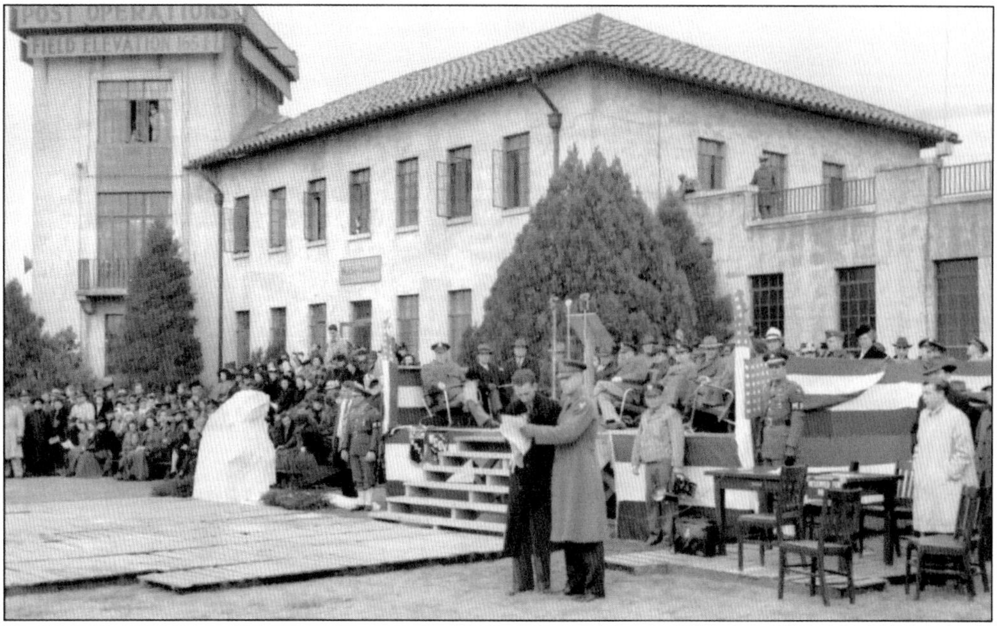

Flying activity at the Wright school ended abruptly on May 26, 1910, as a result of a broken propeller chain. Because the school was slated to be closed soon, a repair of the machine was not considered feasible. Within days, the camp was closed and the school relocated to Dayton. In December 1943, a two-ton marble monument was unveiled at Maxwell Field to commemorate the nation's first civilian flying school.

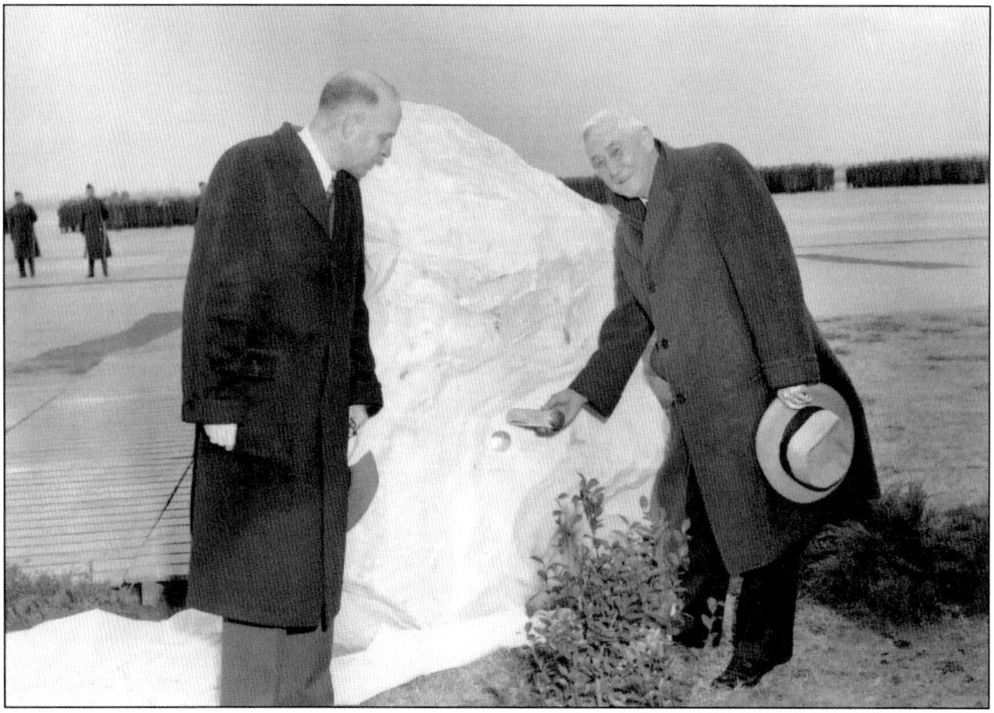

A time capsule is placed in the marble monument commemorating the site of the nation's first civilian flying school and the establishment of Maxwell Field.

Two

TAYLOR FIELD

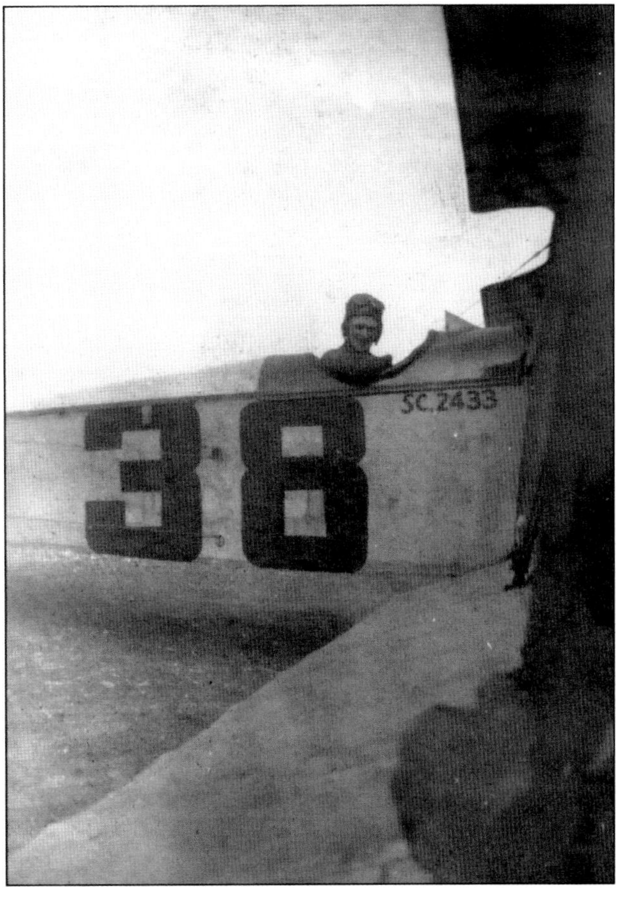

In July 1917, Congress appropriated $64 million for the production of aircraft and the construction of primary training fields needed to produce 6,000 military aviators for service in the war in Europe. Like the Wright brothers before them, military inspectors believed the mild weather conditions and flat, open terrain of central Alabama made Montgomery an ideal location for the establishment of a flying training field. (Mark Pace collection.)

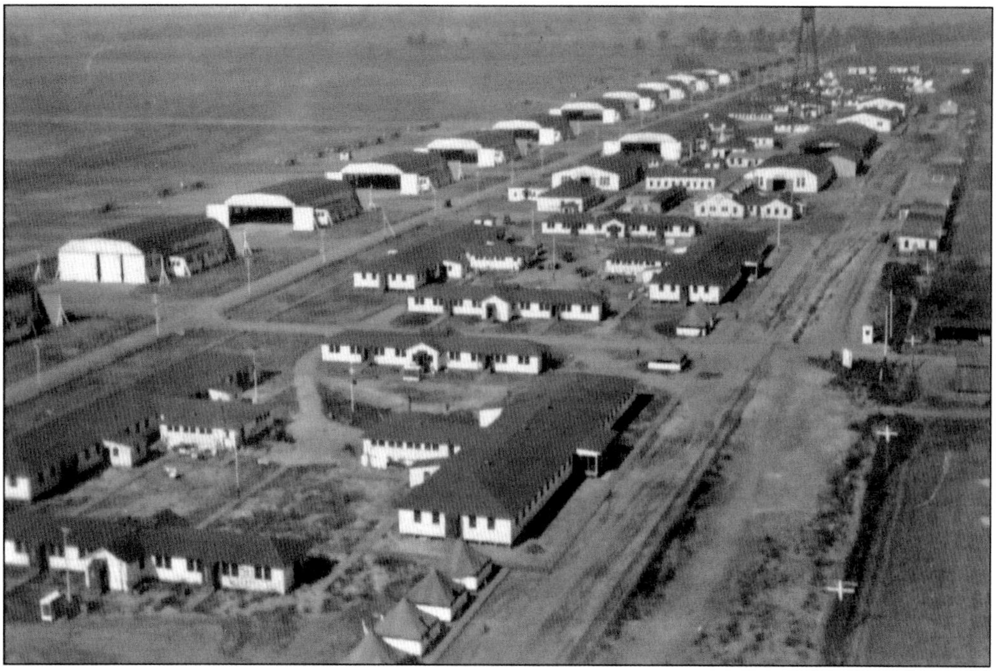

Established in December 1917, Taylor Field was located in the Pike Road community southeast of Montgomery. The 800-acre facility included 16 hangars, repair shops, barracks, a swimming pool, and a hospital. Taylor Field was named for Capt. Ralph L. Taylor of Stanford, Connecticut, a member of the Signal Corps who lost his life in an aviation accident in August 1917 over Mineola Field, New York. (Mark Pace collection.)

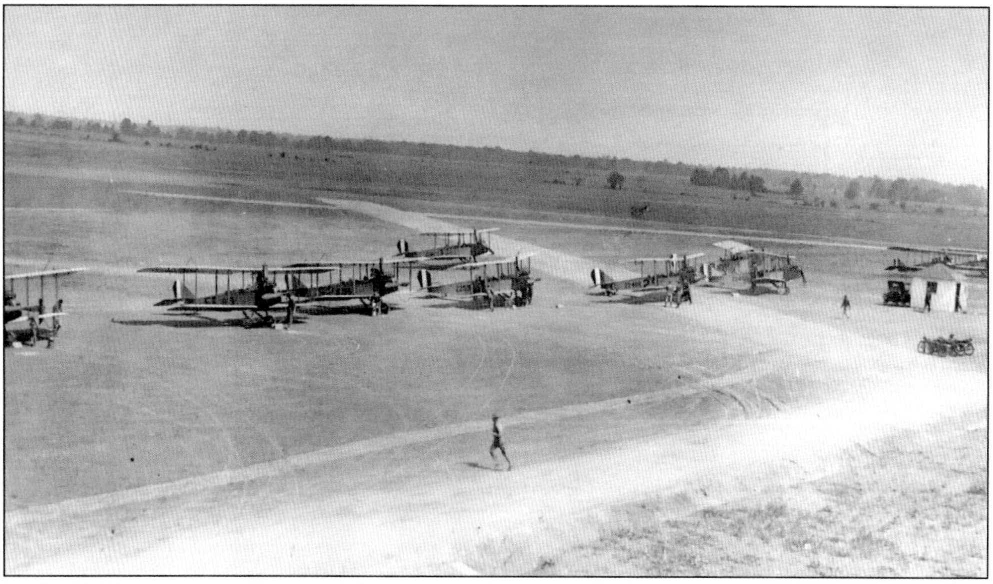

Taylor Field was reportedly one of the most ideal training facilities in the nation. The flying field was described as being "as level as a floor," and the climate allowed training to be conducted throughout the year. The intersecting gravel runways visible in this image were constructed for use during periods of wet weather that made large portions of the flying field unusable. (Air University Office of History.)

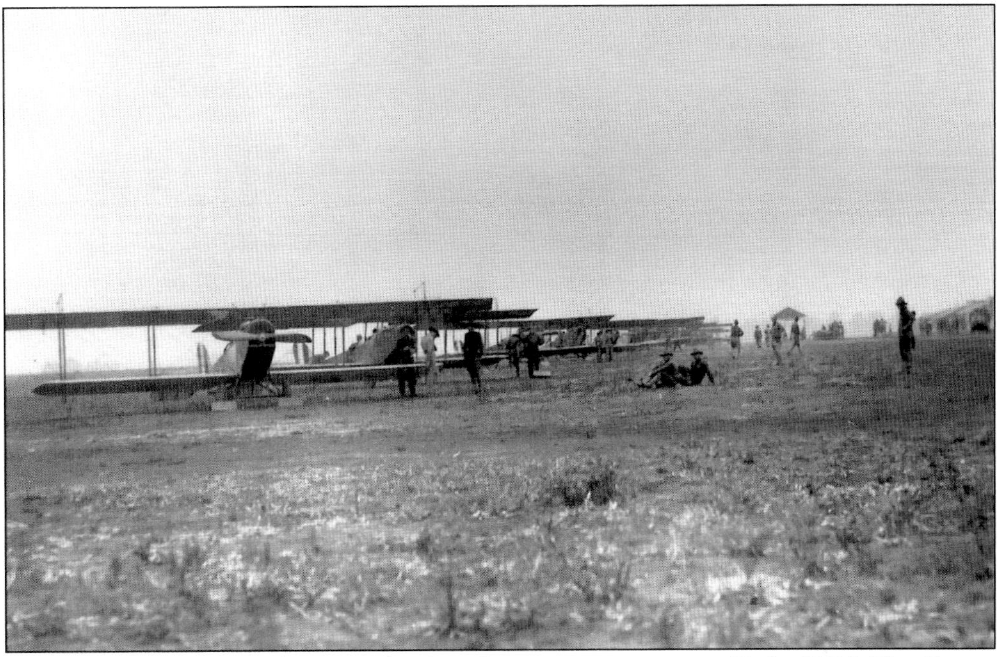

Approximately 200 aircraft were utilized in the training program at Taylor Field. The Curtiss JN-4D, affectionately known as the "Jenny," was powered by a 90-horsepower, water-cooled OX-5 engine. The Jenny had a maximum horizontal flight speed of 75 miles per hour and a rate of climb of 400 feet per minute. (Air University Office of History.)

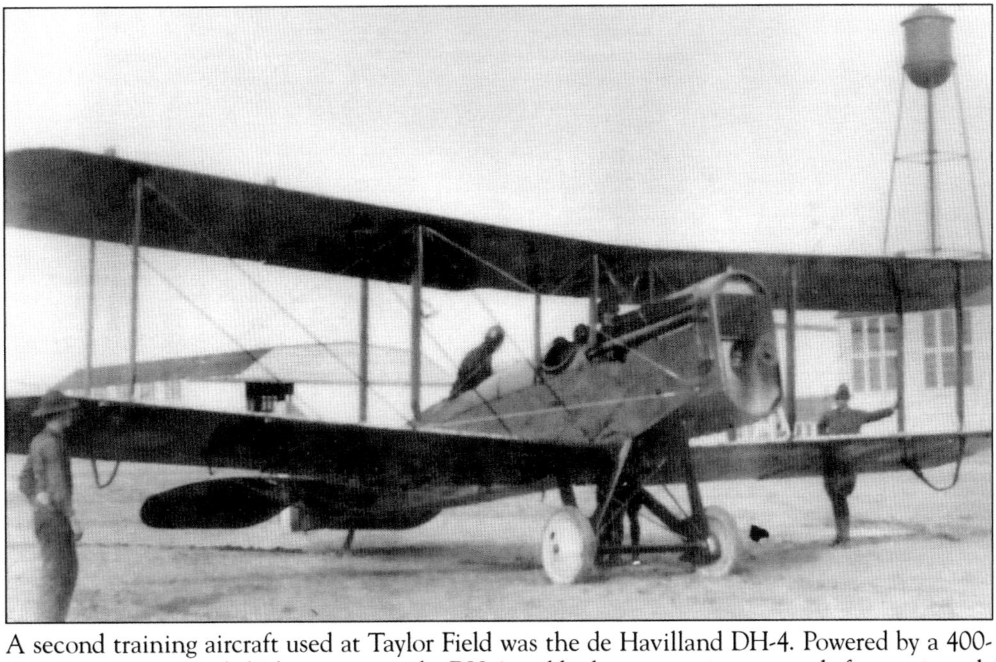

A second training aircraft used at Taylor Field was the de Havilland DH-4. Powered by a 400-horsepower, water-cooled Liberty engine, the DH-4 could achieve a maximum speed of approximately 120 miles per hour. These early aircraft did not have wheel brakes for stopping or steering. Members of the ground crew would assist the pilot in positioning the airplane for takeoff. (Air University Office of History.)

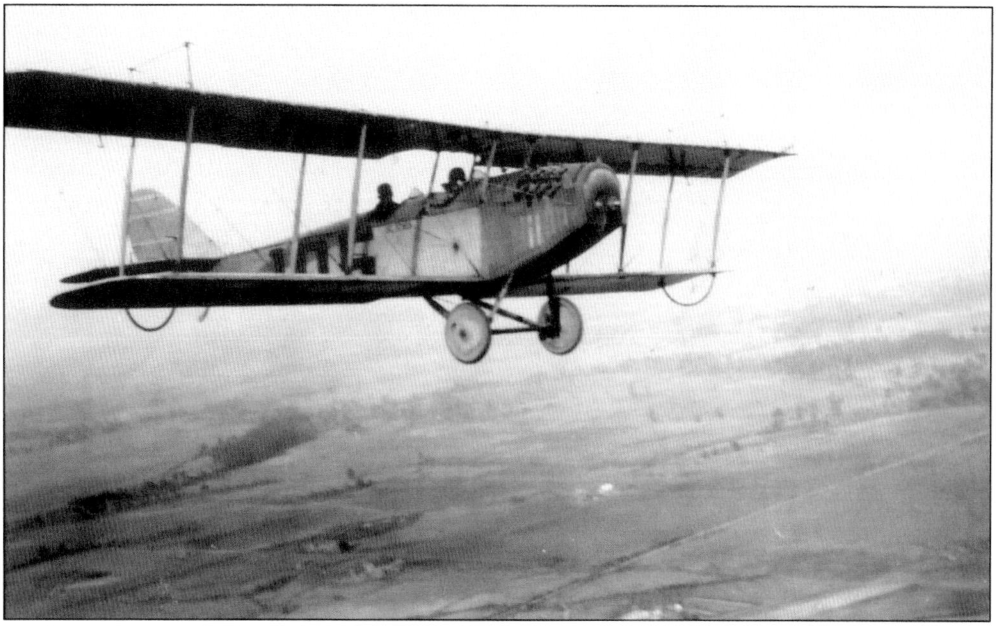

Student aviators at Taylor Field and other primary flying schools received 40 to 50 hours of flight training. The first 8 to 10 hours of flight time were spent with an instructor learning the use and function of the flight controls and how to perform maneuvers. Because the aircraft were not equipped with communication radios, the instructor and student communicated by means of hand signals. (Mark Pace collection.)

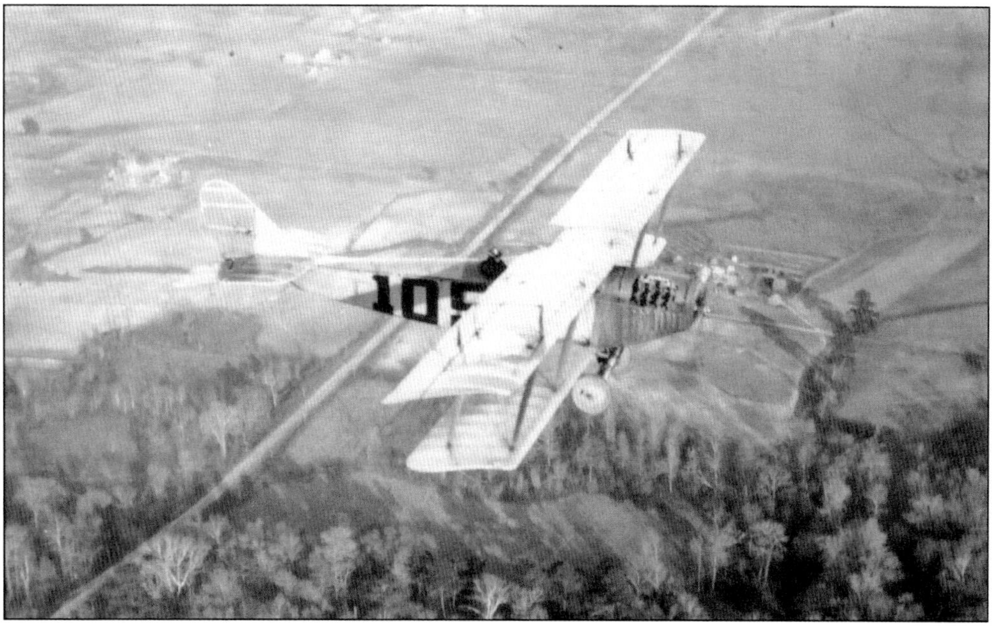

After demonstrating proficiency in basic flight maneuvers, cadets progressed to the cross-country phase of training. This course consisted of three flights around a triangular course of specified distance, followed by longer round-trip flight to a destination at least 75 miles from the departure point. Rudimentary maps, nonexistent navigational aids, and a lack of prepared landing fields made this one of the more challenging aspects of the training program. (Mark Pace collection.)

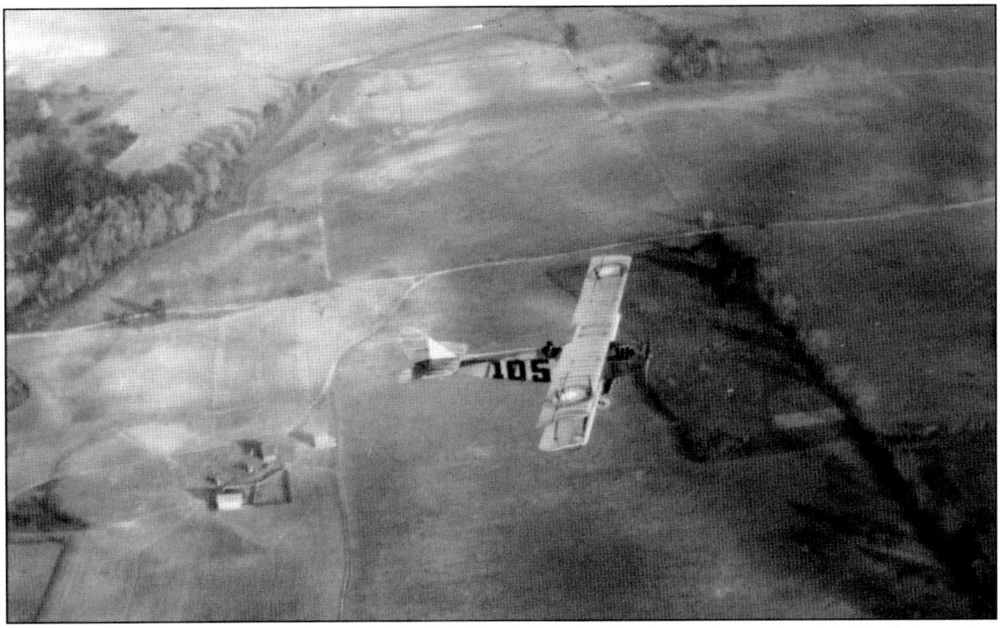

The final phase of primary flight training consisted of instruction in aerobatics. Students were trained to recover from stalls and spiral dives and to perform loops. After becoming proficient in these maneuvers, cadets practiced formation flying in groups of three to six aircraft. Successful completion of the Reserve Military Aviator's test at the conclusion of training entitled the cadet to wear the wings of a military aviator. (Mark Pace collection.)

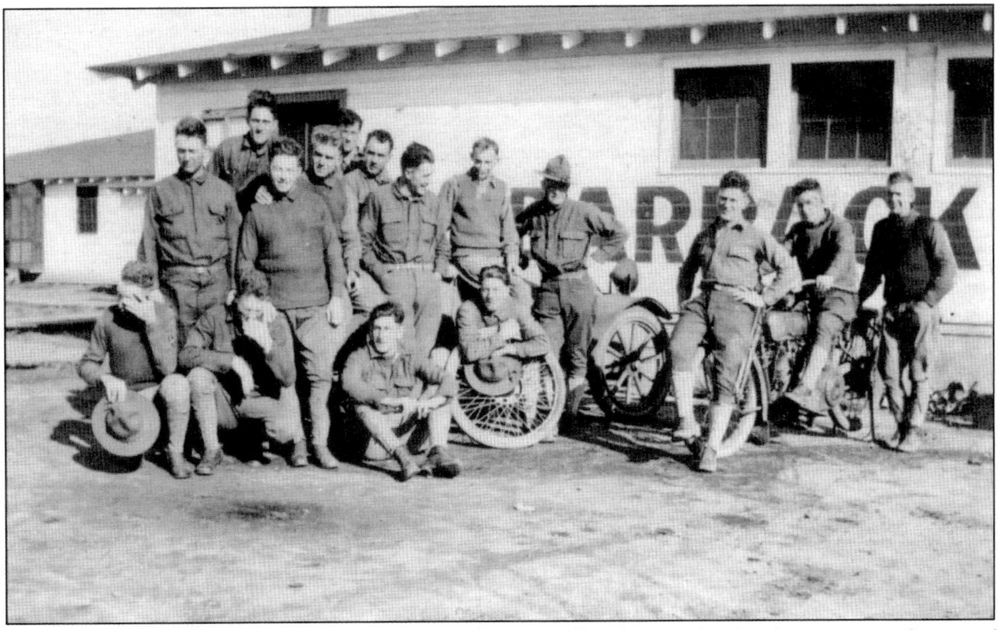

Before beginning primary flight training, cadets completed ground-school courses in theory of flight, operation and maintenance of aircraft engines, weather, and other subjects at one of eight designated colleges or universities. Upon completion of primary training, cadets were assigned to an advanced training school. One hundred and thirty-nine flying cadets completed the eight-week course at Taylor Field. (Mark Pace collection.)

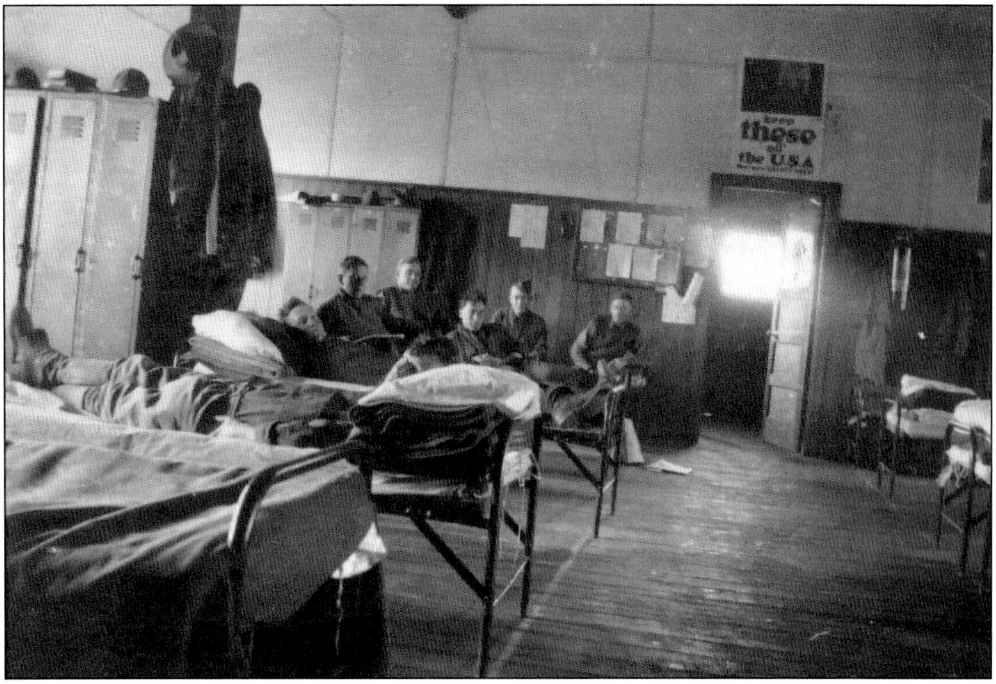

Flying cadets relax in one of the barracks buildings at Taylor Field. The poster above the door promotes the sale of Liberty Bonds. (Mark Pace collection.)

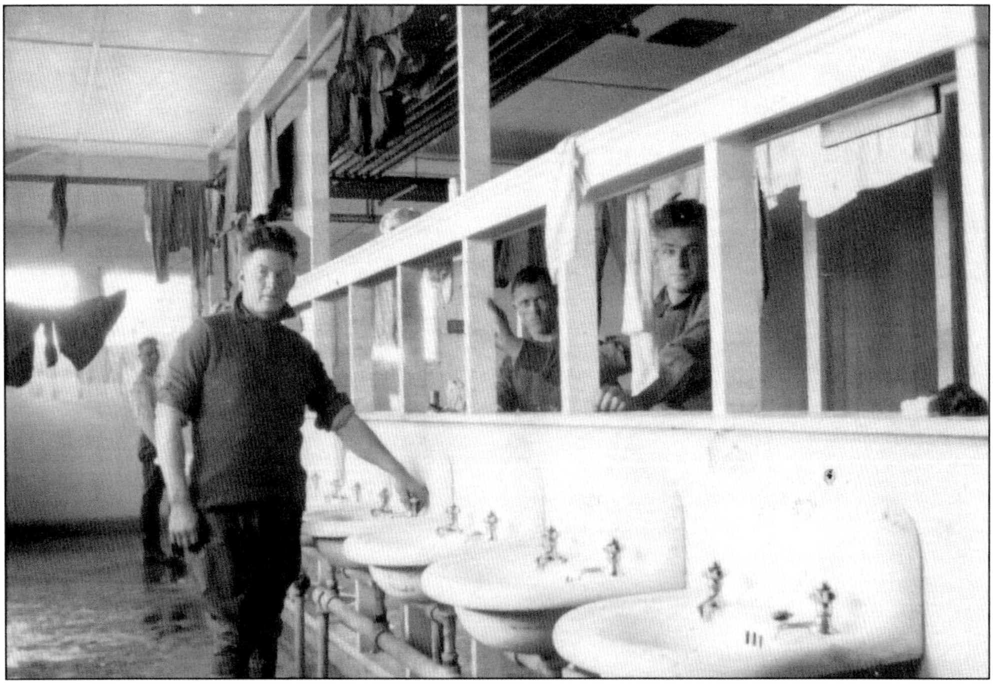

Taylor Field was described as being a "model little city with every city convenience." Running water and indoor plumbing were available at the field at a time when many residents of the surrounding area were not able to enjoy these luxuries. (Mark Pace Collection.)

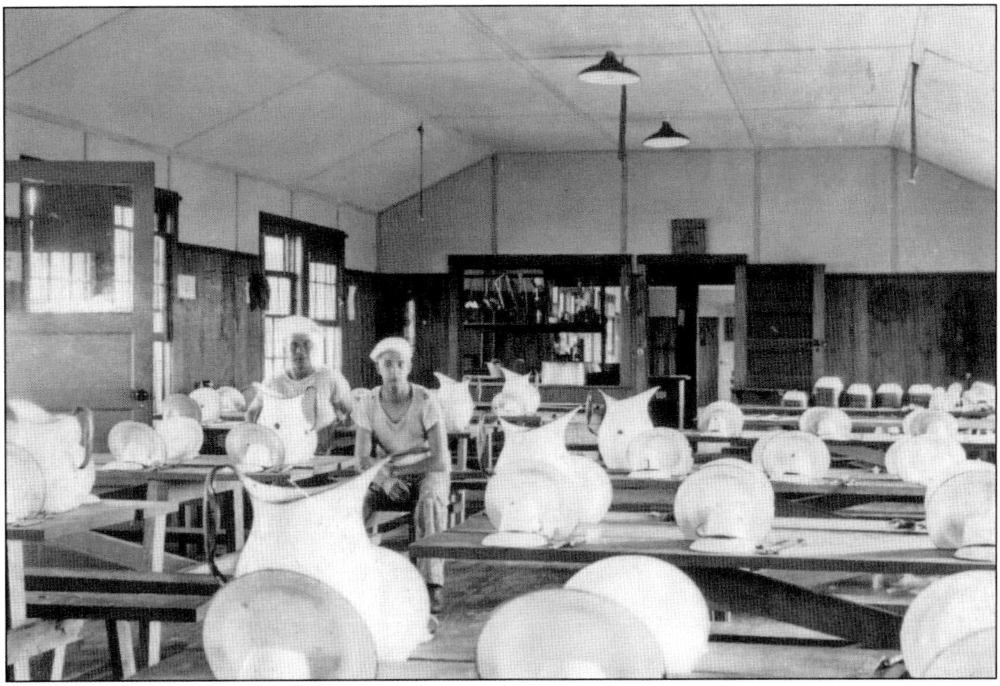

Members of the kitchen staff prepare the dining area to serve personnel of Taylor Field. (Mark Pace collection.)

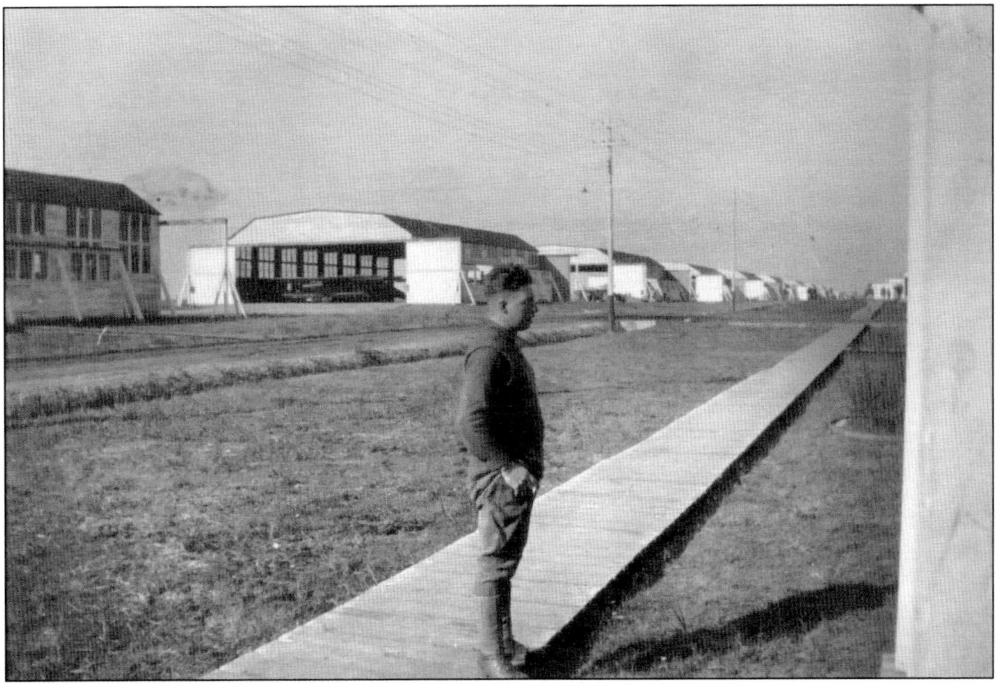

An aviation cadet stands along the wooden walkway located between the hangar line and other buildings on Taylor Field. (Mark Pace collection.)

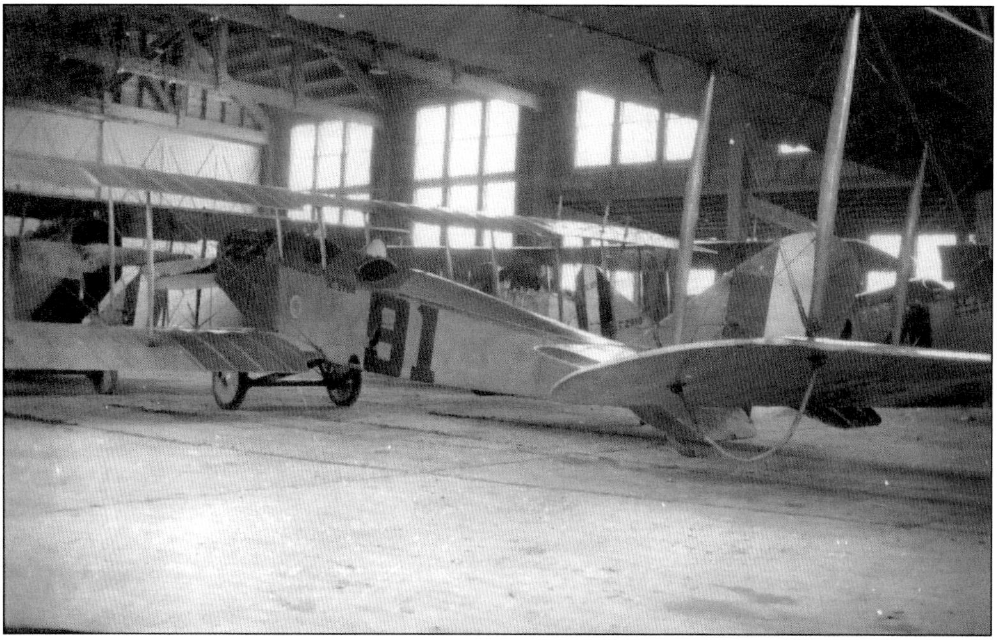

The training aircraft assigned to Taylor Field were stored in 16 large, wood-frame hangars built on concrete foundations. Each hangar had enough floor space to store several aircraft. Multiple window sections provided an abundance of natural lighting. Large sliding doors were installed at each end of the hangar to facilitate the movement of airplanes to or from the structure. (Mark Pace collection.)

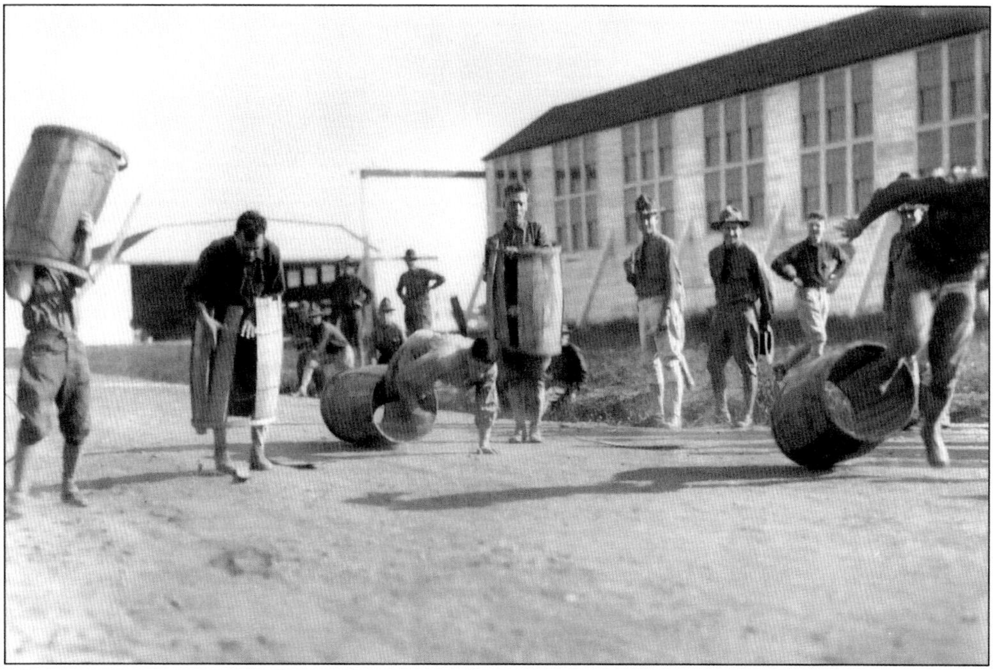

The training course at Taylor Field was not all work and no play. Cadets take time for some old-fashioned fun with barrel races along one of the service roads adjacent to the hangar row. Some of the cadets appear to be having trouble with their barrels. (Air University Office of History.)

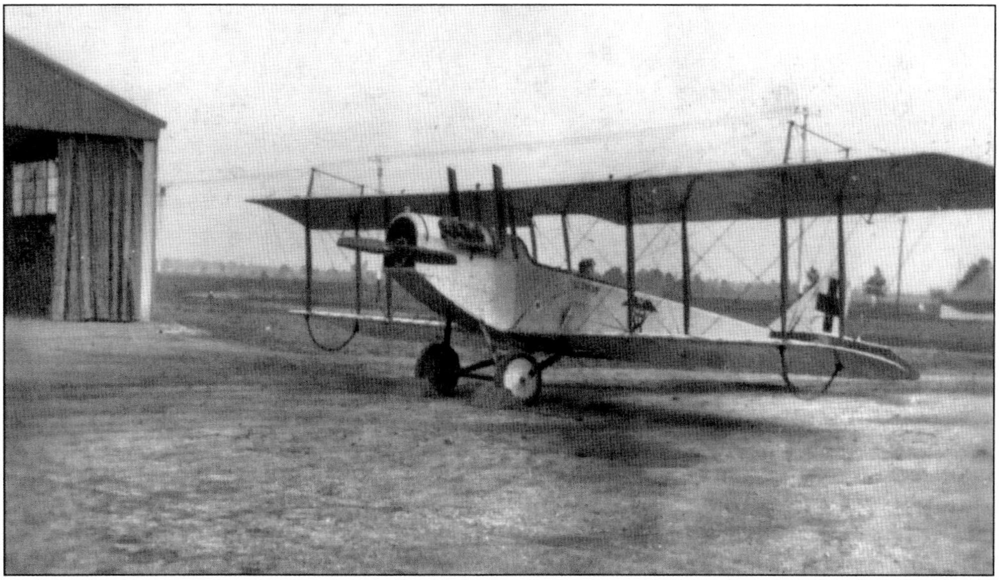

This Curtiss JN-4D Jenny has been converted into a hospital ship. These modified aircraft were painted white and kept at the training fields in case of emergencies. The rear deck behind the cockpit would be removed and the patient placed on a stretcher mounted in the fuselage. This aircraft has vertical exhaust stacks behind the engine to keep exhaust fumes out of the face of the pilot. (Mark Pace collection.)

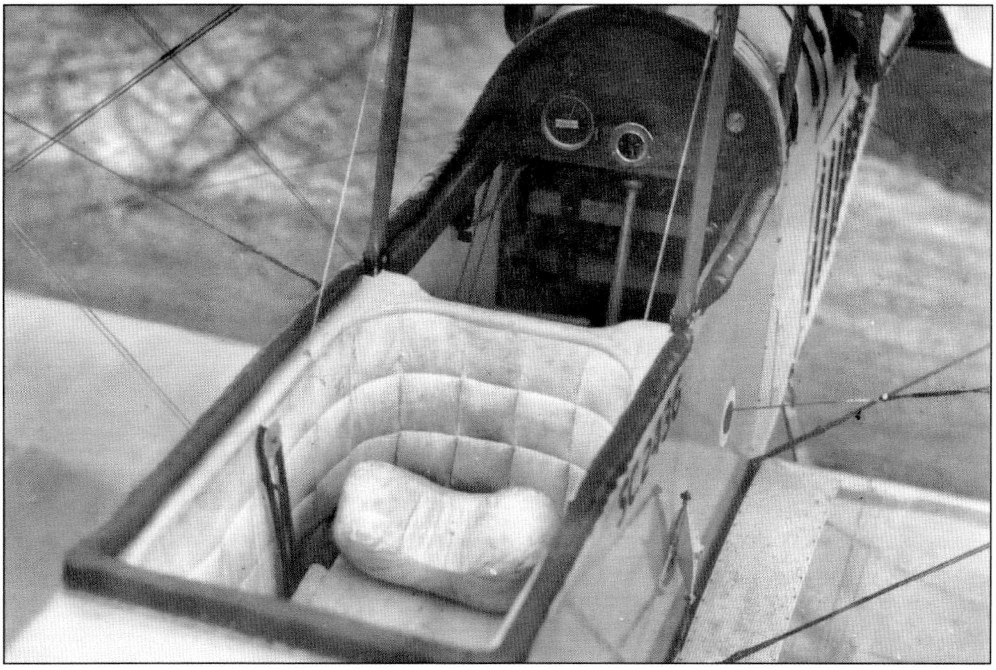

The instrument panel of the Jenny contained five instruments: an altimeter, airspeed indicator, water-temperature and oil-pressure gauges, and tachometer. The control stick, visible in the center of the cockpit below the instrument panel, is similar in appearance to a baseball bat. This Jenny has been converted into a hospital ship, complete with a stretcher and headrest in what was formerly the rear cockpit. (Air University Office of History.)

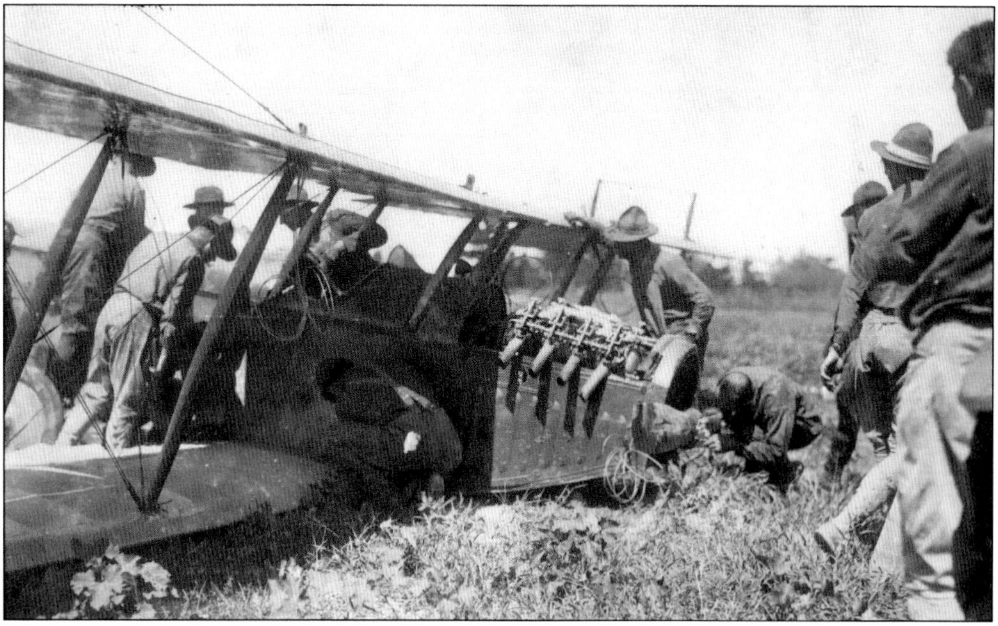

The combination of inexperienced cadets and underpowered aircraft often resulted in accidents. Damaged aircraft were repaired at woodworking shops on Taylor Field or the Montgomery depot. Mechanics could fabricate or repair almost every wooden part of the airplane, including the propeller and internal components of the wing and fuselage. Aircraft damaged beyond repair would be salvaged for serviceable parts to be used on other aircraft. (Mark Pace collection.)

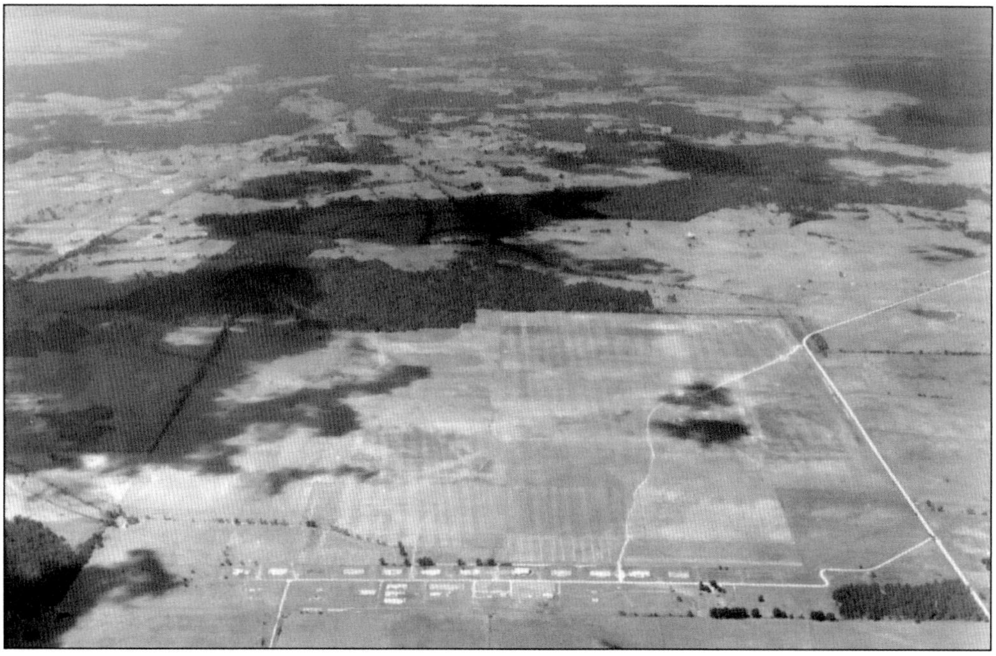

Taylor Field was closed in April 1919, after less than two years of operation. The field was utilized again during the Second World War as Gunter Auxiliary Landing Field No. 5. It was closed for a second and final time in July 1946, and the property was returned to the original owners. (USAFHRA.)

Three

Gunter Field

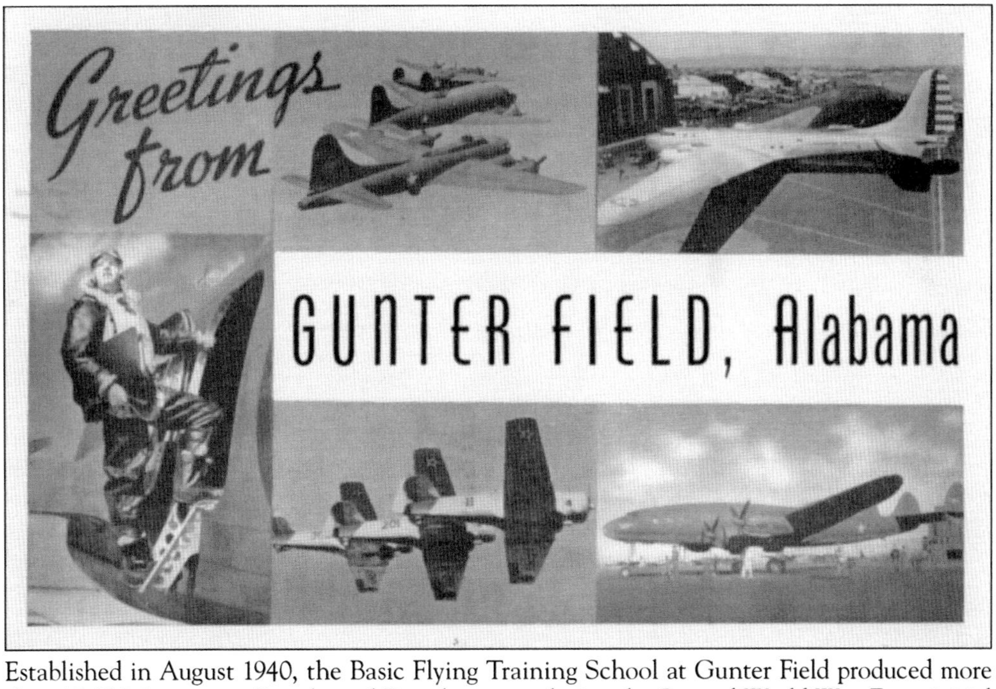

Established in August 1940, the Basic Flying Training School at Gunter Field produced more than 12,000 American, British, and French airmen during the Second World War. From initial construction to termination of the training program, the history of the school spanned a period of less than five years, but it represented one of the most remarkable periods in the history of aviation in Montgomery. (Author's collection.)

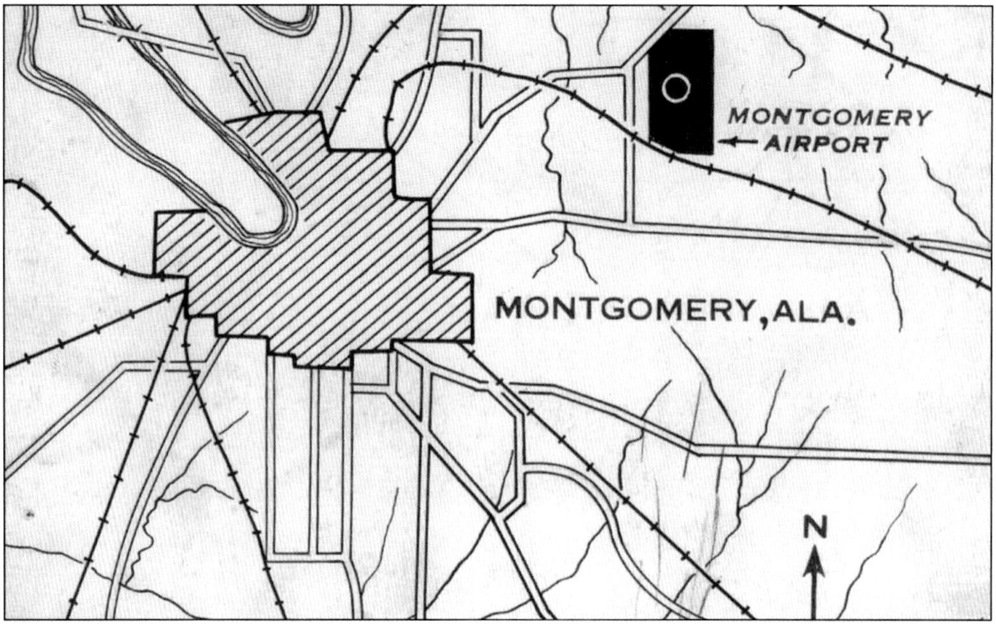

Dedicated in August 1929, the Montgomery Municipal Airport was located three miles northeast of the city on the Upper Wetumpka Road. Determined to develop commercial aviation in the city, Mayor William A. Gunter believed construction of a municipal airport would attract passenger and airmail service to Montgomery. (Alabama Department of Archives and History, Montgomery, Alabama.)

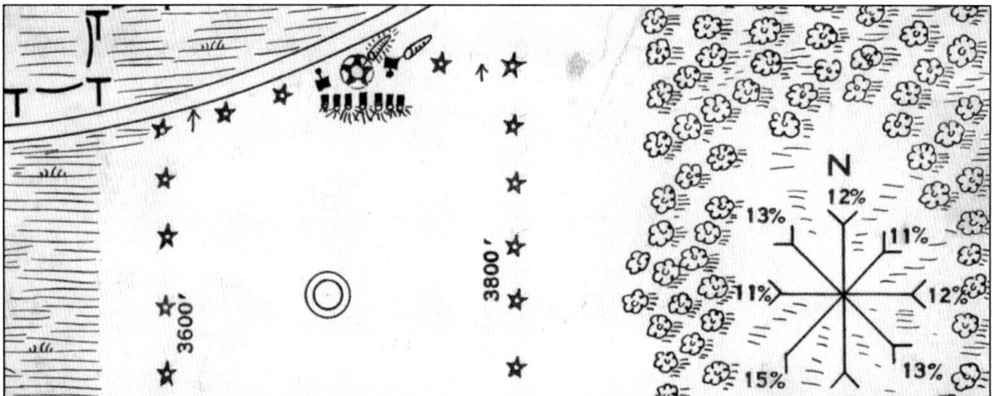

The 600-acre municipal airport consisted of a sod landing area with a white circular field marker located in the center. Beacon, boundary, obstruction, and landing area floodlights for night operations were available on request. Since Maxwell Field was not lighted, military aviators would use the municipal airport to fulfill their night-flying requirements. (Alabama Department of Archives and History, Montgomery, Alabama.)

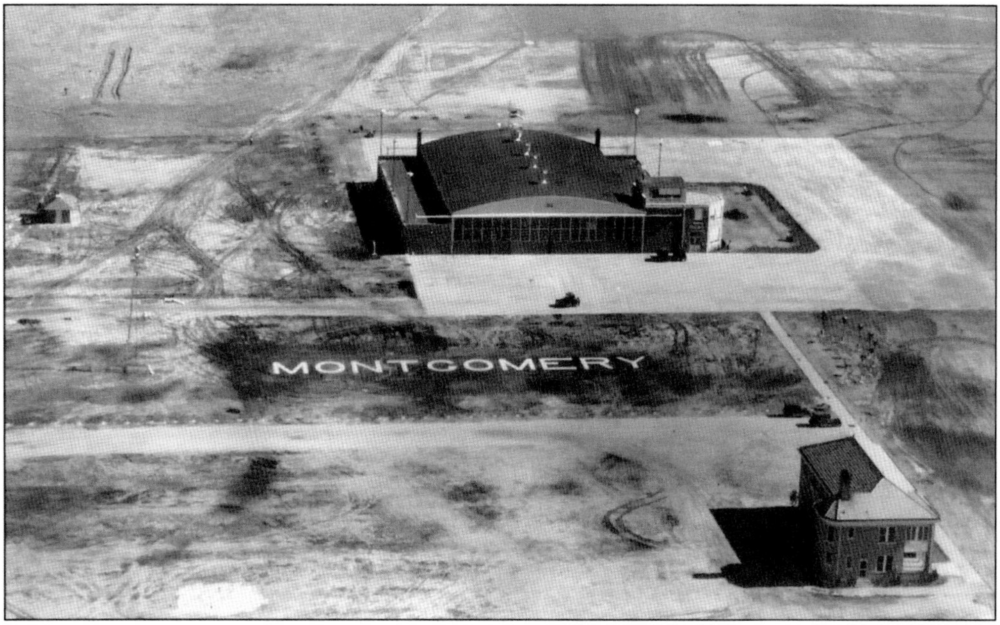

The municipal hangar was located on the northern edge of the flying field. A two-story brick-veneer building located adjacent to the hangar served as a hotel and restaurant for transient pilots and passengers. The name of the city is prominently displayed to assist pilots flying overhead in verifying their geographical position. Today these structures are located in the Gunter Industrial Complex. (Air University Office of History.)

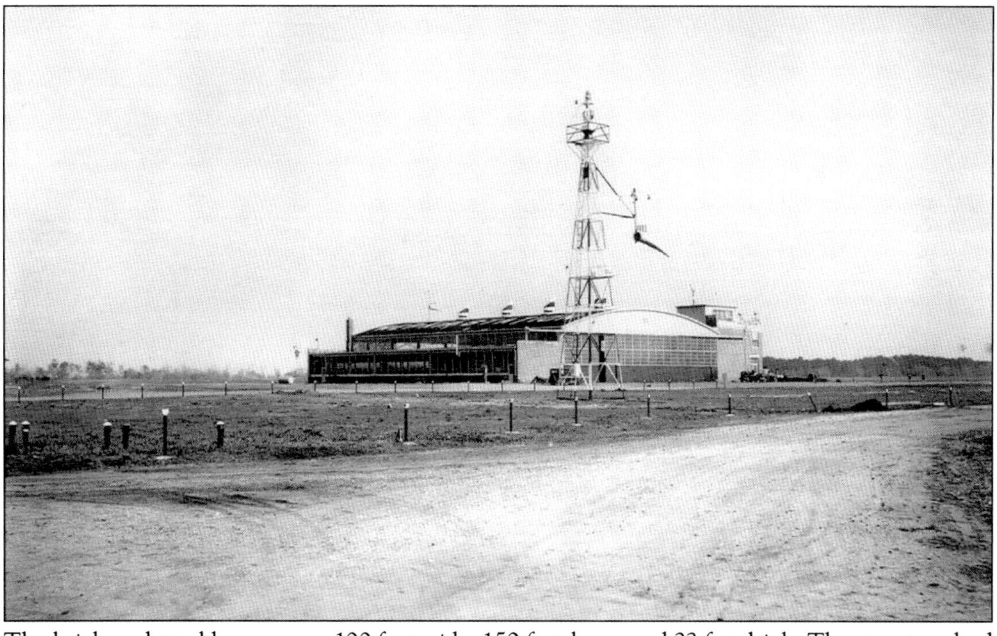

The brick-and-steel hangar was 100 feet wide, 150 feet long, and 22 feet high. The structure had additional rooms attached to both sides for use as workshops, classrooms, and offices. An aerial beacon assisted pilots in locating the field at night. A wind cone mounted on the beacon tower was used in determining wind direction and velocity. (Alabama Department of Archives and History, Montgomery, Alabama.)

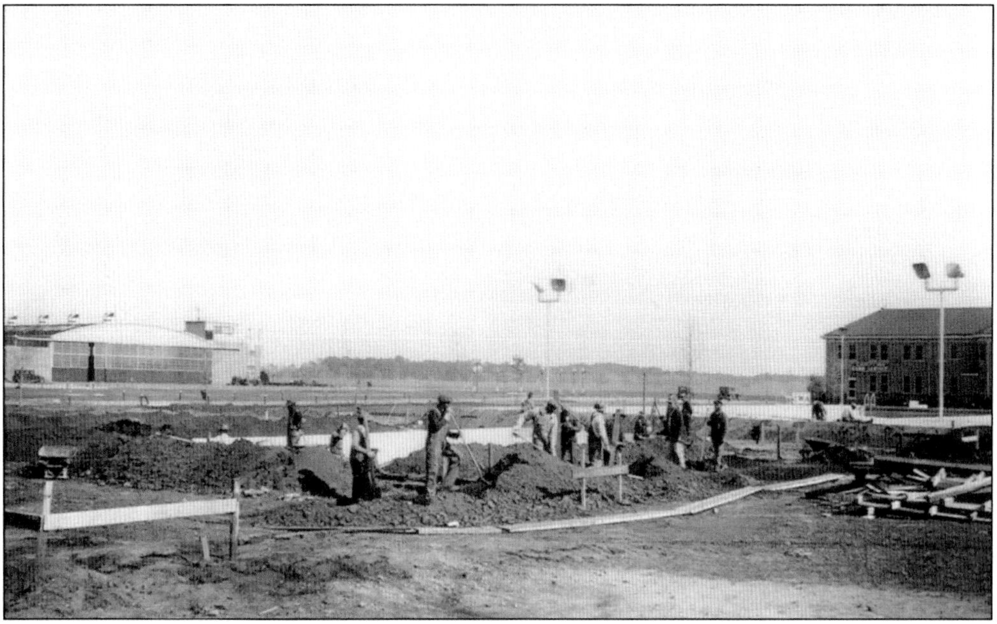

Combining aeronautical and recreational facilities in a central location allowed the Montgomery Municipal Airport to be of interest and service to the entire community. This design preceded the Alabama Air Park Plan, in which community swimming pools, golf courses, and other recreational activities were included in the airport layout. (Alabama Department of Archives and History, Montgomery, Alabama.)

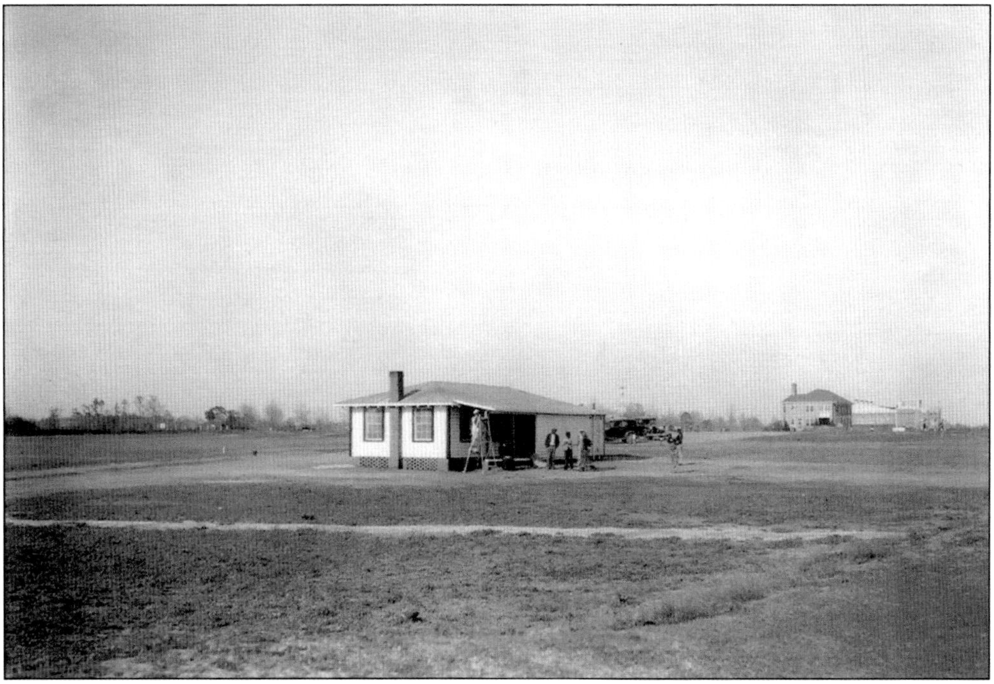

An 18-hole golf course was located adjacent to the flying field. The hotel building and hangar are visible behind the caddy house. (Alabama Department of Archives and History, Montgomery, Alabama.)

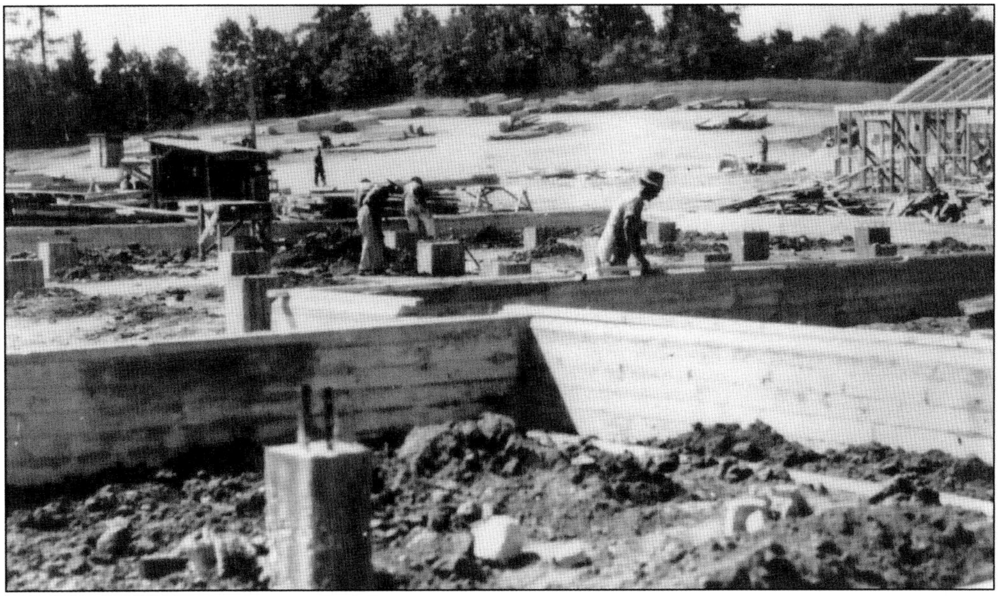

In August 1940, the federal government entered into an agreement with the City of Montgomery to lease the municipal airport for the establishment of an Army Air Corps basic flying training school. Initial plans designated 54 buildings, including barracks, officer's quarters, mess halls, and classrooms. Civilian workers employed through the Works Progress Administration labored as carpenters, plumbers, painters, and in other capacities during construction. (Air University Office of History.)

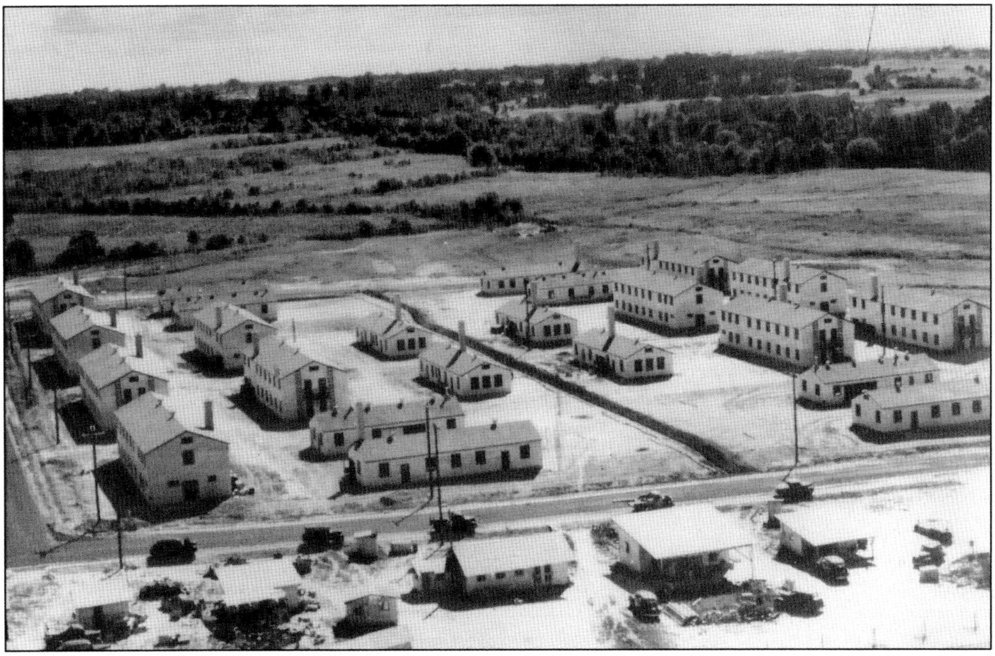

Projected strength of the new flying school included 63 officers, 316 cadets, and 1,073 enlisted men. Subsequent revisions to this requirement increased the number of military personnel on the base. Construction of additional barracks, officers' quarters, and other buildings was required to accommodate the increase in personnel. (Air University Office of History.)

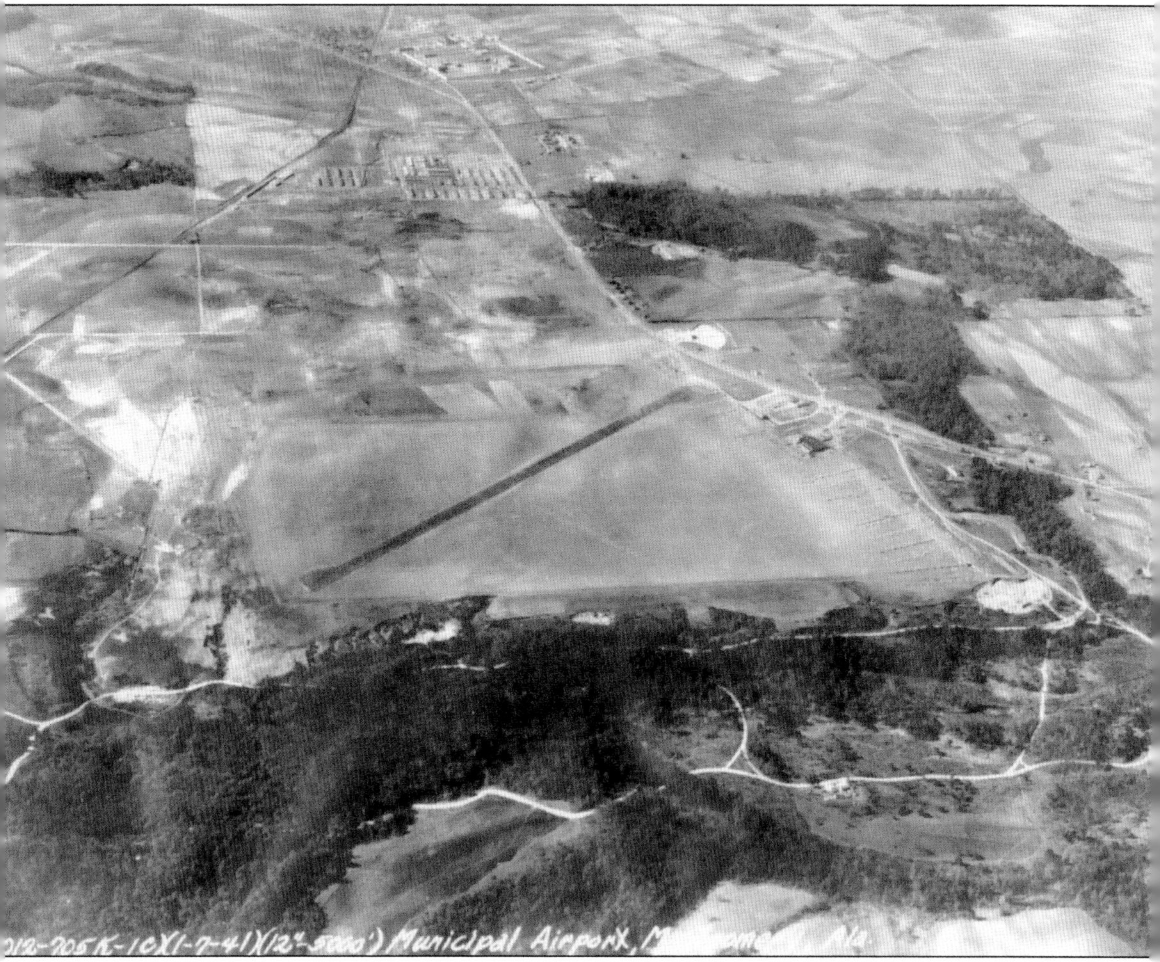

A 1941 aerial view of the former municipal airport shows the macadam runway that had been completed three years earlier. The 3,500-foot runway was orientated in a northwest-southeast direction. The need for a hard-surface runway became evident when Eastern Air Lines refused to operate newer Douglas DC-3 aircraft on the sod landing area. After the military leased the municipal airport site, Eastern was allowed to continue using the field to provide passenger and airmail service to the city. As training activity increased, the field became too congested to permit regular commercial airline operations. Eastern was allowed to use some of the facilities at Maxwell Field to prevent a disruption of air service. (USAFHRA.)

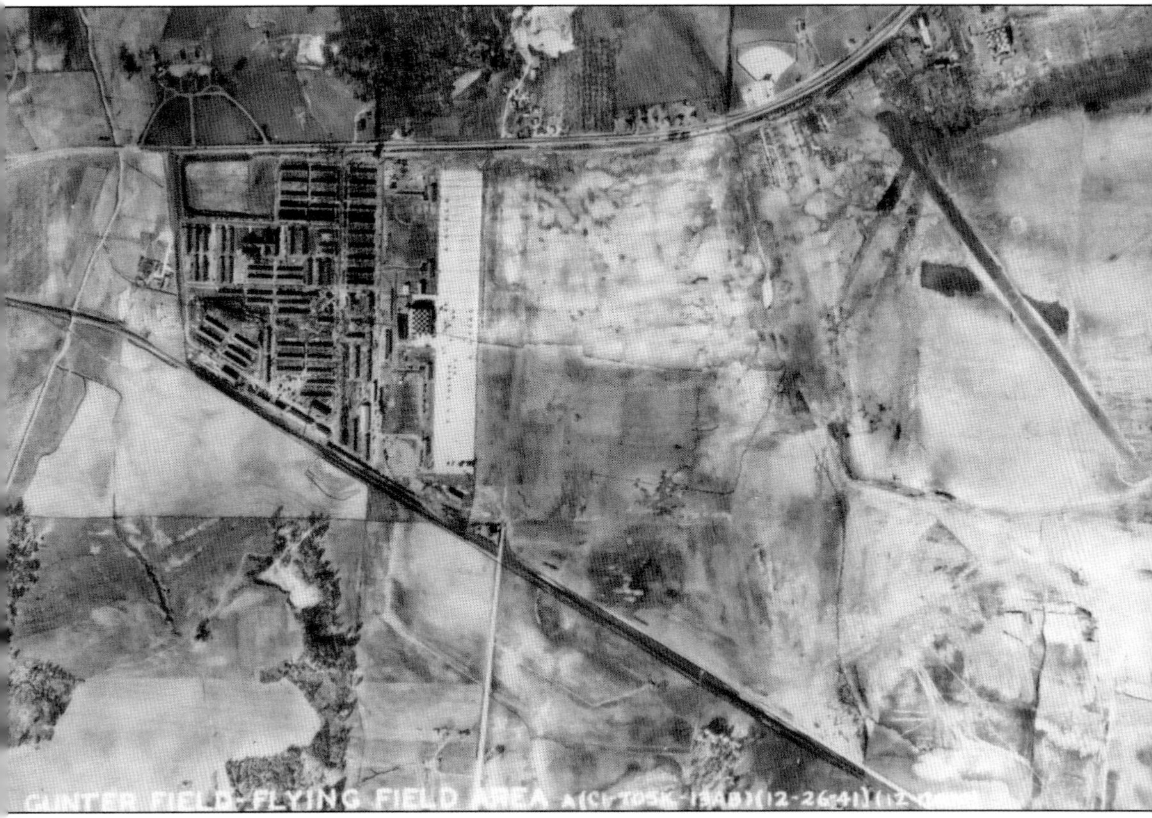

By July 1941, construction of the basic flying school at Gunter Field was essentially completed. In less than one year, the former municipal airport had been converted into a military airfield. During preparation of the flying field, grading machines were shutdown only long enough for refueling, lubrication, and to change operators. The paved runway of the former municipal airport is visible in the right-hand portion of this image. Eventually the field would contain four paved runways: the original northwest-southeast runway, an east-west runway, and two parallel north-south strips. Today the Gunter industrial complex is located on the former system of runways. (USAFHRA.)

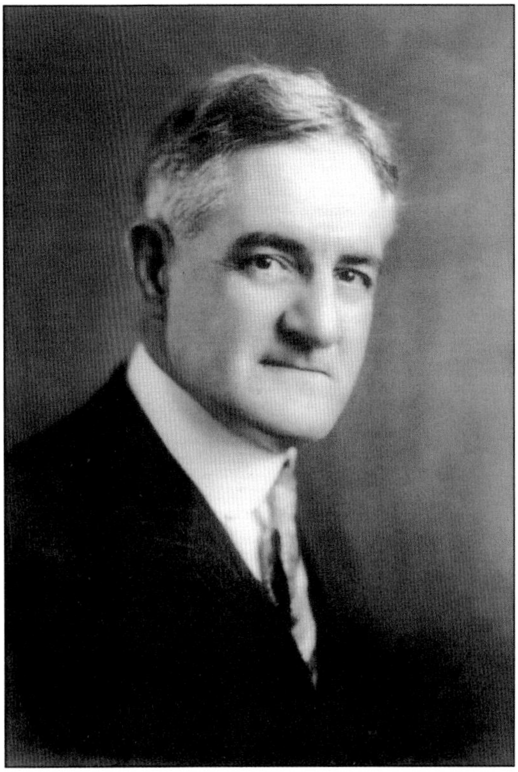

Mayor William Adams Gunter was a strong proponent of aviation and was instrumental in the development of the Montgomery Municipal Airport. During his 27-year career as mayor, Gunter worked tirelessly to promote and support aviation in the city. After his death in December 1940, the former municipal airport was named in his honor. (Alabama Department of Archives and History, Montgomery, Alabama.)

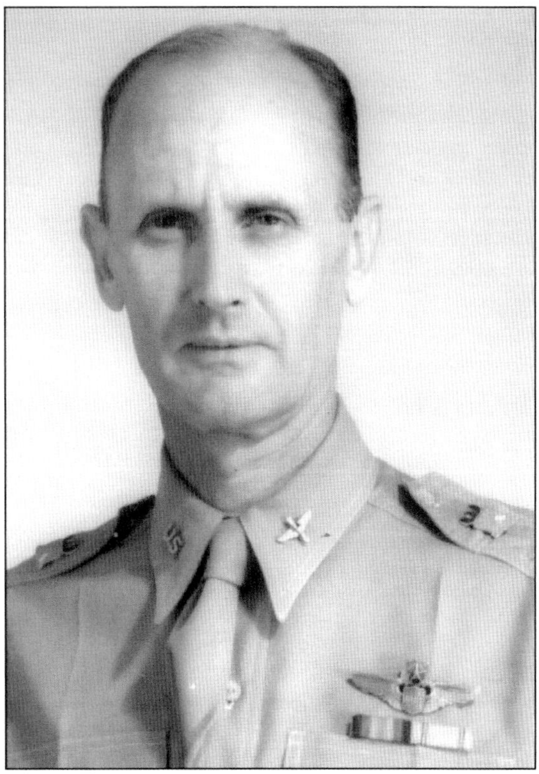

Aubrey Thomas Hornsby was born in Eclectic, Alabama. During the First World War, Hornsby served as an aerial observer with the American Expeditionary Forces in Europe. In 1940, Colonel Hornsby was appointed to supervise the conversion of the Montgomery Municipal Airport into an Army Air Corps basic flying school. He would later serve as the first base commander of Gunter Field. (USAFHRA.)

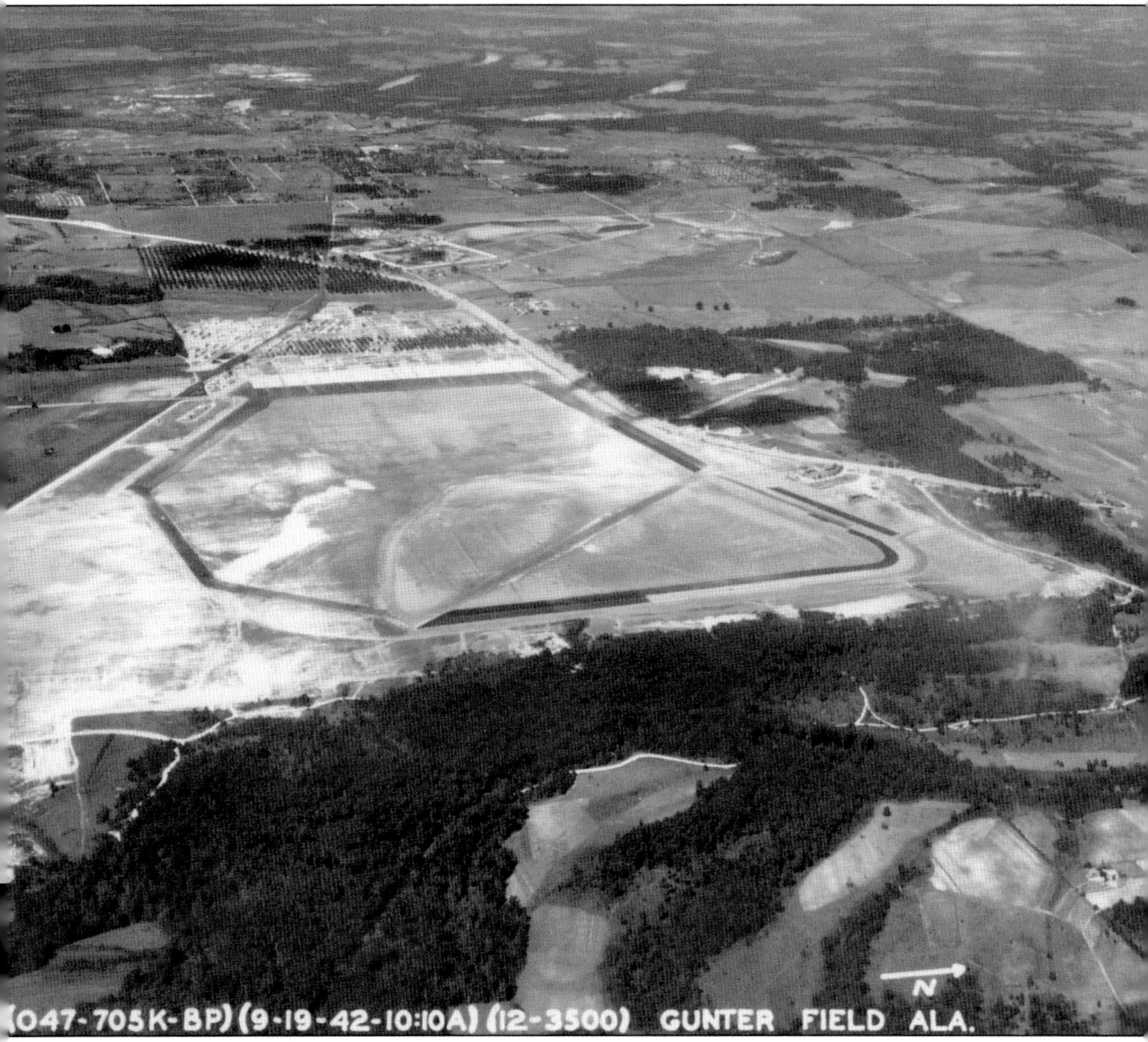

In July 1942, the federal government entered into a lease with the City of Montgomery for an additional 200 acres of land for the expansion of Gunter Field. This increased the size of the post to approximately 1,150 acres. In this September 1942 aerial view of the post, the surface area of the flying field had been expanded to more than two times its original size, and permanent structures built to accommodate military personnel had been erected on the western edge of the field. The macadam runway of the original municipal airport transverses the eastern corner of the flying field. In April 1971, the federal government returned 771 acres of land to the City of Montgomery. This parcel included the former site of the municipal airport. (USAFHRA.)

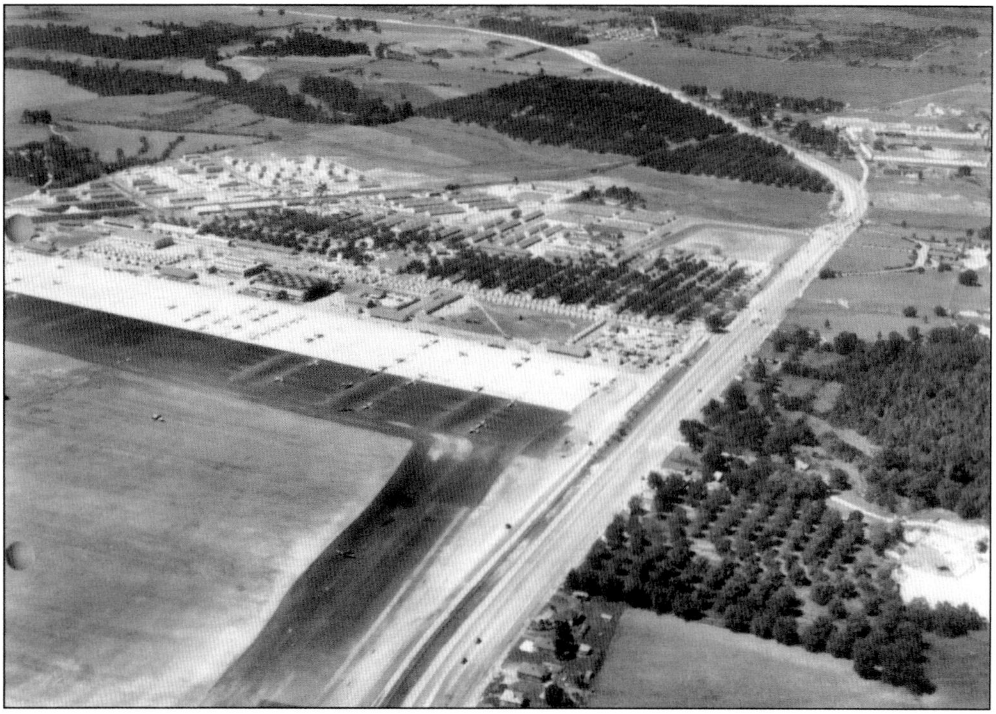

The building area at Gunter Field included administration buildings, classrooms, officer's quarters, mess halls, barracks, warehouses, a hospital, and other structures necessary to support the initial cadre of 2,000 men assigned to the base. The pecan grove visible in the building area was saved by careful planning during construction of the facility. The Upper Wetumpka Road bordered the field to the north. (USAFHRA.)

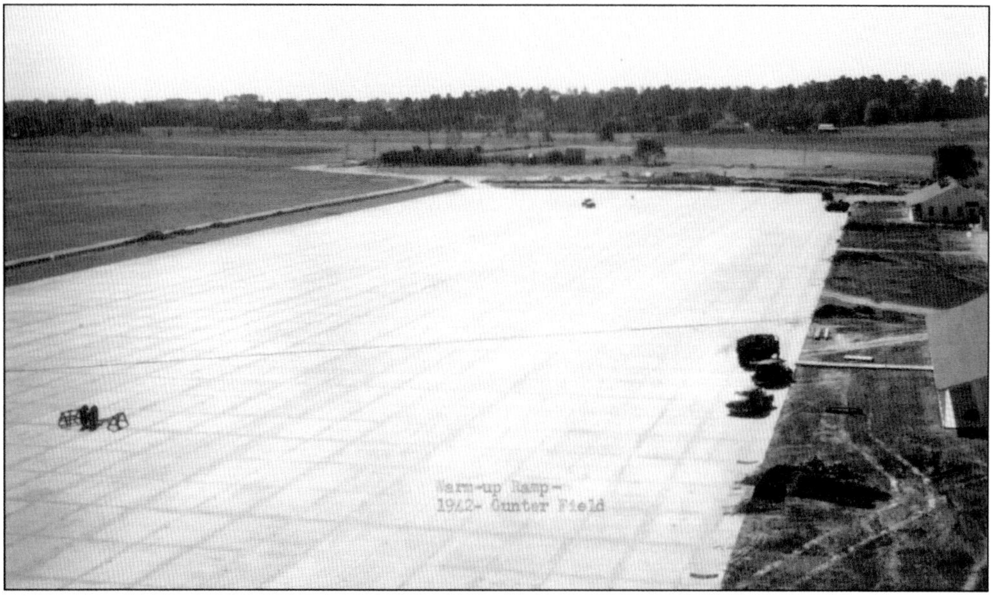

The concrete warm-up ramp, located adjacent to the flying field, provided an area for parking and routine maintenance of training aircraft based at Gunter Field. In 1944, during the peak of training activity, approximately 400 aircraft were assigned to the field. (USAFHRA.)

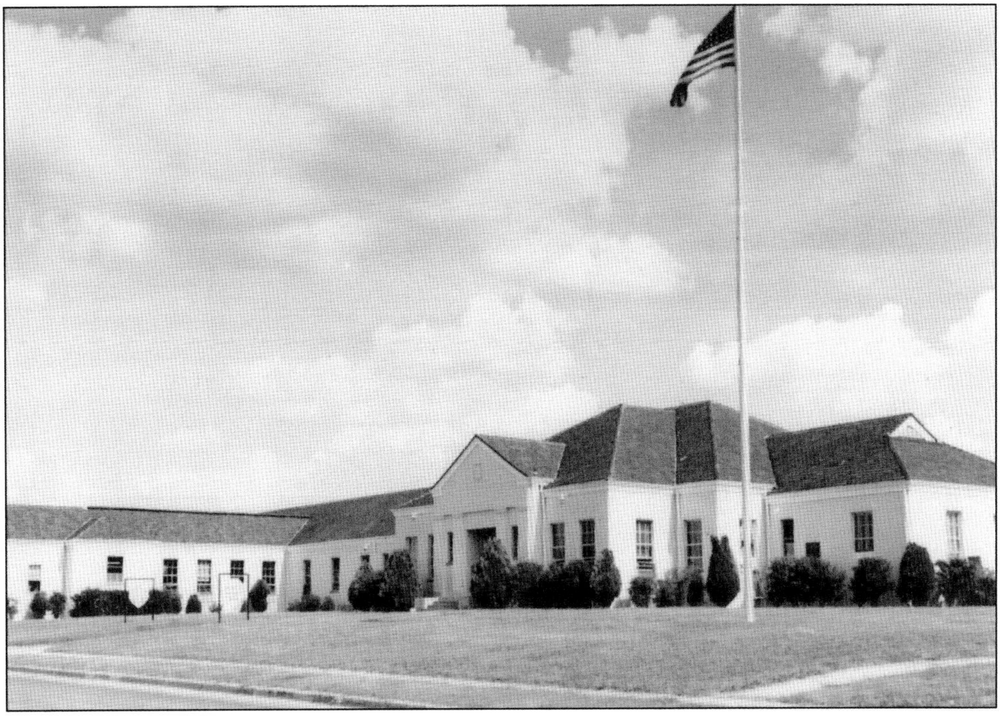

This building served as the Post Headquarters, United States Army Air Forces Basic Flying School, Gunter Field. (USAFHRA.)

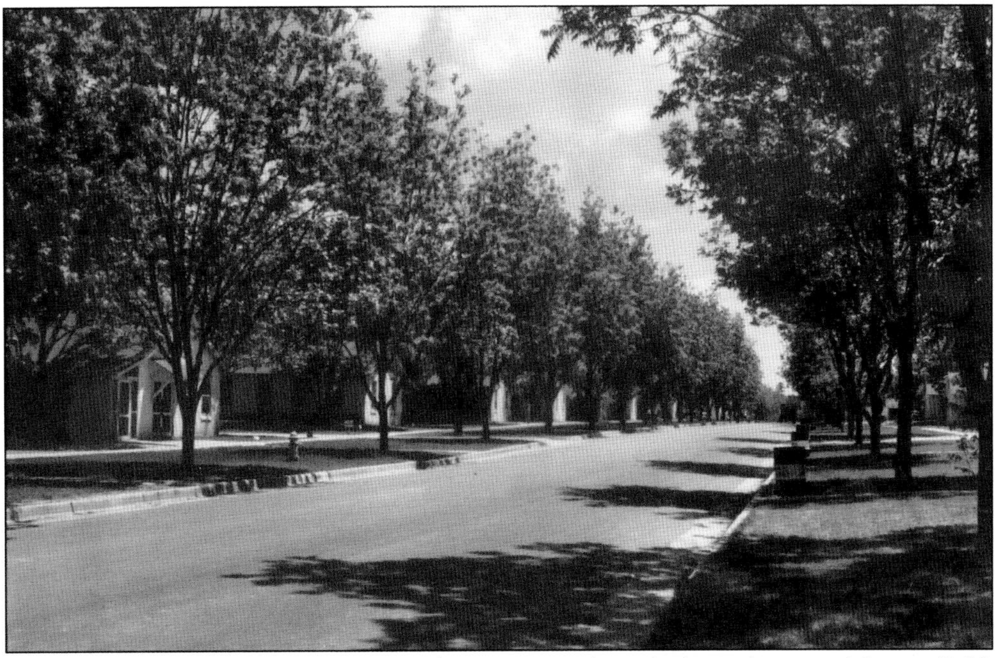

This 1943 photograph illustrates a typical street scene along the barracks area of Gunter Field. During construction, Colonel Hornsby, project officer at the field, directed that buildings be laid out in a manner that preserved the magnificent rows of pecan trees. Because of this effort, only six pecan trees were taken down during construction. (USAFHRA.)

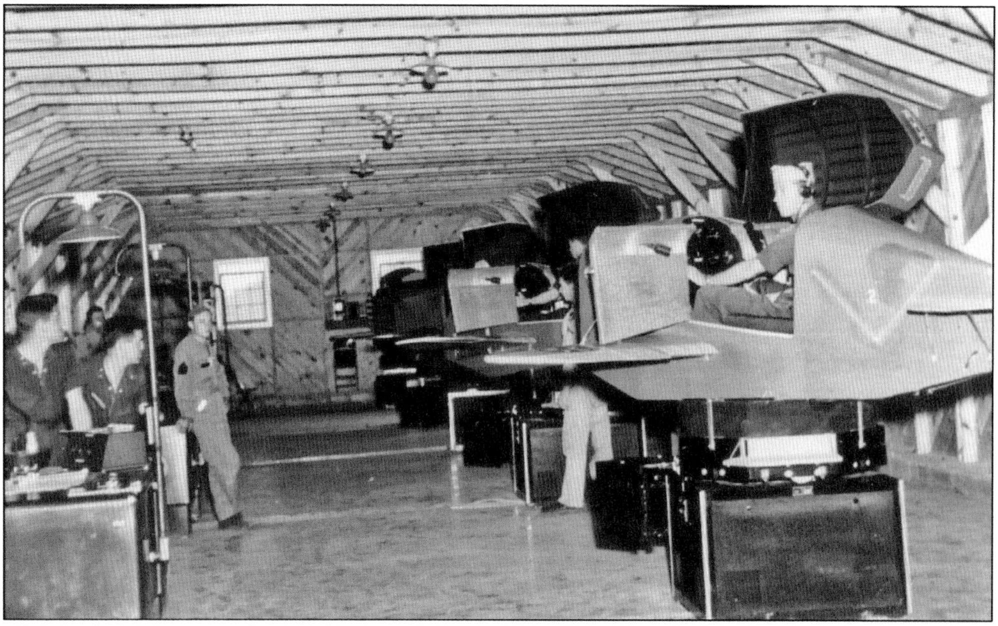

The Link trainer was designed to provide cadets with the ability to maneuver and navigate an airplane solely by reference to cockpit flight instruments. Seated in the trainer, a hood was pulled over the student to simulate reduced-visibility conditions. At a workstation nearby, the instructor would create navigation problems for students to solve using only the navigation and flight instruments in the Link device. (USAFHRA.)

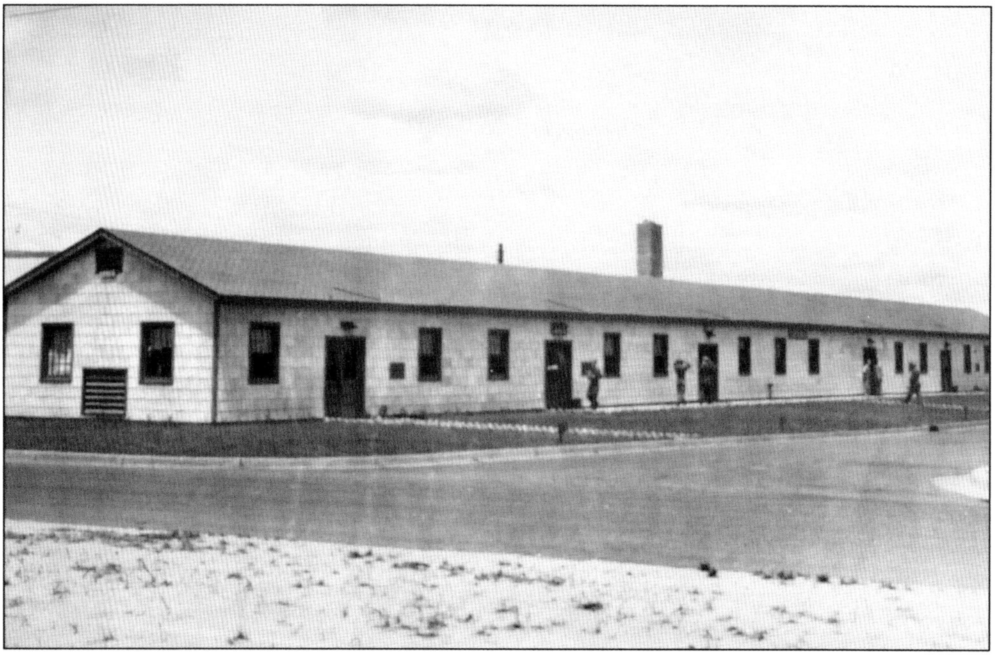

In November 1941, the Link trainer became part of the basic flying training program at Gunter Field. Initially the Link trainer building held only three of the training devices. In December 1941, a school for Link trainer instructors was opened at the field, and by December 1944, eighteen of the devices were in use. (USAFHRA.)

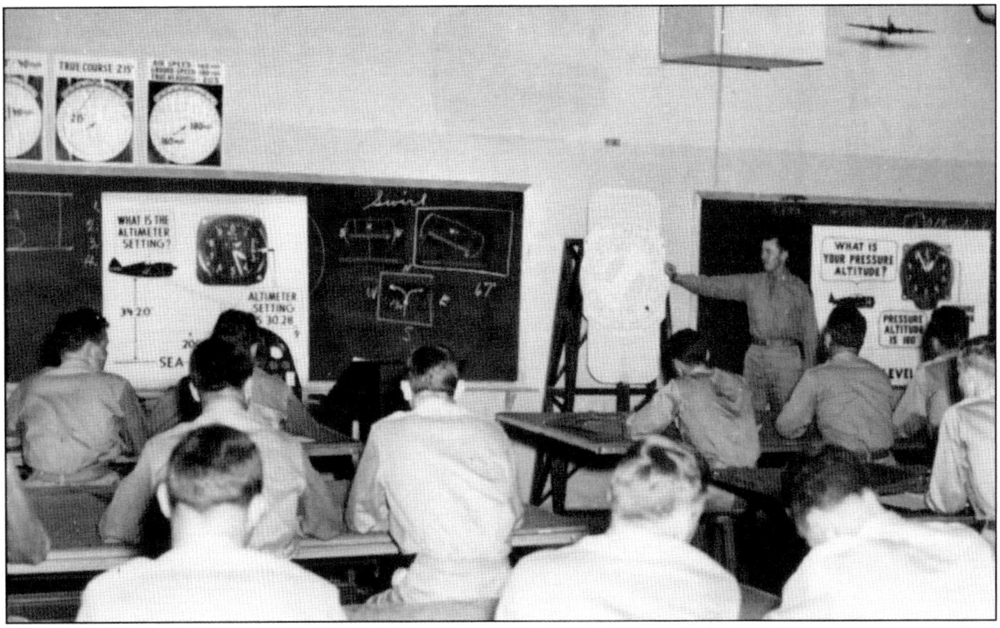

In addition to flight training, academics were an important part of the training program. Cadets completed ground-school courses in navigation, meteorology, radio communication and code, aircraft systems, and engine operation. In this class, cadets receive instruction in aircraft flight instruments and navigation. A failure of any portion of ground or flight training resulted in the cadet being "washed-out" of the program. (USAFHRA.)

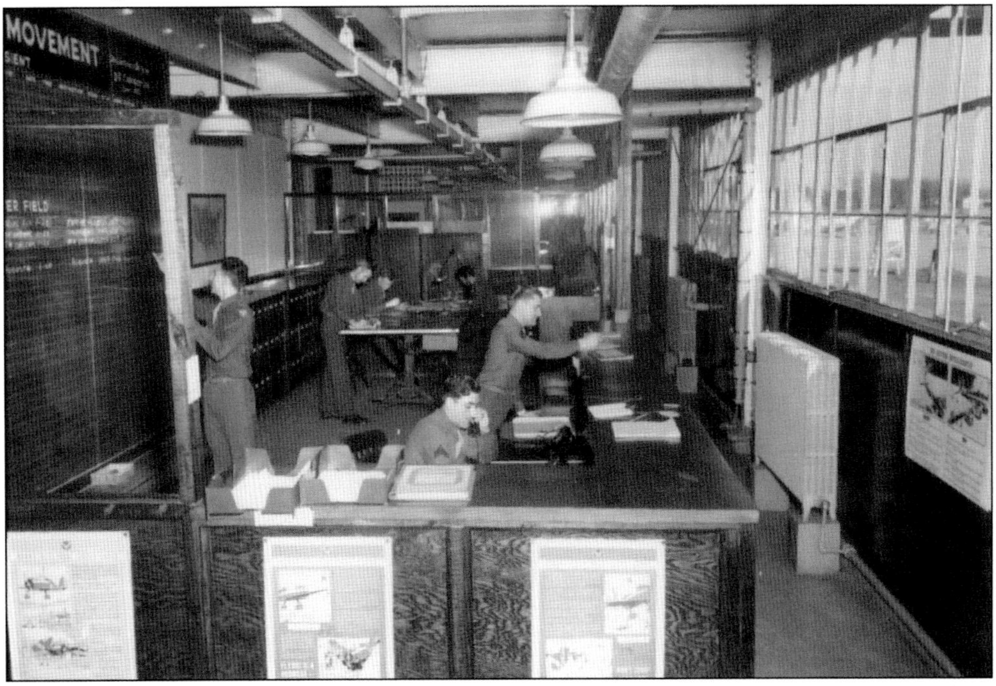

The Dispatch Office coordinated aircraft operations at Gunter Field and its associated auxiliary landing fields in the Montgomery area. With approximately 400 aircraft based at the field in 1944, there was seldom a lull in activity at the Dispatch Office. (USAFHRA.)

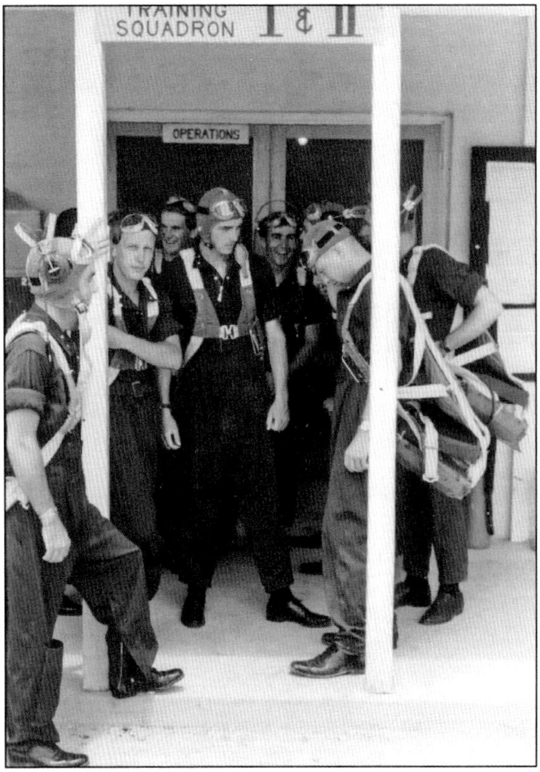

Aviation cadets of the Basic Flying Training School at Gunter Field gather outside of the operations building as they prepare for a training sortie. (USAFHRA.)

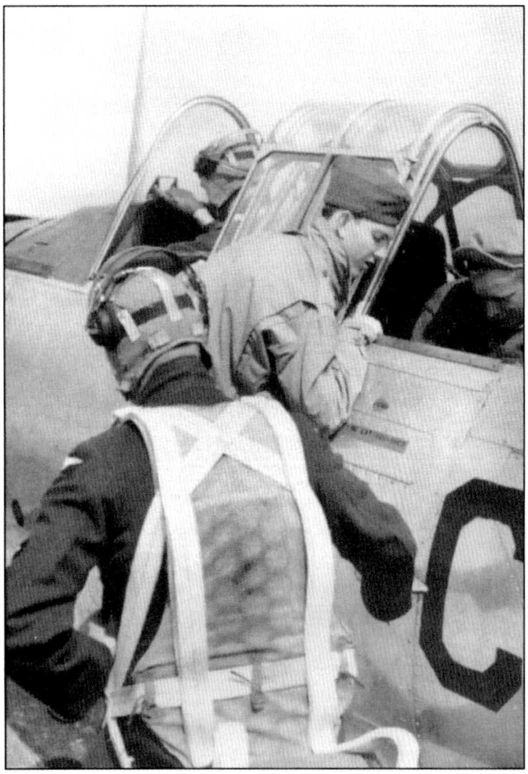

Members of the ground crew assist the student and instructor before a training flight. The BT-13A had a tandem seating arrangement, with the instructor normally occupying the rear cockpit. Both pilots wore a seat-type parachute in the event an in-flight emergency dictated its use. The 10-week basic flying course consisted of 70 hours of flight training. Cadets who successfully completed the basic course graduated to an advanced flying school. (USAFHRA.)

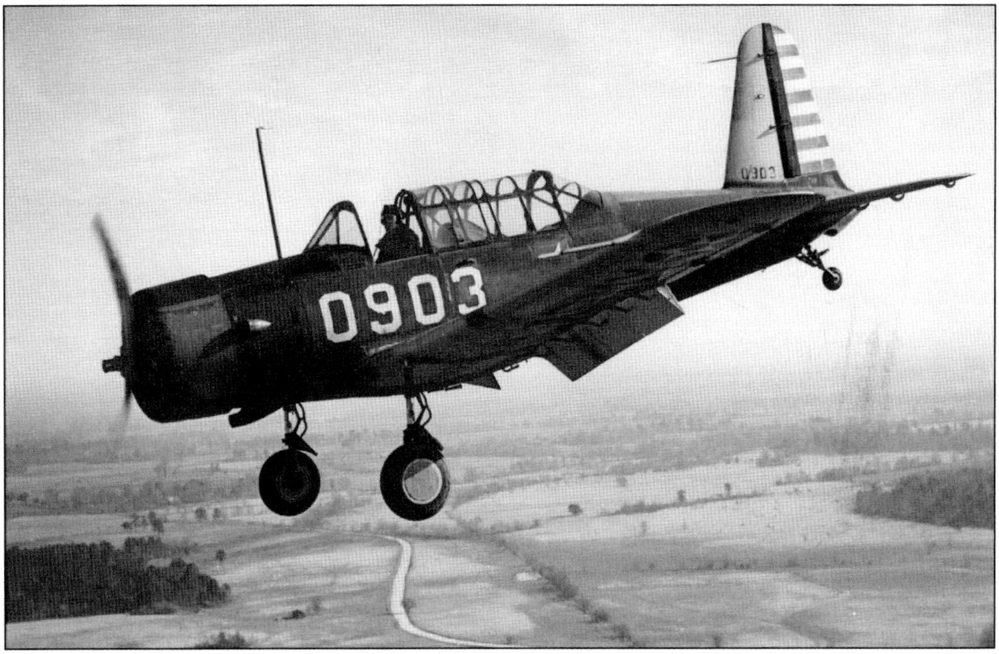

The primary training aircraft used at Gunter Field was the Vultee BT-13A Valiant. Powered by a 450-horsepower Pratt and Whitney Wasp engine, the aircraft had a top speed of 180 miles per hour. The aircraft was known by cadets as the "Vultee Vibrator" because of a tendency for the canopy to vibrate during certain maneuvers. (USAFHRA.)

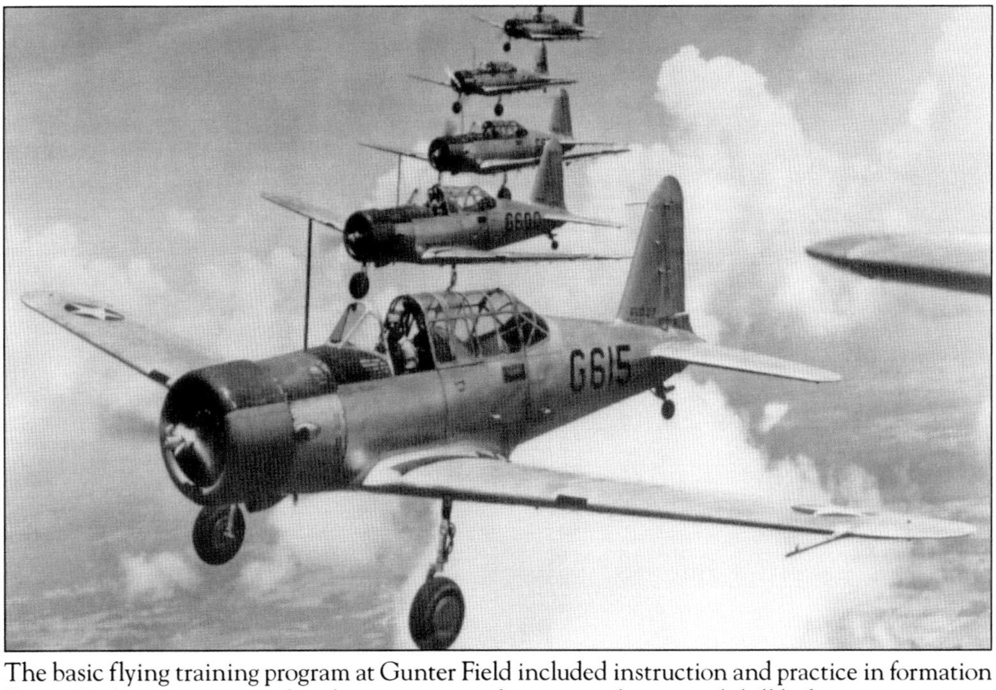

The basic flying training program at Gunter Field included instruction and practice in formation flying. Cadets were required to demonstrate proficiency in this critical skill before progressing to advanced flight training. Many cadets and instructors flew the BT-13A aircraft with the canopy open to ventilate the cockpit during the hot and humid summer months. (USAFHRA.)

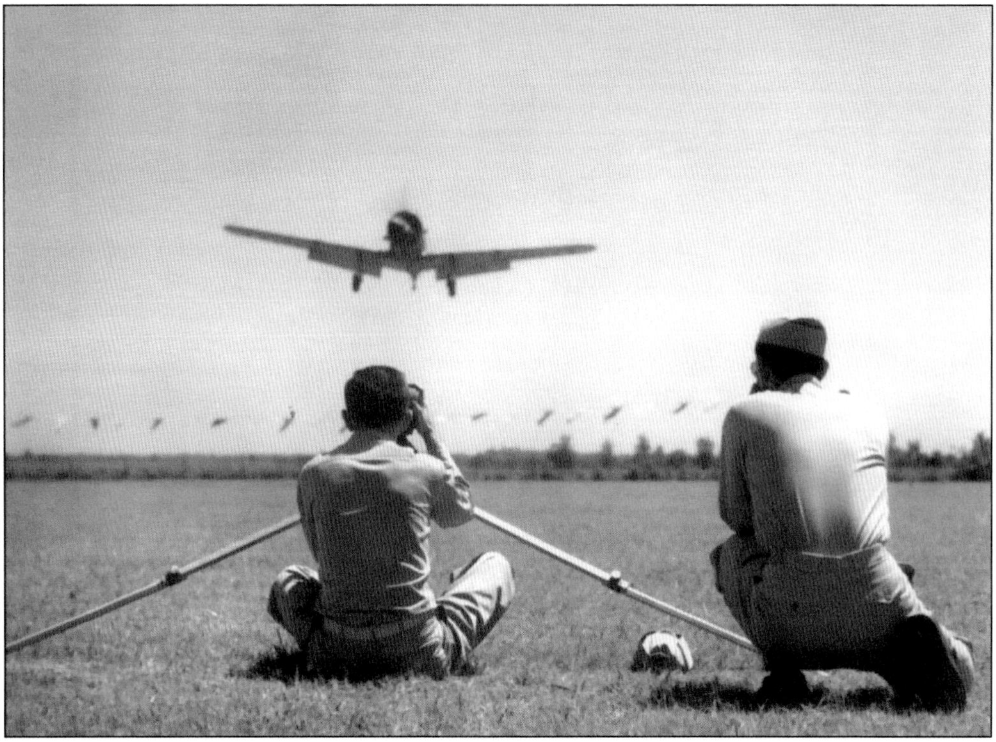

In addition to normal approaches and landings, cadets received instruction in landing over an obstacle, landing on a strange field, and forced landings. In the hurdle stages of landing practice, cadets were evaluated on their ability to fly over a simulated obstacle and land within a specified area. (USAFHRA.)

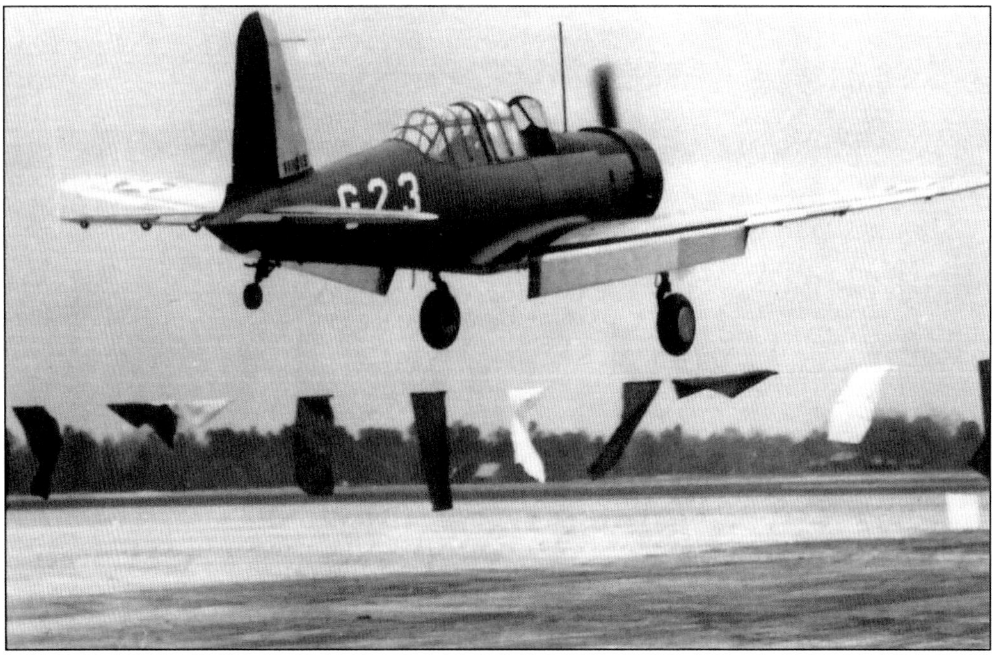

A cadet practices landings approaches over a simulated hurdle at Gunter Field. (USAFHRA.)

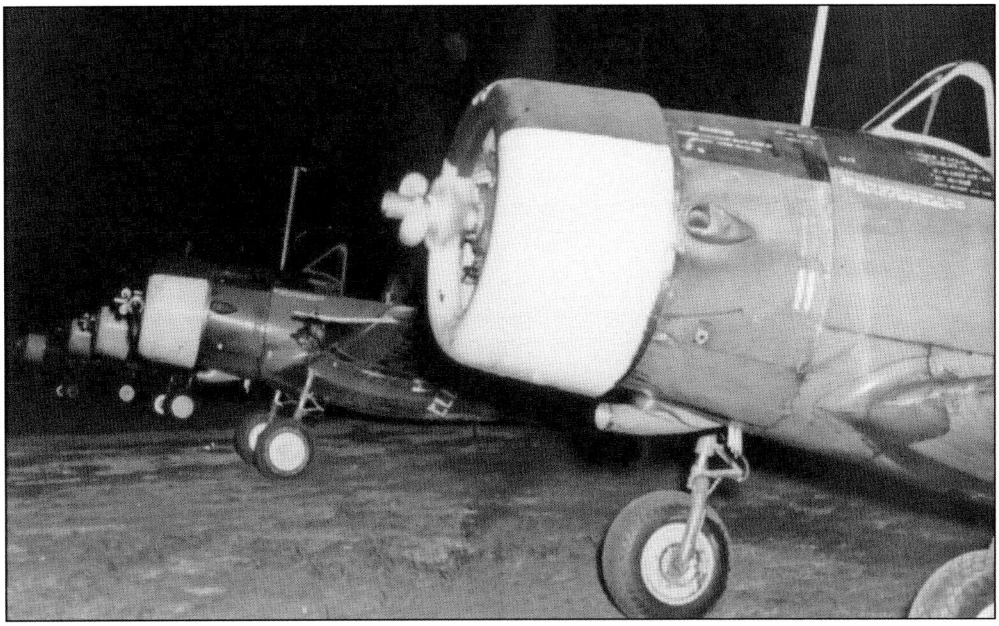

Cross-country flights at night could prove to be challenging and occasionally dangerous. In May 1942, a flight of 35 aircraft flown by United Kingdom students departed Gunter Field on a navigation training flight to Crestview and Mobile. Returning from Mobile on the last leg of the flight, the formation encountered heavy haze and rain showers. Twelve of the training aircraft crashed, resulting in the loss of seven pilots. (USAFHRA.)

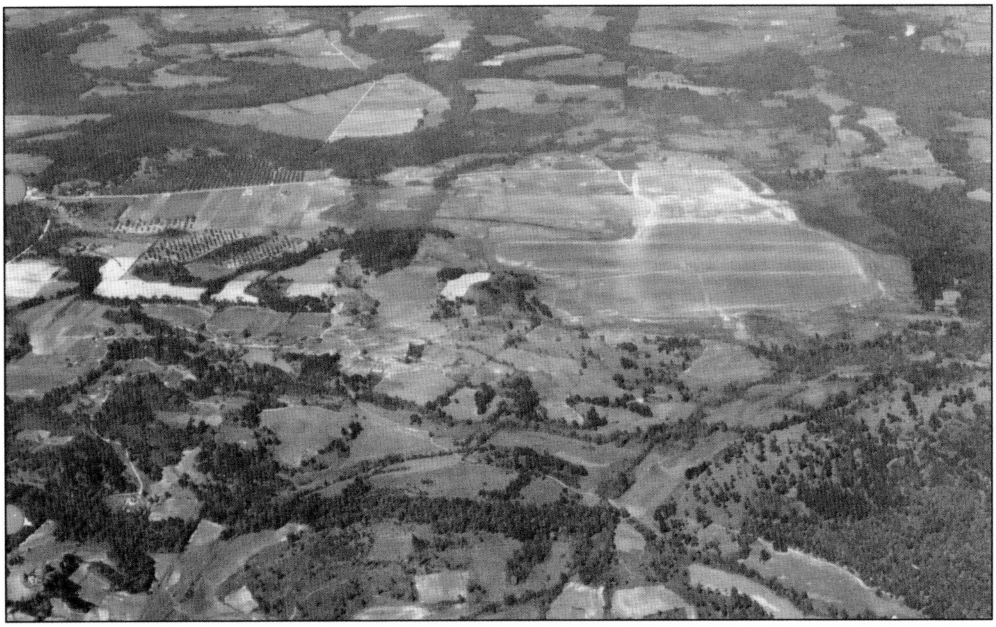

To reduce congestion at Gunter Field, five auxiliary fields were constructed in the Montgomery area. Taylor Field, the former First World War training site, was reopened after more than 20 years of inactivity. Additional fields included Shorter, Mount Meigs, McLemore, and the Elmore Field near Wetumpka. In 1943, the new Montgomery Municipal Airport, Dannelly Field, was utilized as an auxiliary field. (USAFHRA.)

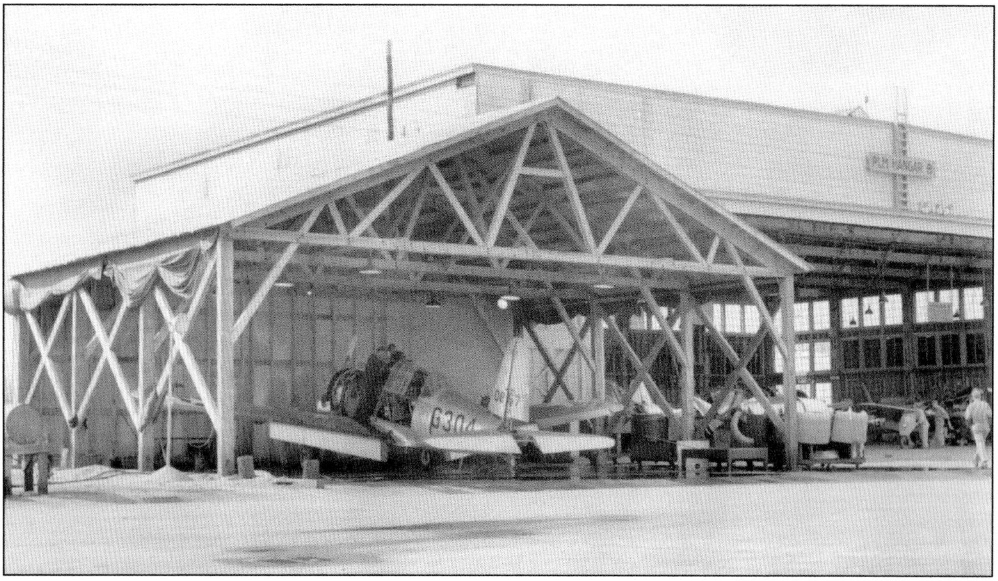

A BT-13A training aircraft is prepared for a periodic maintenance inspection. During this phase, all cowlings and inspection covers were removed from the engine compartment and fuselage. If necessary, aircraft radios were removed for inspection and overhaul in the Gunter Radio Shop. This stage of the inspection was performed by the 22nd Aviation Squadron under the supervision of their noncommissioned officers. (USAFHRA.)

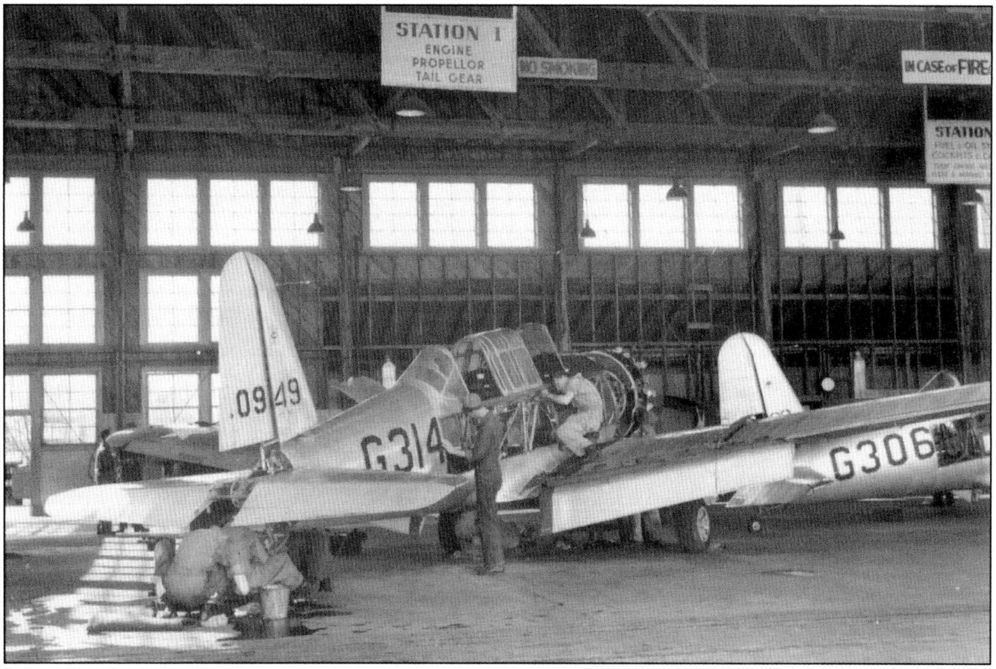

Periodic inspections of aircraft based at Gunter Field were conducted in the Production Line Maintenance hangar. At Station One, mechanics specializing in engines, propellers, and tail gear performed the required inspections and replaced worn parts. The BT-13 aircraft based at Gunter Field were highly utilized. Aircraft No. 311, assigned to the 86th School Squadron, was the first aircraft of this type to accumulate 1,000 hours of flying time. (USAFHRA.)

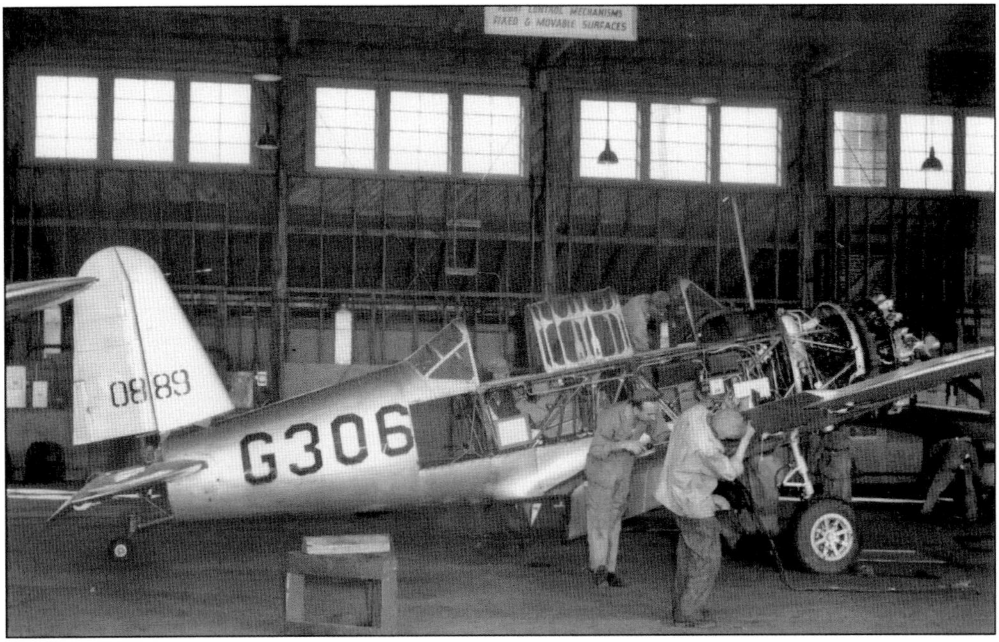

At Station Two, mechanics specializing in fuel and oil systems, cockpits and cabins, flight control mechanisms, and fixed and movable surfaces performed the required inspections and replaced worn parts. (USAFHRA.)

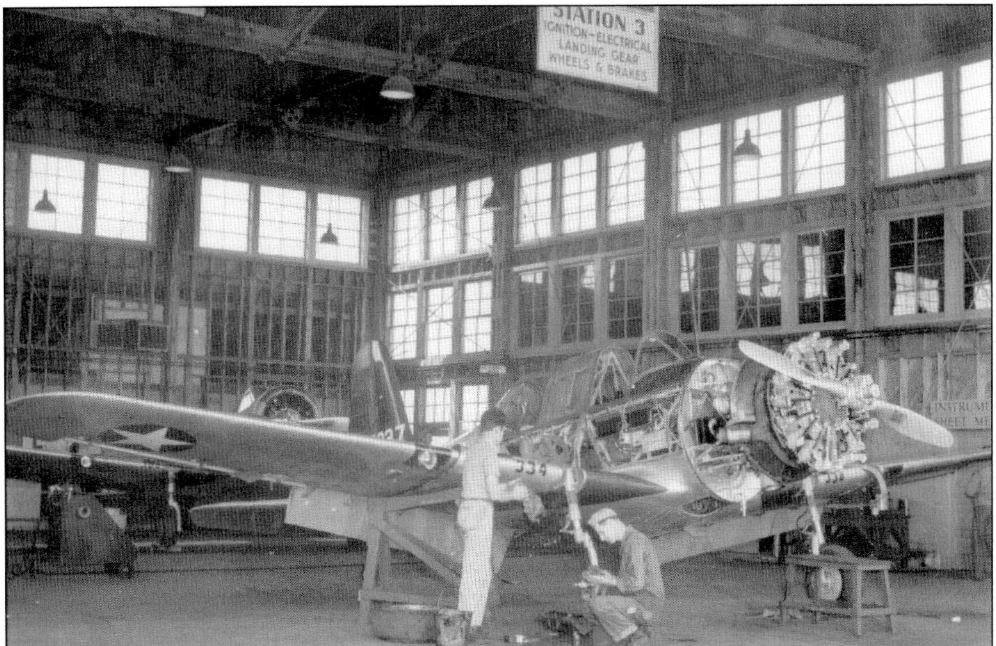

At Station Three, mechanics specializing in ignition, electrical, landing gear, and wheels and brakes performed the required inspections and replaced worn parts. Once this inspection was completed, the post inspector would check the aircraft to determine if all work had been done according to specifications. A satisfactory inspection would allow the airplane to return to service. (USAFHRA.)

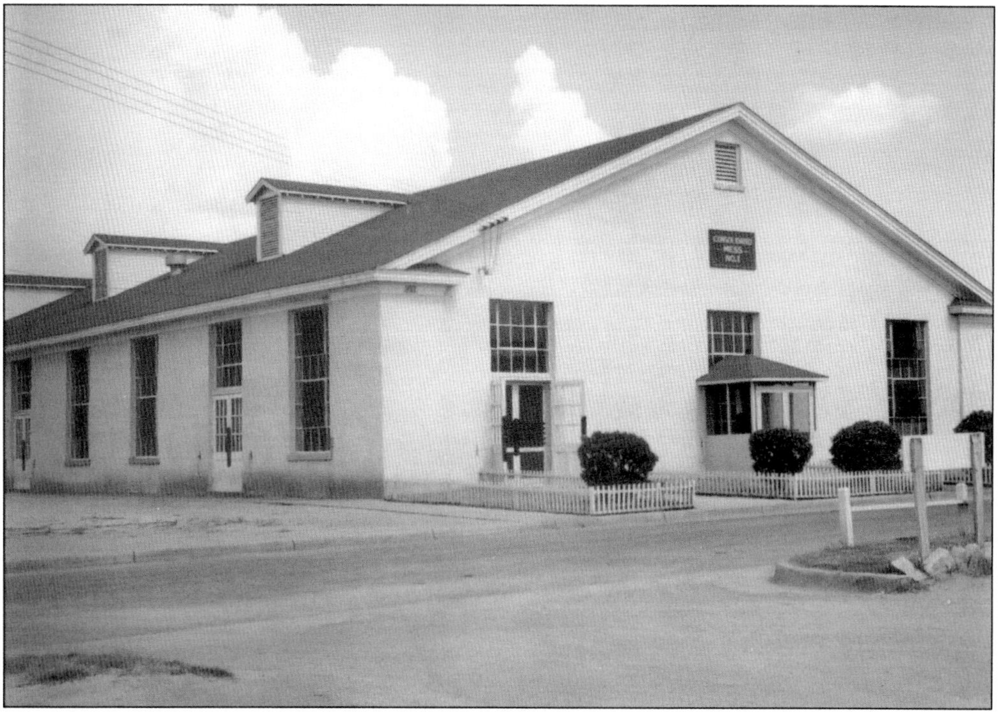

Consolidated Mess Hall No. 1 was opened in May 1943. The building was large enough to accommodate 1,000 men in one seating. (USAFHRA.)

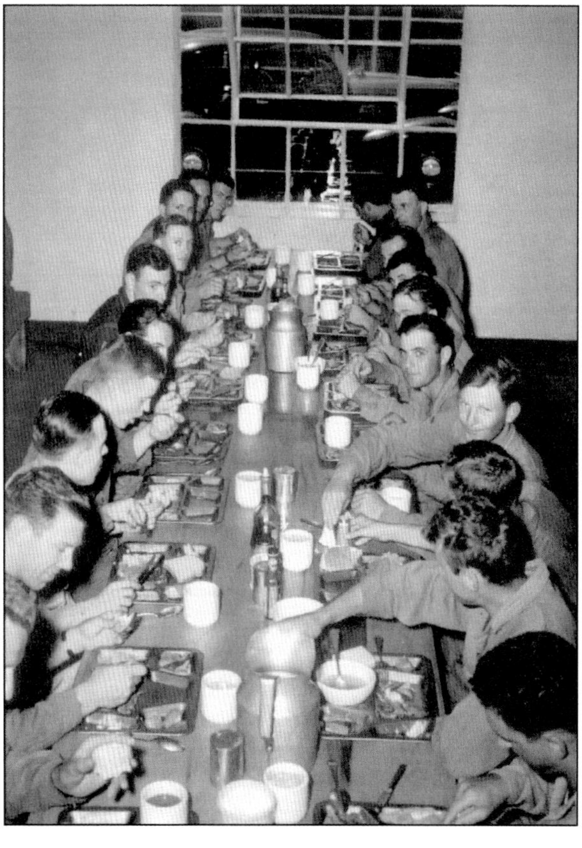

Gunter Field personnel enjoy a typical meal in Consolidated Mess Hall No. 1. (USAFHRA.)

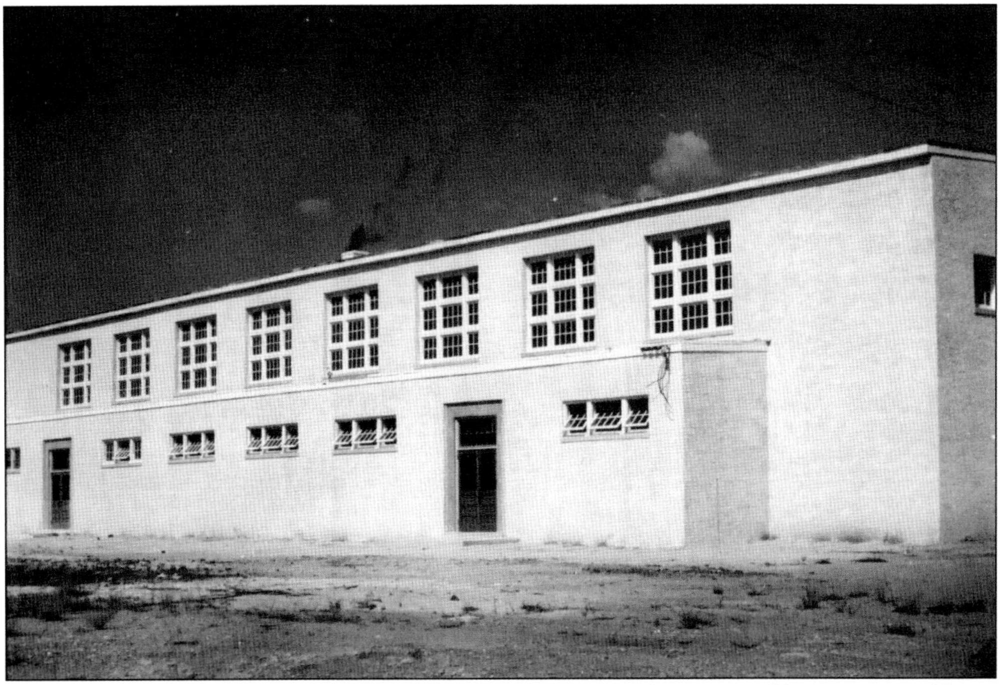

Completed in October 1943, the Gunter Field gymnasium served a variety of functions. In addition to its primary role as a physical training facility, the gymnasium was also used for the presentation of shows sponsored by the USO, for dances, and for regular sporting events. (USAFHRA.)

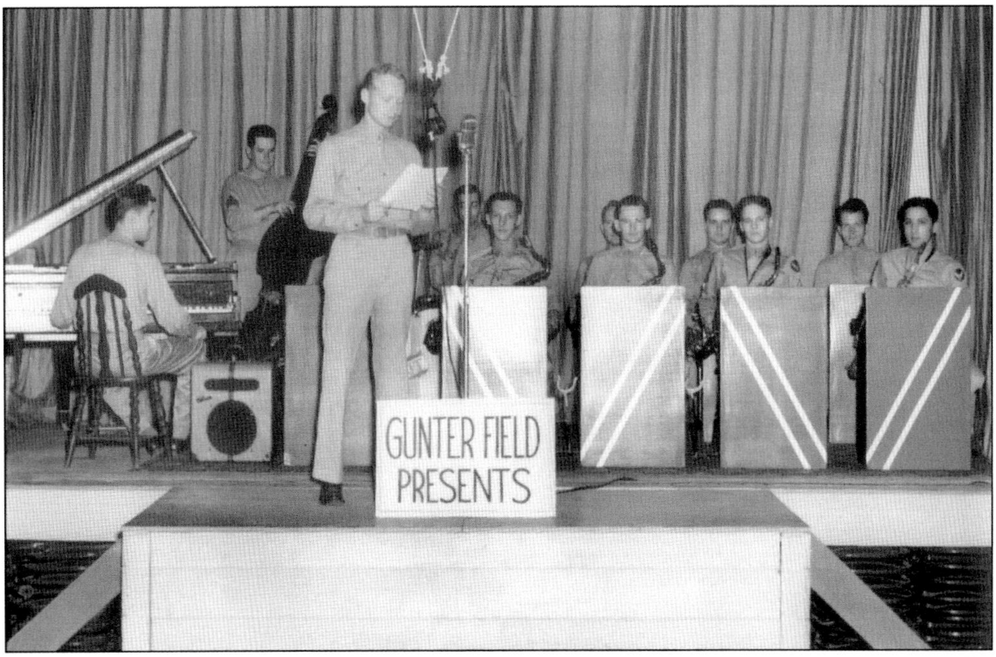

The 602nd Army Band performs their weekly radio broadcast on Montgomery station WSFA from the gymnasium at Gunter Field. In addition to performing at USO shows and other military installations, the band was featured in concerts, parades, dances, and church services in communities across the state. (USAFHRA.)

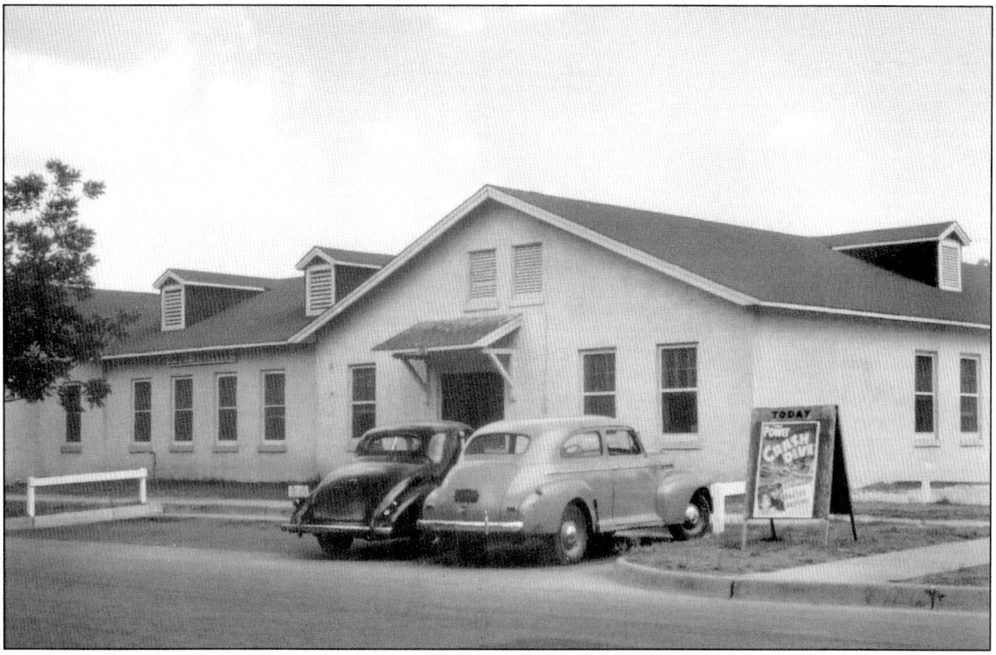

Tyrone Power stars in *Crash Dive* at the Gunter Field Theater. Other forms of entertainment were available to personnel at the base, including a nearby open-air theater that offered reduced rates for servicemen. On Sundays, transportation was provided to students who wanted to attend church services in the local area. (USAFHRA.)

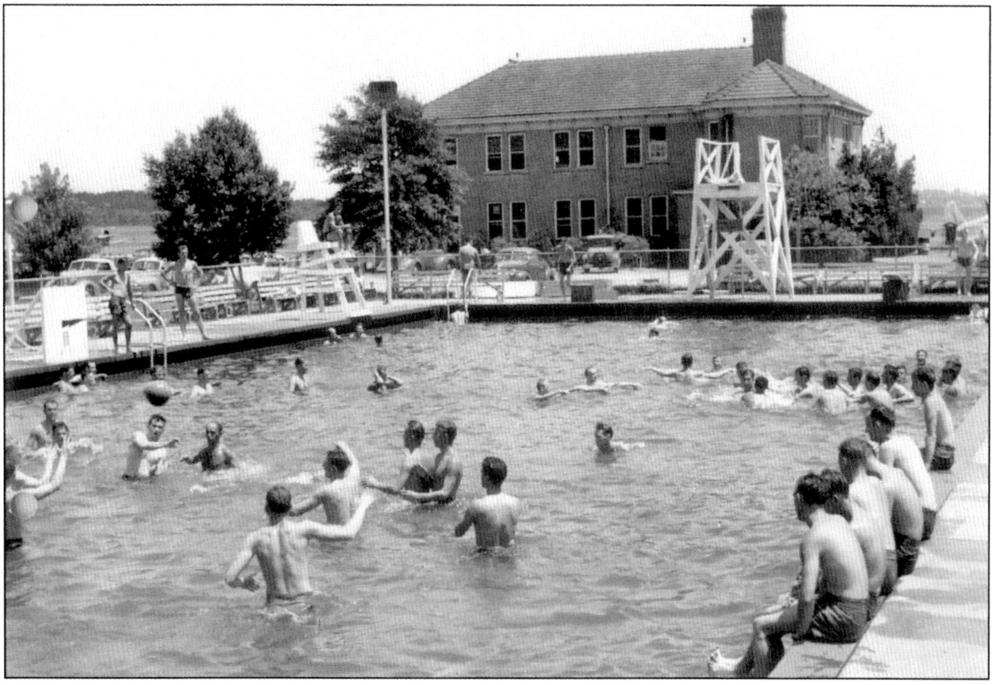

The swimming pool for enlisted personnel was part of the former municipal airport facility. The two-story, brick-veneer building in the background was the former airport hotel and restaurant. (USAFHRA.)

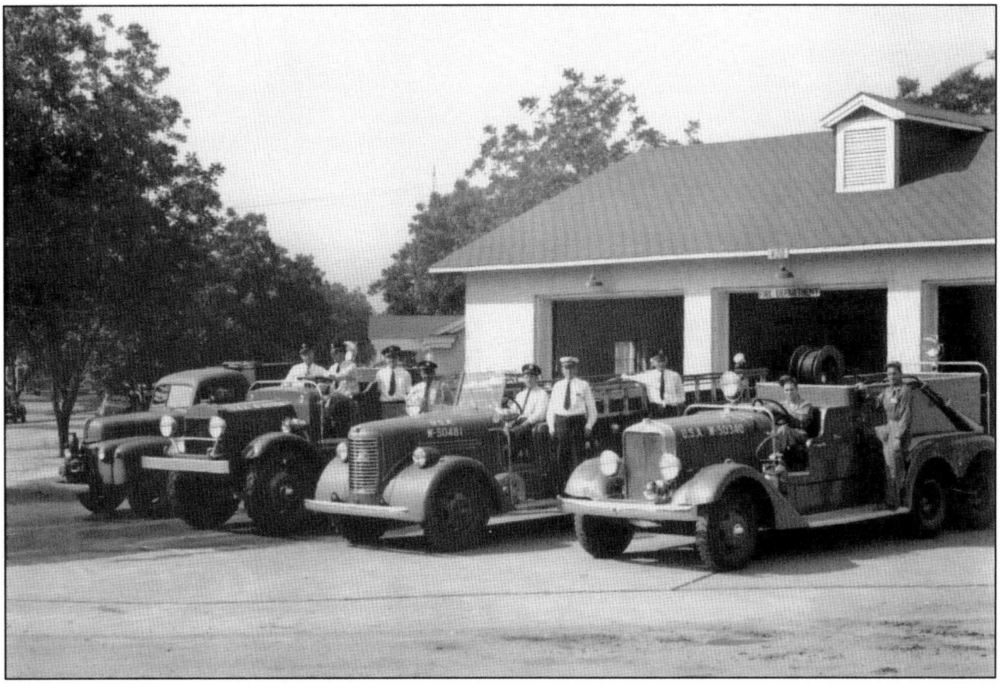

The Gunter Field Fire Department provided emergency services for the military and civilian personnel of the Army Air Forces Basic Flying Training School. (USAFHRA.)

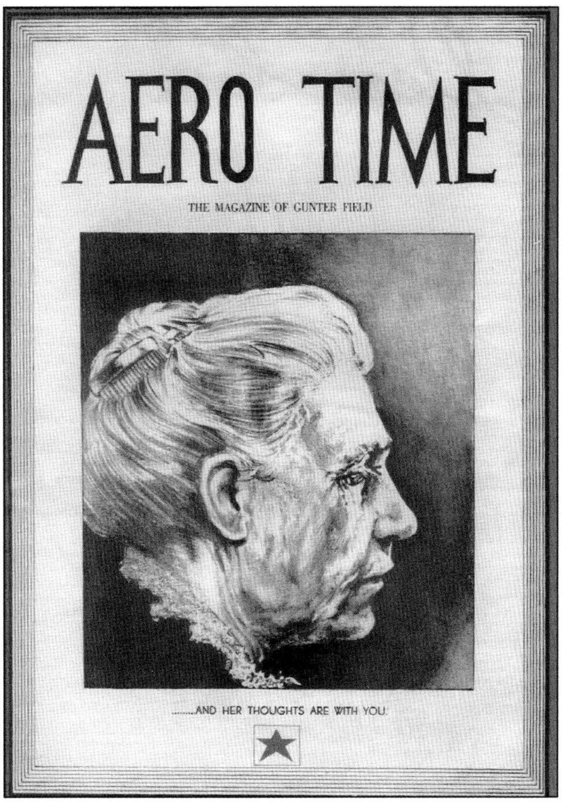

Aero Time, the magazine of Gunter Field, was published monthly by the officers and enlisted men of the Army Air Forces Basic Flying School. The magazine was a feature issue of the *Aero Gram*, the weekly base newspaper. This April 1944 issue commemorates Mother's Day. (Author's collection.)

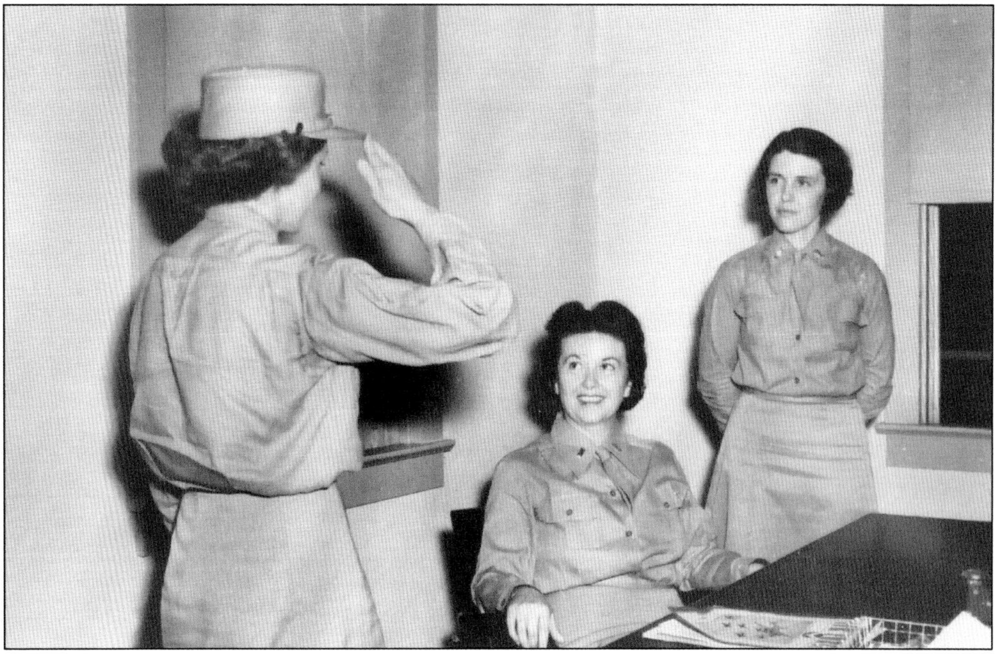

Cpl. Frances Bankert (left) reports for duty before Lt. Beatrice Landry (seated) and Lt. Irene Jennings. In July 1943, these women were among the first contingent of the Women's Army Corps (WACs) to arrive at Gunter Field. The WACs were assigned to non-flying aviation positions, including Link trainer instructors, mechanics, parachute riggers, and radio operators. (USAFHRA.)

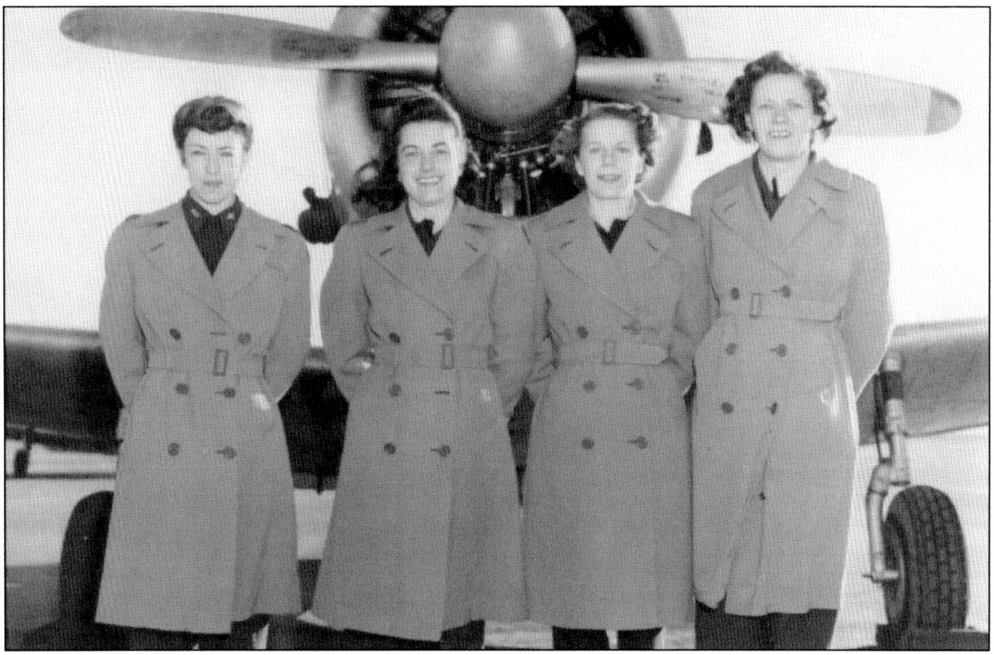

Female pilots of the Women's Airforce Service Pilots (WASP) at Gunter Field served as utility and test pilots. During the Second World War, the WASP flew every airplane in the inventory of the U.S. Army Air Forces. Although trained as military pilots, members of the WASP were never made part of the Army Air Forces. (USAFHRA.)

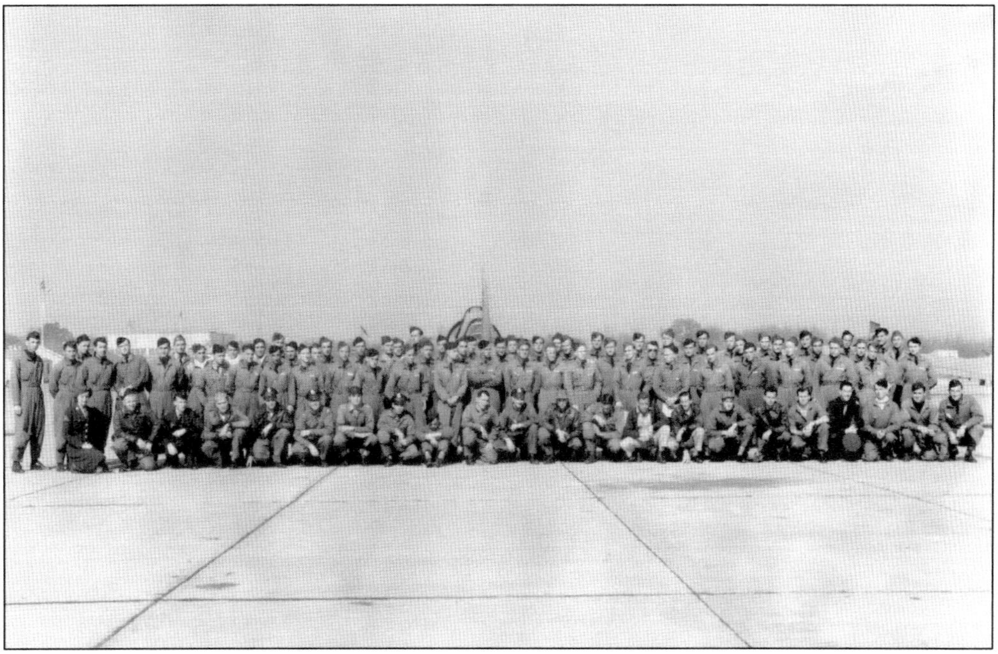

The French Detachment at Gunter Field is pictured with its flight officers and interpreter in November 1943. From September 1943 until the last class graduated in September 1945, exactly 1,414 French aviation cadets were trained at Gunter Field. The last class of cadets to receive training at the basic flying school at Gunter Field was composed entirely of French students. (USAFHRA.)

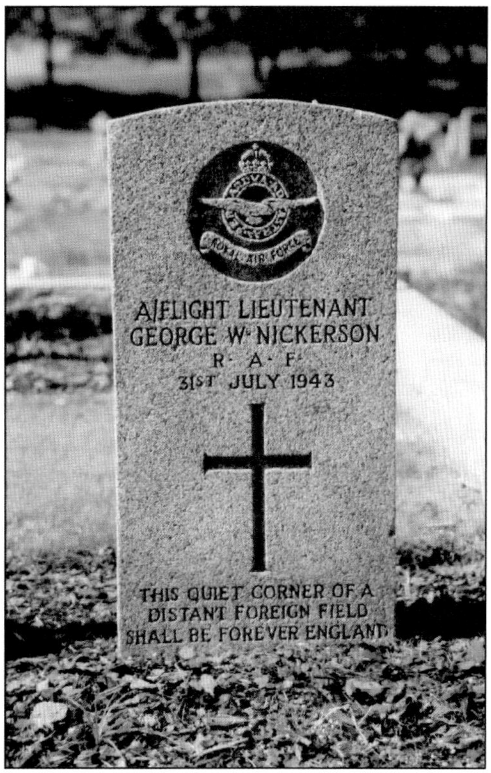

"This quiet corner of a distant foreign field shall be forever England." This distant foreign field is the Oakwood Cemetery in Montgomery. Flight Lt. George W. Nickerson is one of 78 members of the Royal Air Force who lost their lives while attending training in Montgomery during the Second World War. Twenty French airmen are buried in an adjacent area of the cemetery. (Author's collection.)

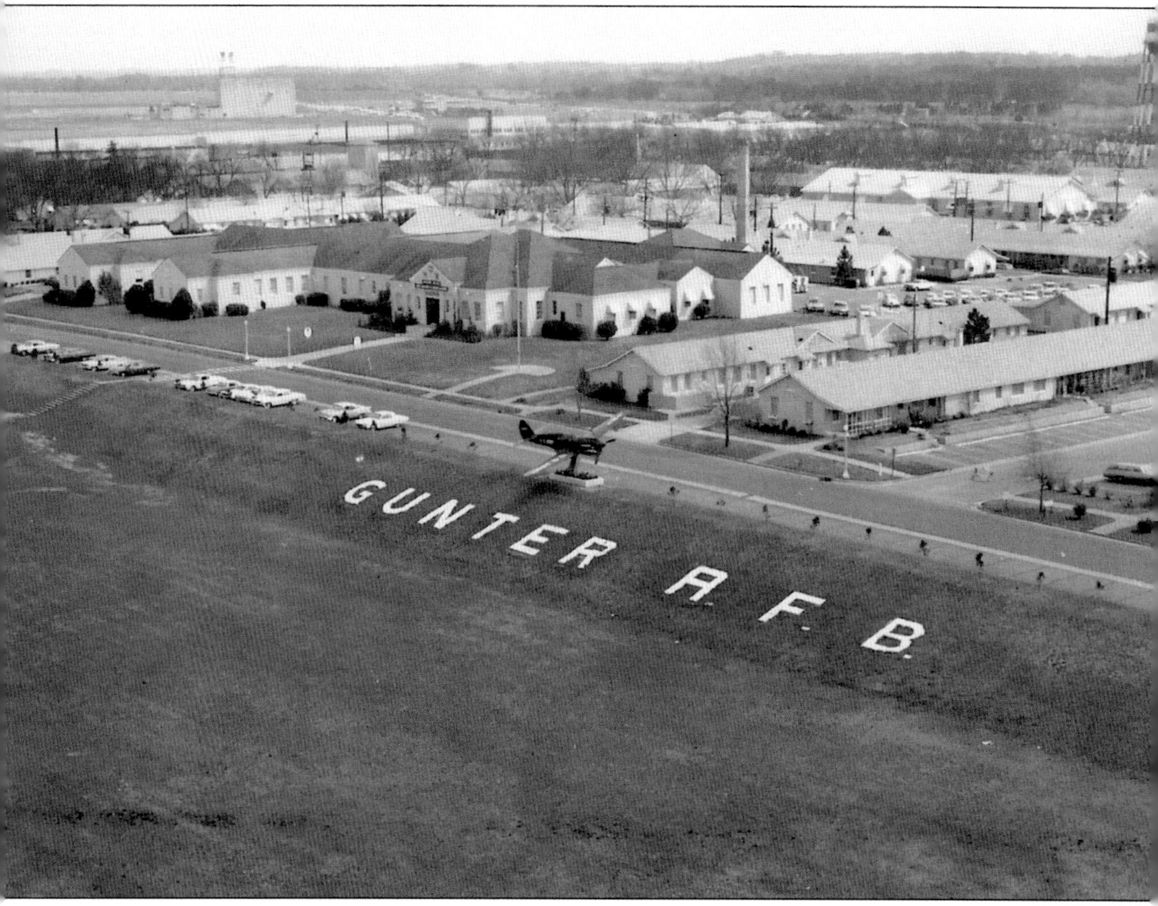

In September 1945, the Basic Flying School at Gunter Field was closed. Although limited flying activity would continue at the base during subsequent years, the end of the Second World War culminated a remarkable chapter in the history of the field. In January 1948, the former training field was renamed Gunter Air Force Base to reflect the creation of the air force as an independent branch of the armed forces. The relocation of the School of Aviation Medicine and Extension Course Institute to Gunter in 1950 marked the beginning of the facility's transition into a supplemental educational facility. The Extension Course Institute, the correspondence school of the U.S. Air Force, provides courses of instruction to as many as 300,000 students at military bases around the world. (Air University Office of History.)

Four

MAXWELL FIELD

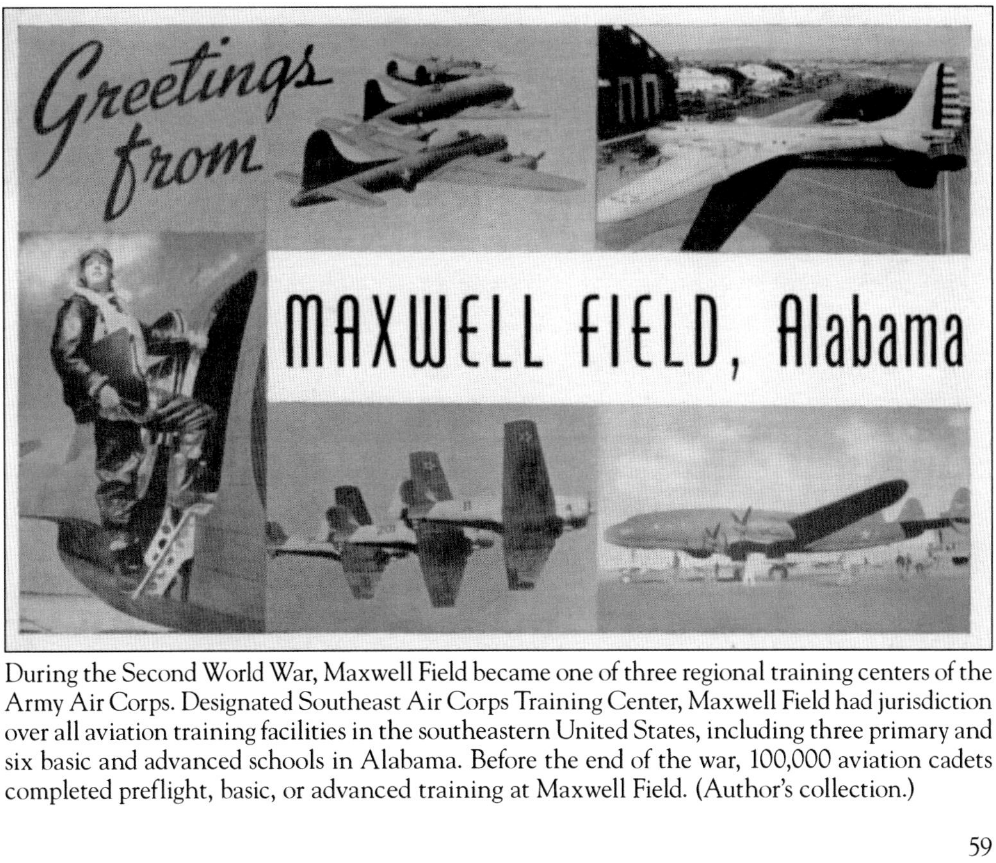

During the Second World War, Maxwell Field became one of three regional training centers of the Army Air Corps. Designated Southeast Air Corps Training Center, Maxwell Field had jurisdiction over all aviation training facilities in the southeastern United States, including three primary and six basic and advanced schools in Alabama. Before the end of the war, 100,000 aviation cadets completed preflight, basic, or advanced training at Maxwell Field. (Author's collection.)

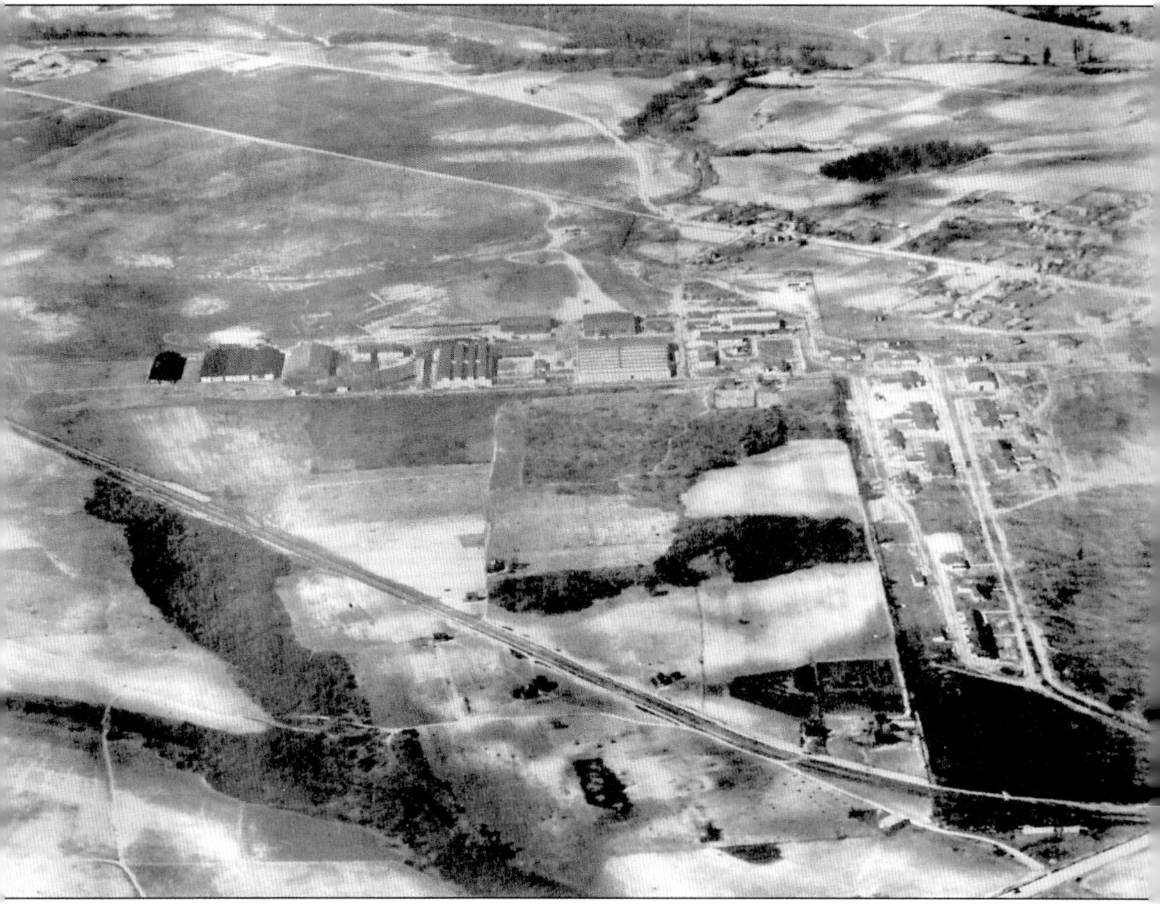

In April 1918, inspectors of the Aviation Section of the U.S. Signal Corps selected Montgomery as the site of an engine and repair depot to support flight training activities at Taylor Field and five other pilot training schools in the Southeast: Gerstner Field, Lake Charles, Louisiana; Payne Field, West Point, Mississippi; Souther Field, Americus, Georgia; Door and Carlstrom Fields, Arcadia, Florida; and Taylor Field, Montgomery. The 302-acre tract of land selected for the depot included the field once used by the Orville and Wilbur Wright to establish the nation's first civilian flying school. (Air University Office of History.)

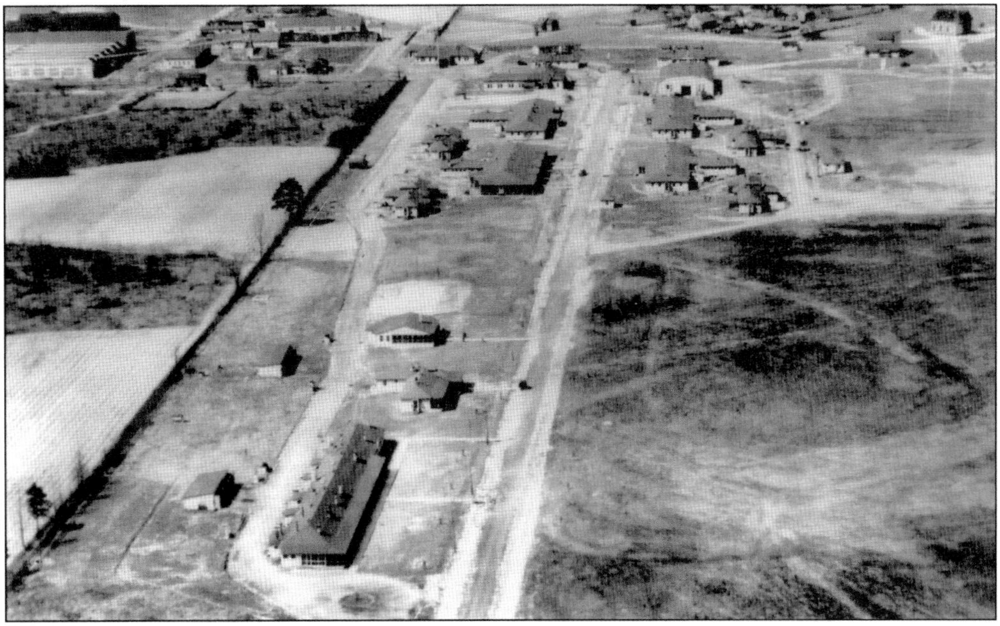

Light, water, and rail services for the Engine and Repair Depot were extended from Montgomery. Ninety days after construction began, 52 buildings consisting of barracks, hangars, a post exchange, a commissary, and an infirmary were completed and released to the military. The $819,000 project included installation of approximately 3 miles of Tarvia-surfaced roads and preparation of the 203-acre flying field. (Air University Office of History.)

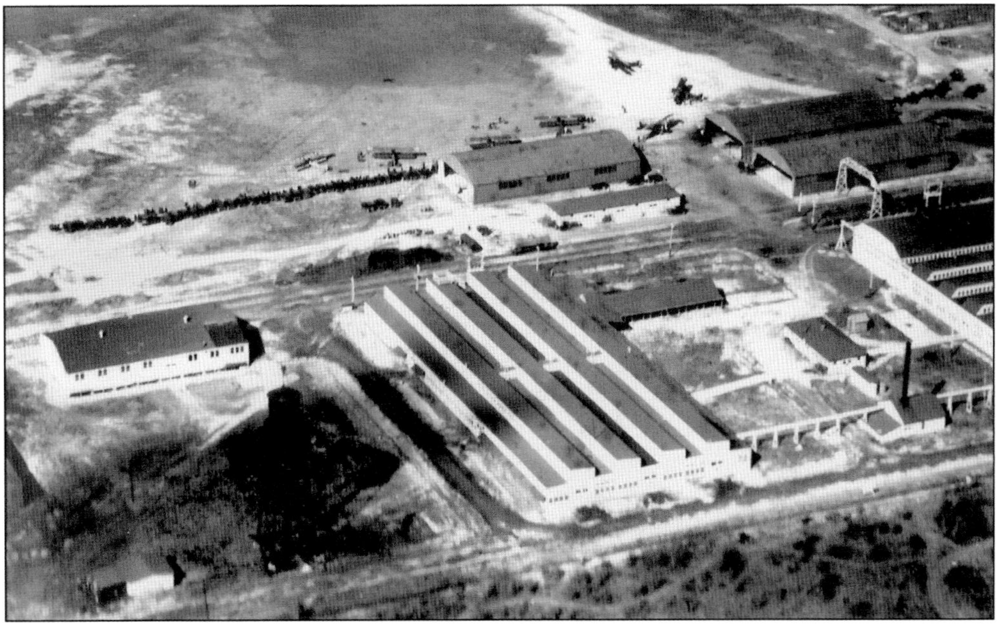

The workshops of the depot were equipped to produce or repair virtually every component of the most common training aircraft of the Air Service, including the Curtiss JN-4D and de Havilland DH-4 aircraft based at Taylor Field. After an aircraft was rebuilt or repaired, a pilot assigned to the depot would conduct a test flight to verify that it operated and handled normally. (Air University Office of History.)

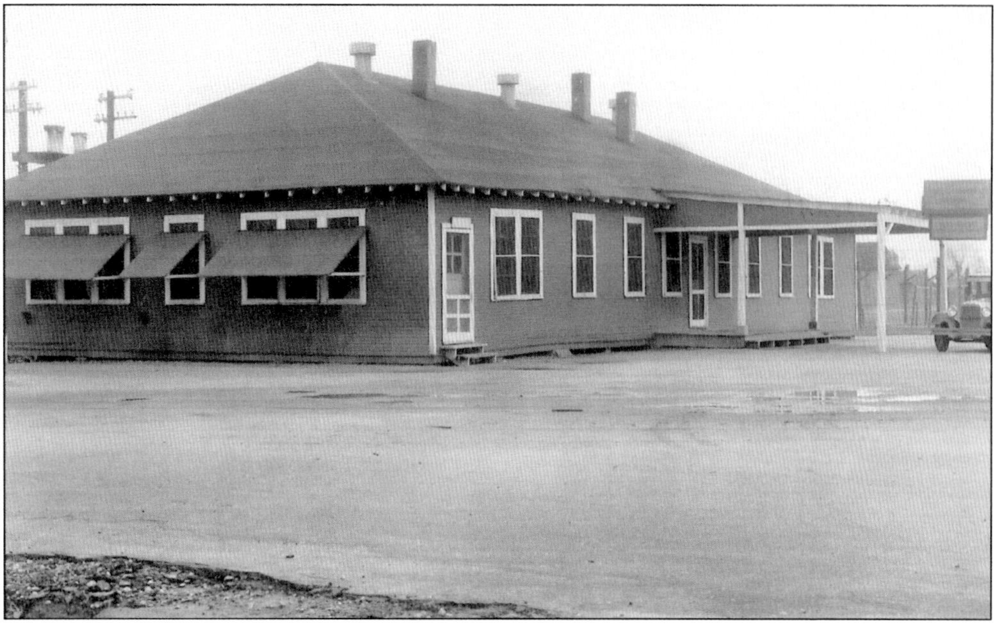

Pictured is the Post Headquarters building of the Montgomery Engine and Repair Depot. In September 1918, the Engine and Repair Depot was renamed Engine and Plane Repair Depot No. 3. In March 1919, the name was changed to Aviation Repair Depot–Montgomery, or ARDMONT as it was known by post personnel. In 1921, the facility became the Montgomery Air Intermediate Depot. (Air University Office of History.)

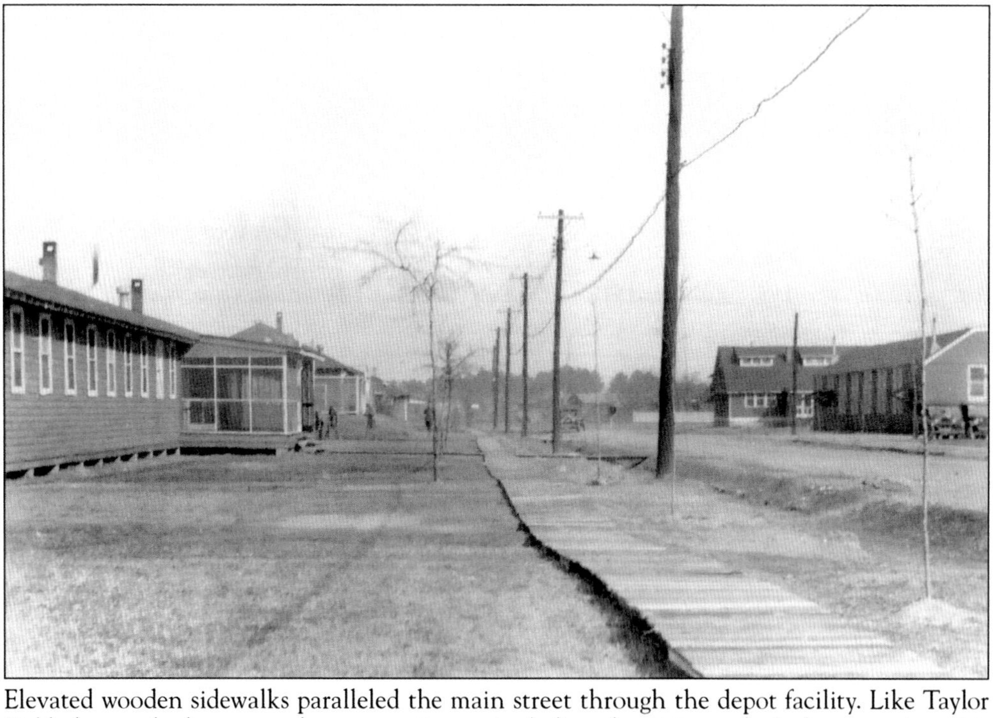

Elevated wooden sidewalks paralleled the main street through the depot facility. Like Taylor Field, the post had many modern conveniences, including electricity and telephone service. (Air University Office of History.)

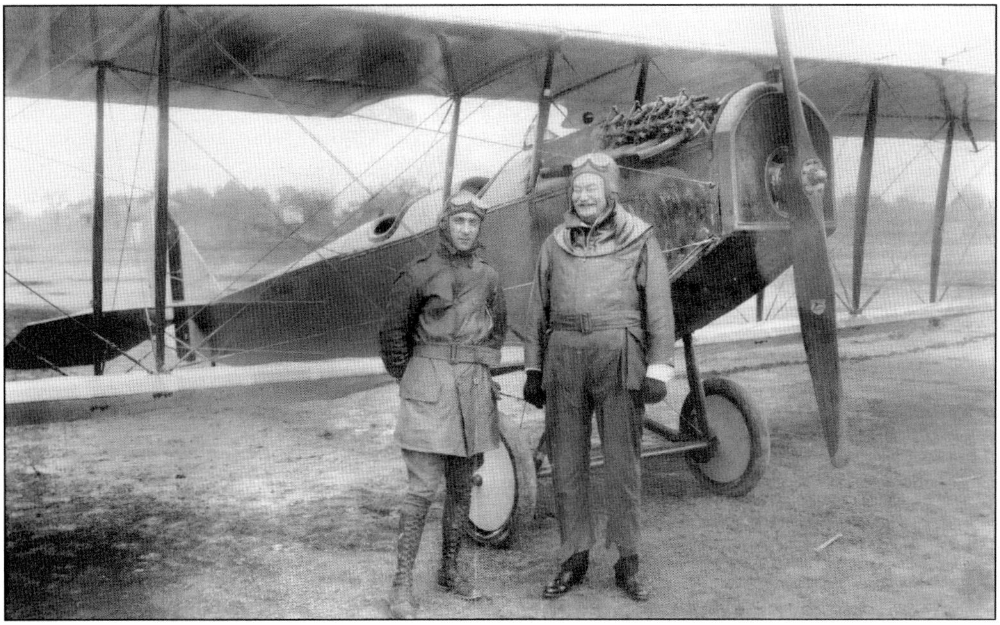

On September 20, 1918, a flag-raising ceremony marked the official opening of the Montgomery facility, one of only three aviation repair depots in the United States. Alabama governor Charles Henderson attended the ceremony and addressed members of the audience. Henderson (right) and flyer Ross L. Smith pose in front of a Curtiss JN-4D Jenny following the governor's first airplane flight. (Alabama Department of Archives and History, Montgomery, Alabama.)

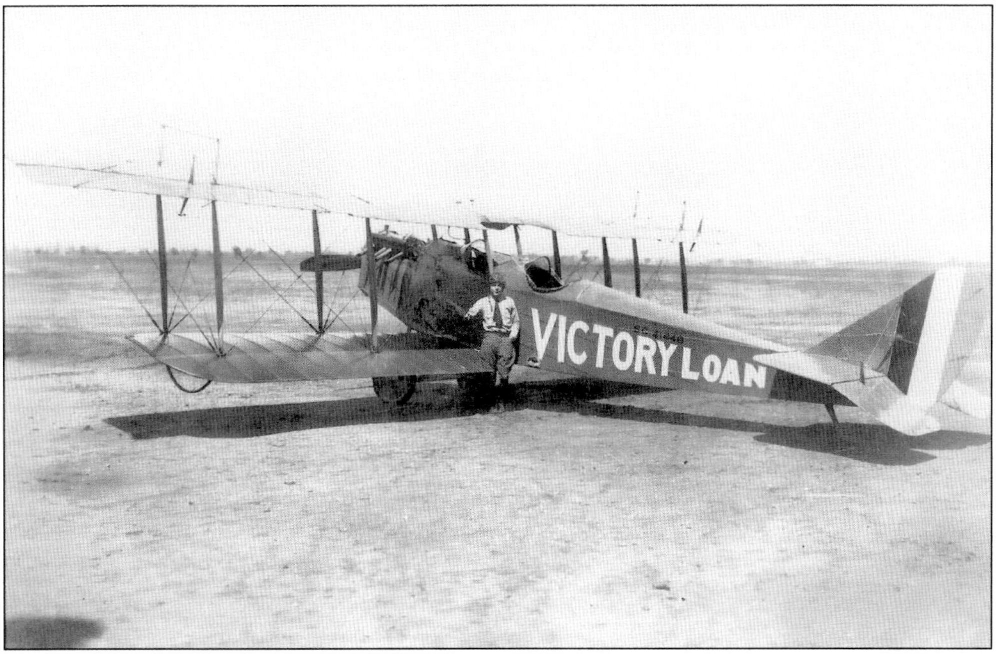

Lt. J. G. Nall served as the officer in charge of inspecting and testing at the Aviation Repair Depot. In addition to his duties as an aircraft inspector, Nall visited communities in surrounding states to promote the Victory Loan Drive. At each rally, Nall and his fellow fliers would perform stunts and other maneuvers to energize the crowd. (Southern Museum of Flight.)

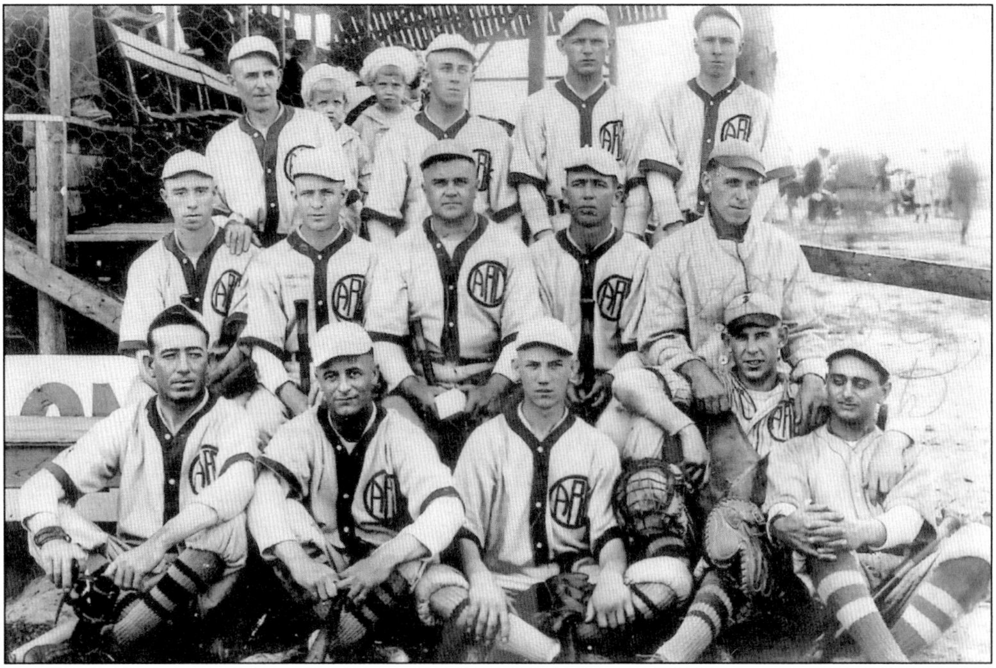

Sporting events were especially popular among personnel at military posts in the Montgomery area. Teams from the Aviation Repair Depot competed against those from Taylor Field and Camp Sheridan. After the war, ARDMONT teams competed against high schools, colleges, and military bases in the vicinity of Montgomery. This 1920 team appears to have recruited the two young members in the back row. (Air University Office of History.)

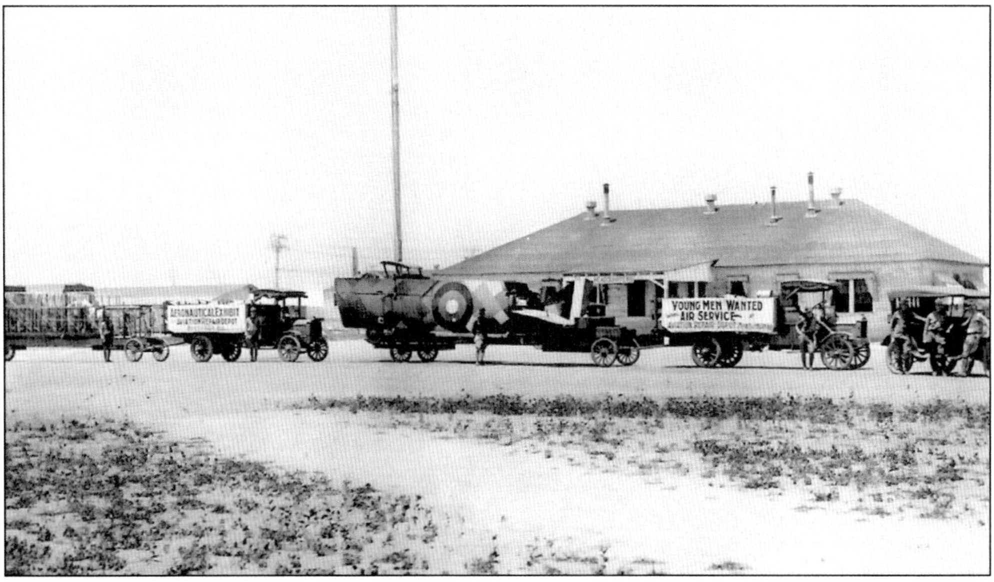

To support the retention of the Montgomery depot during the demobilization of the armed forces after the war, post officials and local dignitaries devised a plan to encourage enlistment in the Air Service. In addition to local publicity, a caravan that included an aircraft static display toured communities in Alabama to inform young men of the advantages of a career in the Air Service. (Air University Office of History.)

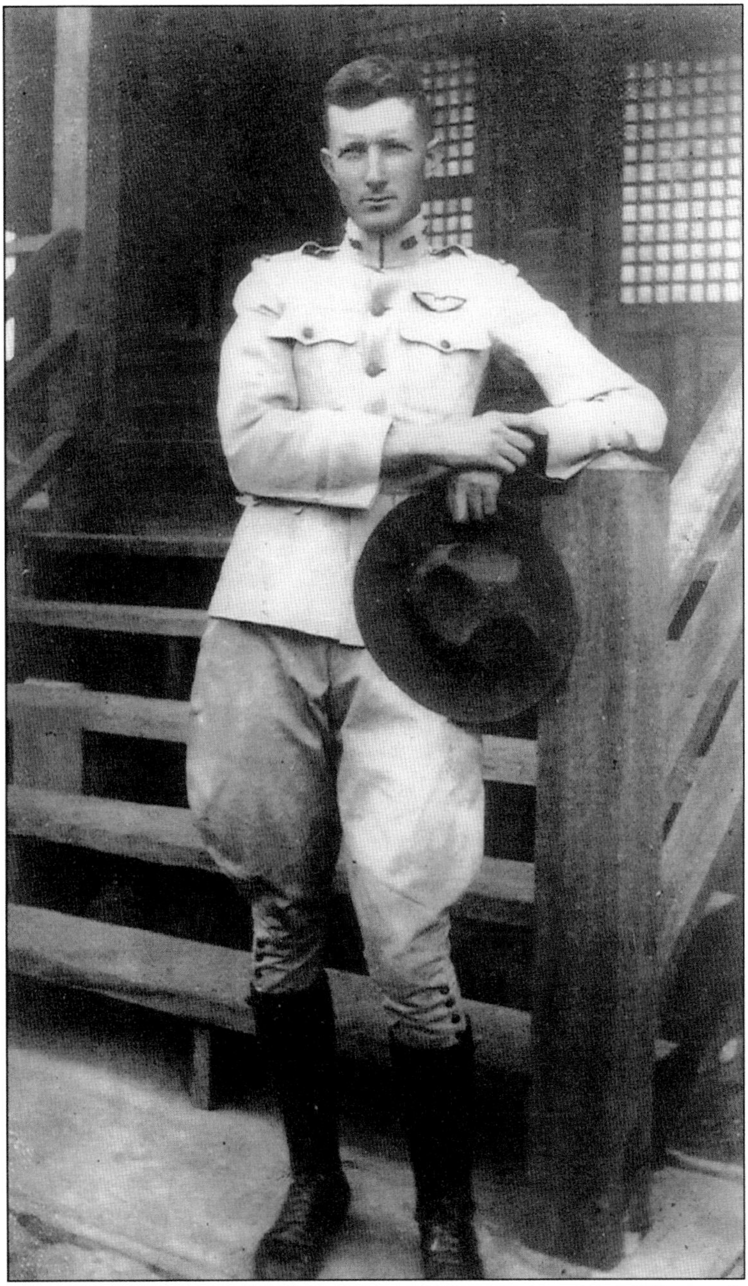

Born in Natchez, Mississippi, on November 9, 1892, William Calvin Maxwell spent his childhood years in Atmore, Alabama. In May 1917, Maxwell enlisted in the army and attended the School of Military Aeronautics in Atlanta, Georgia. Upon completion of flight training at Kelly Field, Texas, in April 1918, Maxwell received a commission as a lieutenant in the Aviation Section of the U.S. Signal Corps. Maxwell was fatally injured in an accident on August 12, 1920, while serving with the 3rd Aero Squadron in the Philippines. Maneuvering his airplane to avoid hitting a group of children during an emergency landing, the wing of Maxwell's aircraft struck a flagpole hidden by tall sugarcane plants. On November 8, 1922, Maxwell Field was named in his honor. (Alabama Department of Archives and History, Montgomery, Alabama.)

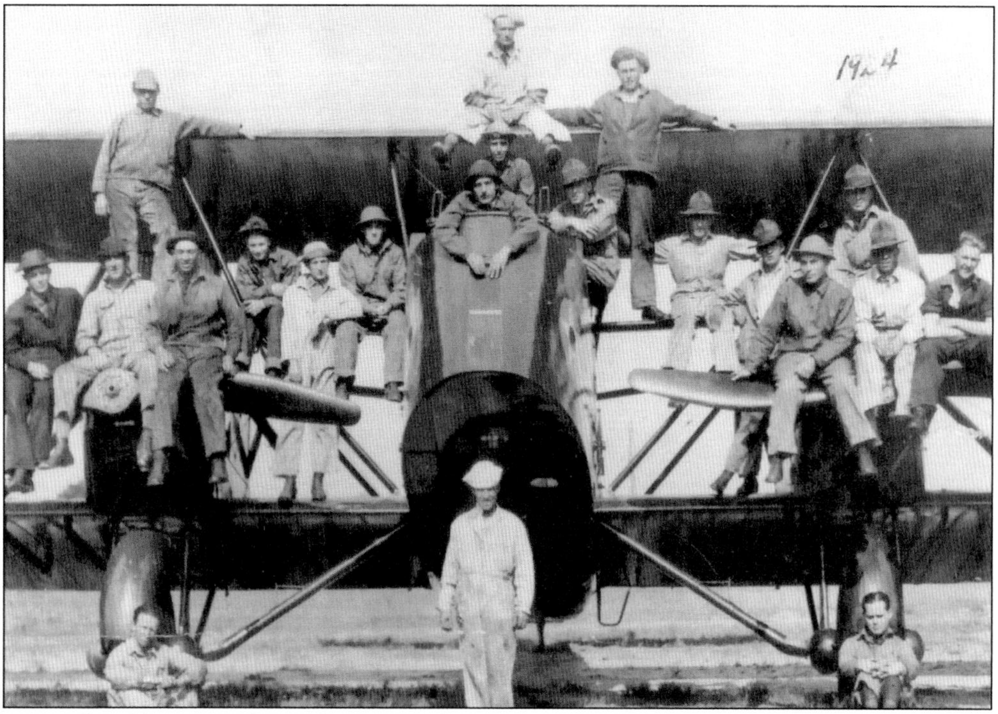

Maxwell Field personnel pose for a 1924 photograph on board a Martin MB-2. Designed by the Glenn L. Martin Company as a short-range night bombardment aircraft, the MB-2 was powered by two 420-horsepower Liberty engines and had a top speed of 99 miles per hour. The huge biplane had a maximum takeoff weight of more than 12,000 pounds. (Air University Office of History.)

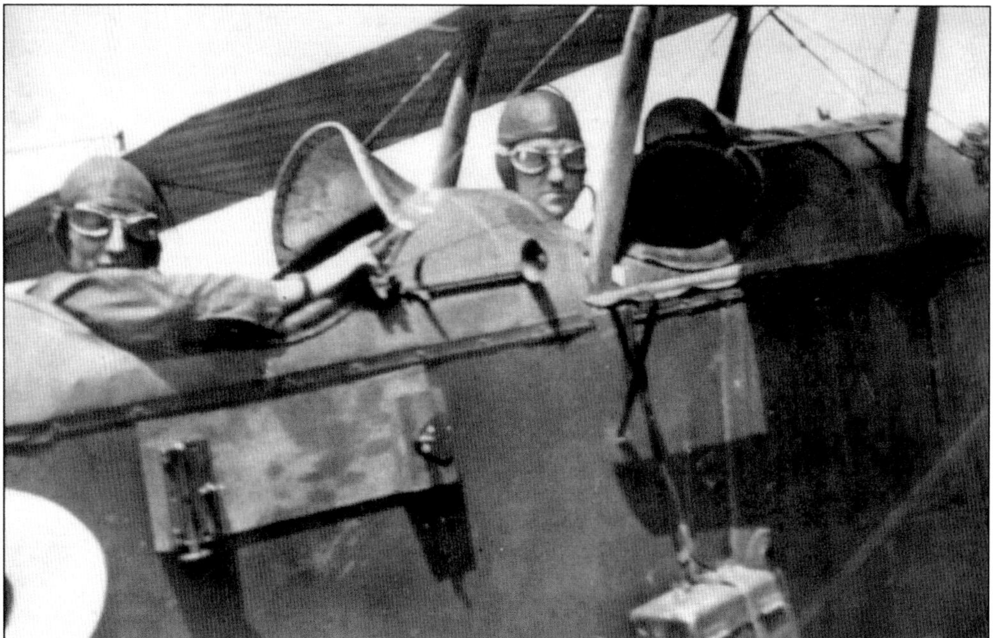

Two pilots prepare for takeoff from Maxwell Field. The lack of an enclosed cockpit necessitated the use of a helmet and goggles. (Air University Office of History.)

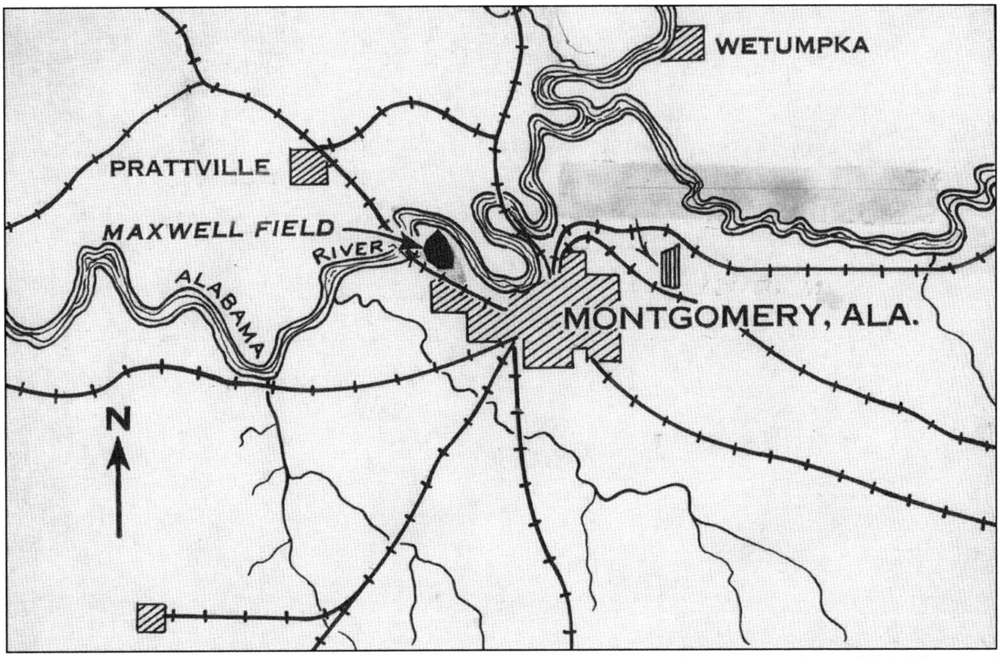

Prior to the August 1929 dedication of the Montgomery Municipal Airport, Maxwell Field served the civilian aviation needs of the City of Montgomery. Although a small airfield was located south of the city on the Norman Bridge Road, the landing area was too small for routine operations of larger aircraft. (Alabama Department of Archives and History, Montgomery, Alabama.)

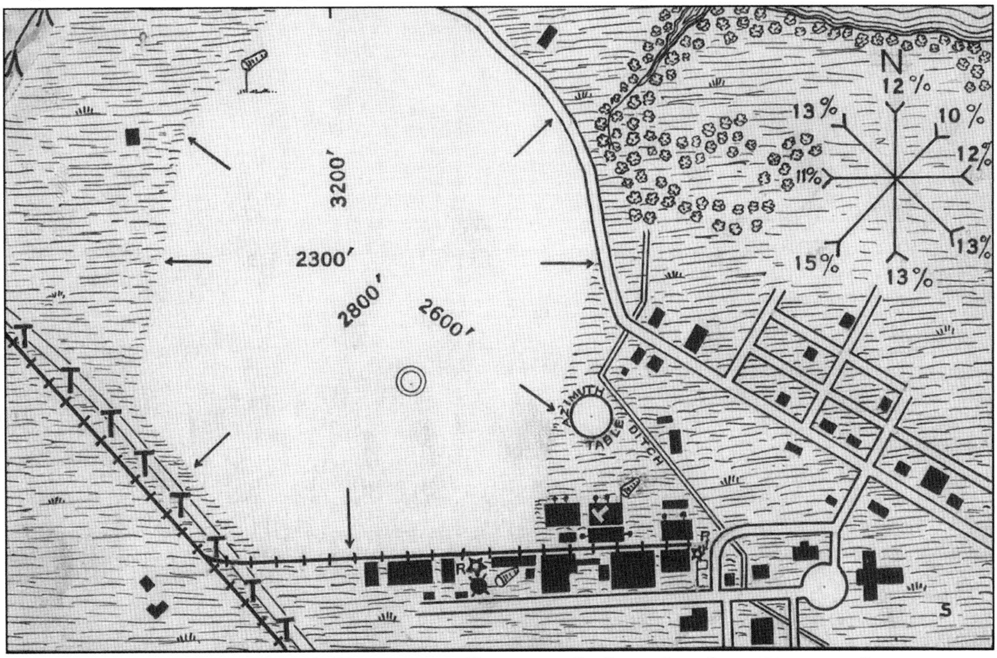

In 1925, the all-over landing field at Maxwell consisted of a sod surface. Because there were no designated runways, pilots could align their aircraft into the prevailing wind for takeoff and landing. Although civilian pilots could land at Maxwell Field, facilities were only available for servicing government aircraft. (Alabama Department of Archives and History, Montgomery, Alabama.)

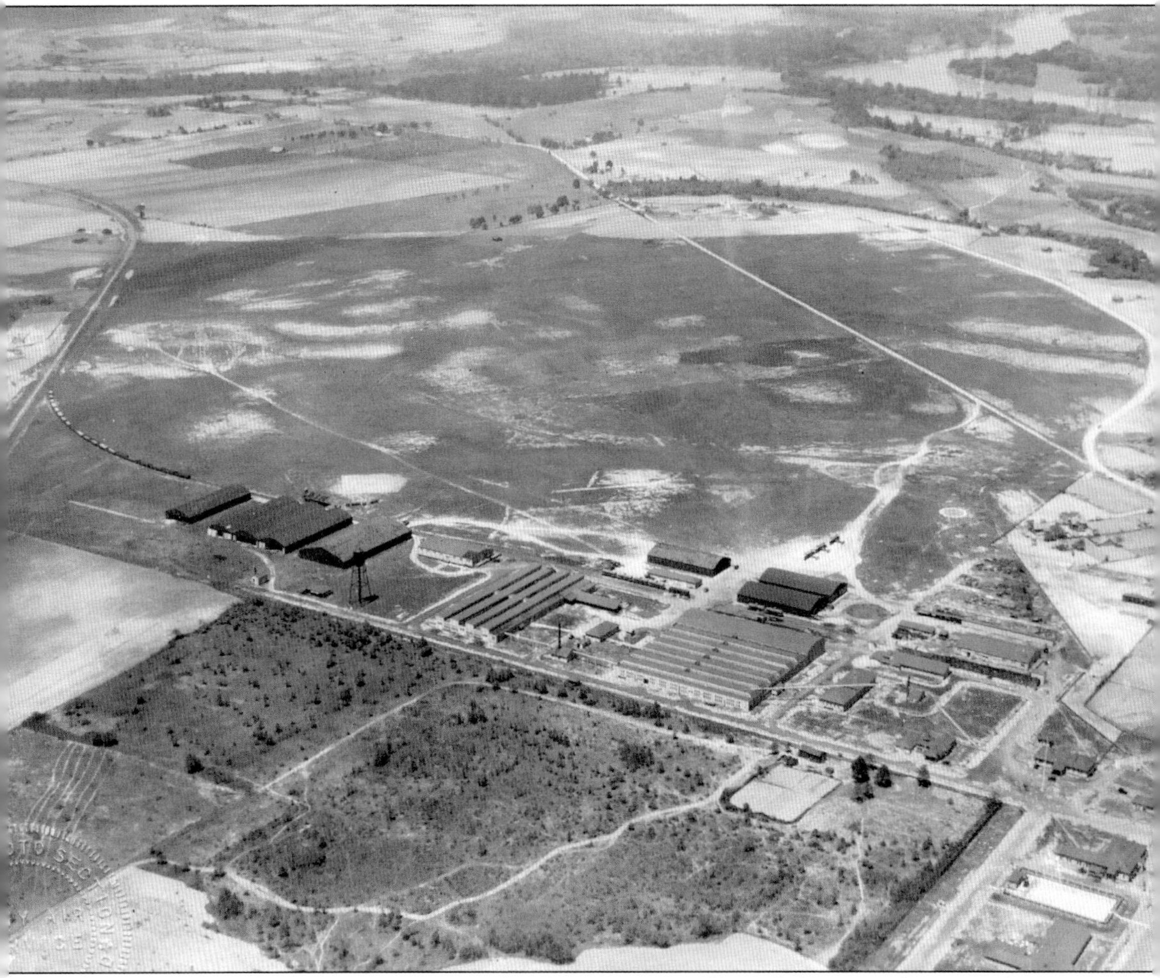

This 1925 aerial view of Maxwell Field depicts the 203-acre flying field, repair shops, and hangars of the former engine and repair depot facility. After years of uncertainty, the permanent status of Maxwell Field was assured in 1925, as Congressman Lister Hill succeeded in obtaining funding for the first permanent structures on the post. The new construction included three barracks for enlisted men, 13 one-story single-family bungalows, and 32 two-story duplexes for noncommissioned officers. The Washington Ferry Road, visible in the right portion of the image, has been rerouted to accommodate the flying field. (Author's collection.)

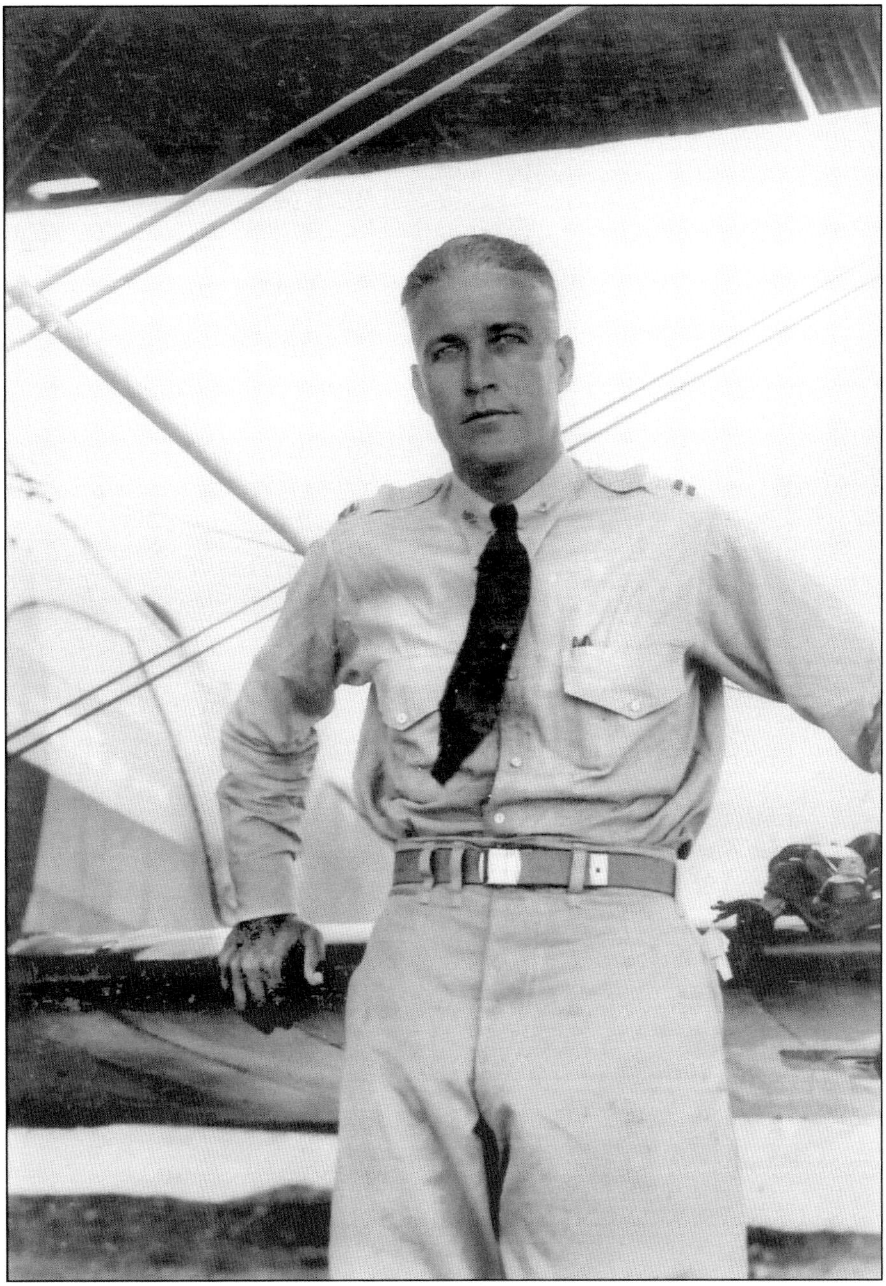

In March 1918, Robert D. Knapp completed military flight training and received a commission as a second lieutenant. In 1923, Knapp was transferred to Maxwell Field, where he flew missions to map the Tennessee River Valley and Mobile Harbor. On April 17, 1925, Knapp and his mechanic, Sgt. J. A. Liner, conducted the first airmail flight into the city of Montgomery. The flight was operated to determine the feasibility of connecting airmail service originating in the Gulf States with the transcontinental service at Chicago. Flying a de Havilland DH-4 aircraft, Knapp and Liner departed New Orleans for Legion Field in Mobile. After picking up five bags of mail, the pair continued to Maxwell Field. Pilots from Roberts Field in Birmingham completed the next leg of the flight from Montgomery to Nashville via Birmingham. (Air University Office of History.)

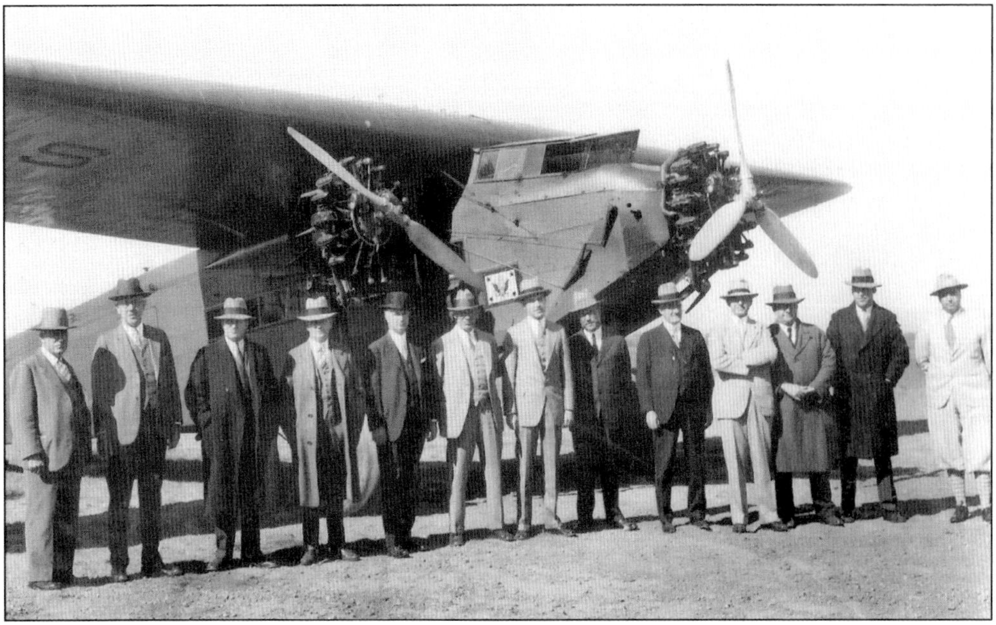

In February 1928, Gen. James E. Fechet, chief of the Air Corps, and members of the U.S. Army Attack Wing Board visited Montgomery to discuss the possibility of locating three pursuit squadrons at Maxwell Field. Fechet was accompanied by Assistant Secretary of War F. Trubee Davison. Representative Lister Hill and Mayor William A. Gunter met with the board at Maxwell Field. (Air University Office of History.)

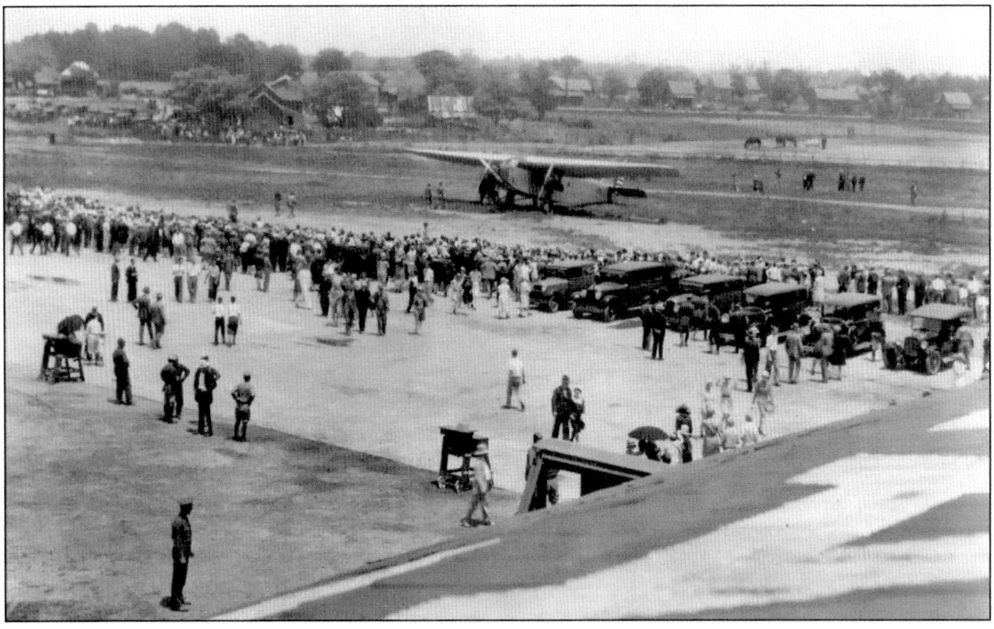

An Atlantic (Fokker) C-2 cargo and transport plane sits among military and civilian personnel at Maxwell Field. The horses visible behind the aircraft were shipped from Nebraska to Maxwell Field in 1929 for use by the officers of the post in keeping fit and to stimulate interest in polo. The houses in the background are part of the small community of Douglasville. (Air University Office of History.)

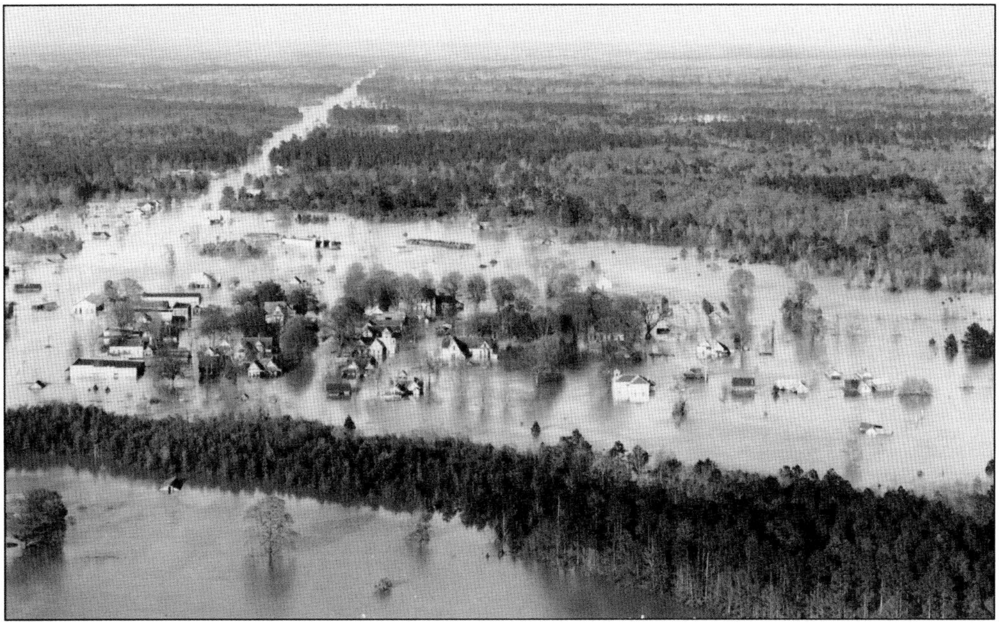

In March 1929, heavy rains caused extensive flooding of towns and communities across south Alabama. Highways and railroads were unusable for recovery efforts, and communications in the affected areas were severed. As thousands of residents attempted to flee the rising water, many became trapped on the roofs of homes and buildings, on hillsides, and in the branches of trees. The flooding killed more than 15 people and left thousands homeless. Five thousand homes and 2,615 other buildings were destroyed by the floodwater. Gov. Bibb Graves contacted Maj. Walter Weaver, post commander of Maxwell Field, to request the assistance of Army Air Corps aircraft in providing relief to victims of the flooding. Weaver declared a state of emergency at Maxwell and pledged every available resource to the relief effort. (Author's collection.)

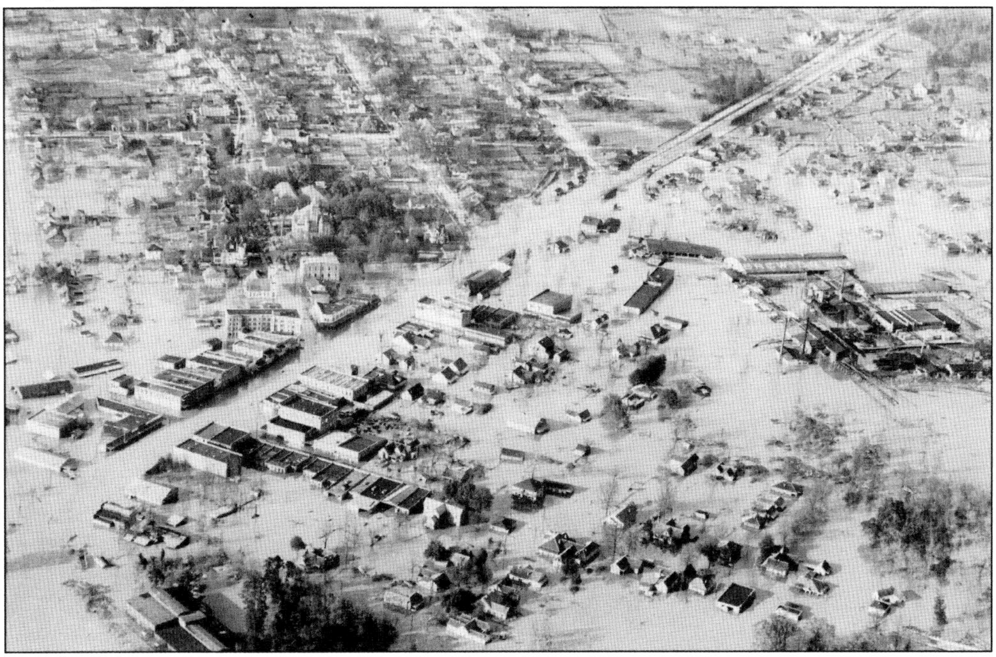

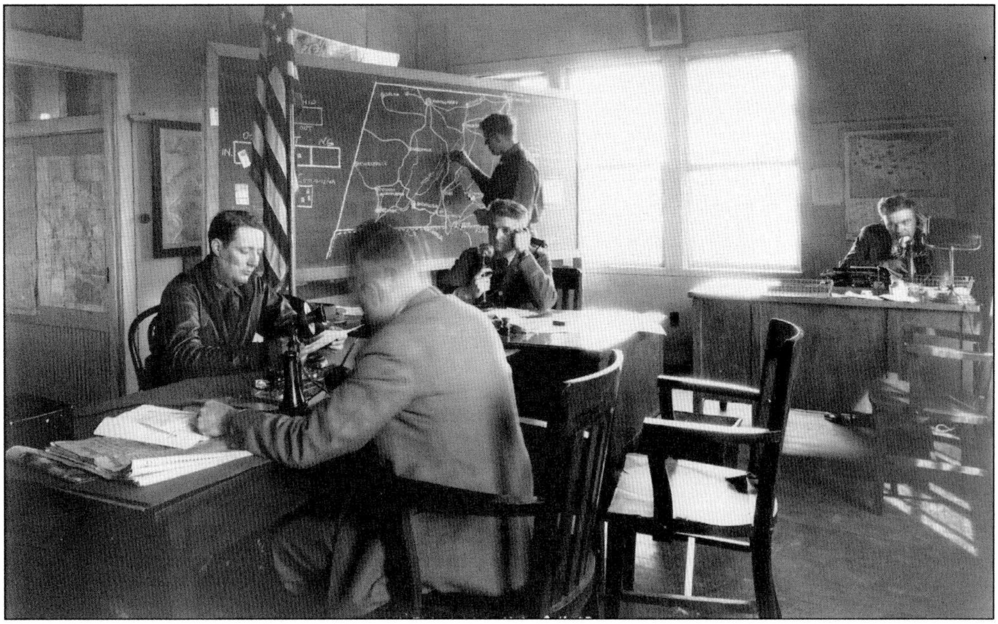

Aircraft from Maxwell Field, Langley Field in Virginia, and the Army National Guard at Roberts Field in Birmingham participated in the relief effort. Pilots provided reconnaissance reports to Flood Relief Headquarters at Maxwell Field for analysis. Supplies could then be air dropped into those areas of greatest need. Aircraft returning from the flood area remained on the ground for only 10 minutes before departing on another relief mission. (Author's collection.)

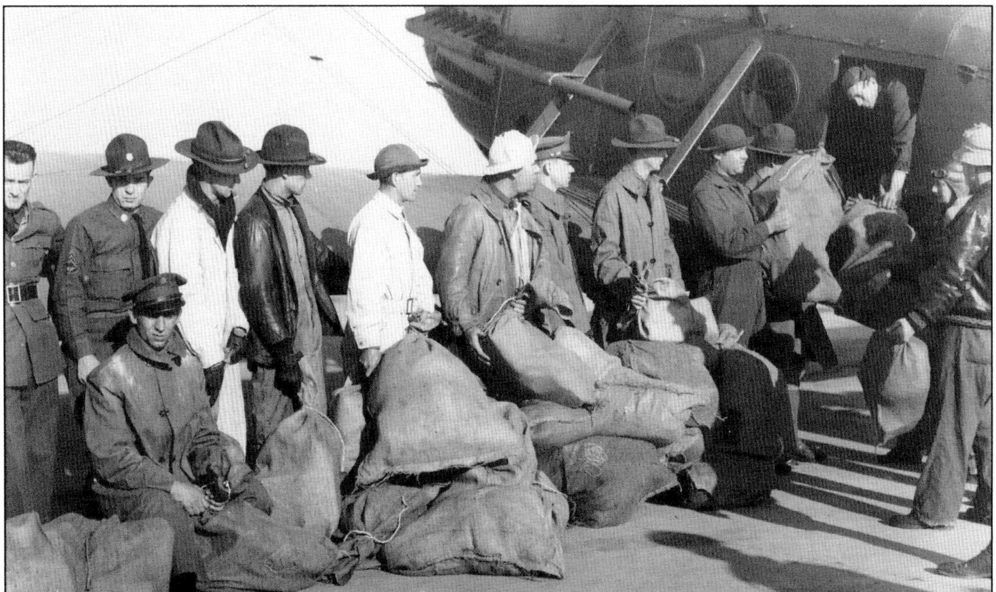

During the five-day relief effort, aircraft from Maxwell Field flew 281 missions and dropped more than 50 tons of supplies. In addition to food, clothing, and medicine, pilots dropped hundreds of copies of a special edition of the Montgomery Advertiser that contained information for signaling and communicating with airplanes. The response of Maxwell Field to this disaster was heralded as the most significant relief effort in the history of the Air Corps. (Author's collection.)

Walter R. Weaver has been called the "Father of Maxwell Field." A graduate of the U.S. Military Academy, Weaver served as post commander from 1927 to 1931. Weaver returned to Maxwell Field in 1939 as post commander and commandant of the Air Corps Tactical School. During 1940–1941, Brigadier General Weaver served as commander of the Southeast Air Corps Training Command at Maxwell Field. (Air University Office of History.)

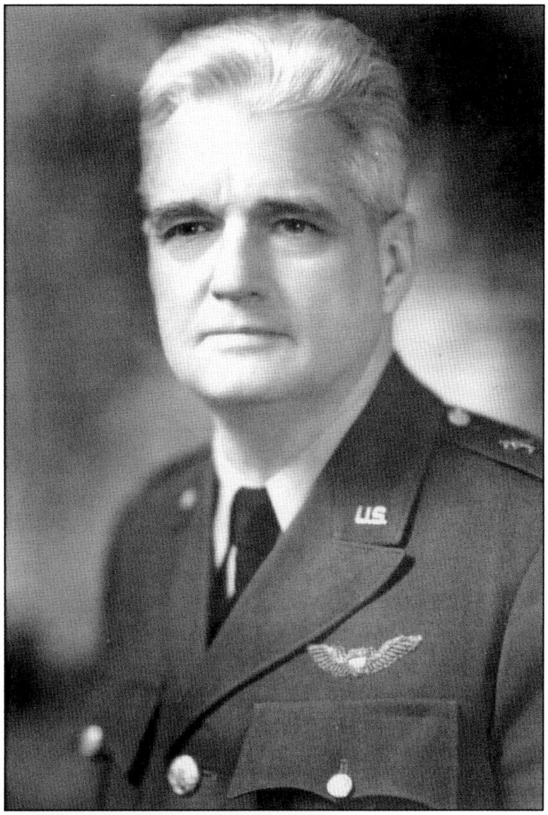

Representing Alabama's 2nd Congressional District, J. Lister Hill (center) became known as the "Godfather of Maxwell Field" for his efforts to keep the post open after the end of the First World War. Hill also worked diligently to ensure the relocation of the Air Corps Tactical School to Montgomery. Elected to the Senate in 1937, Hill remained an ardent supporter of Maxwell Field. (Air University Office of History.)

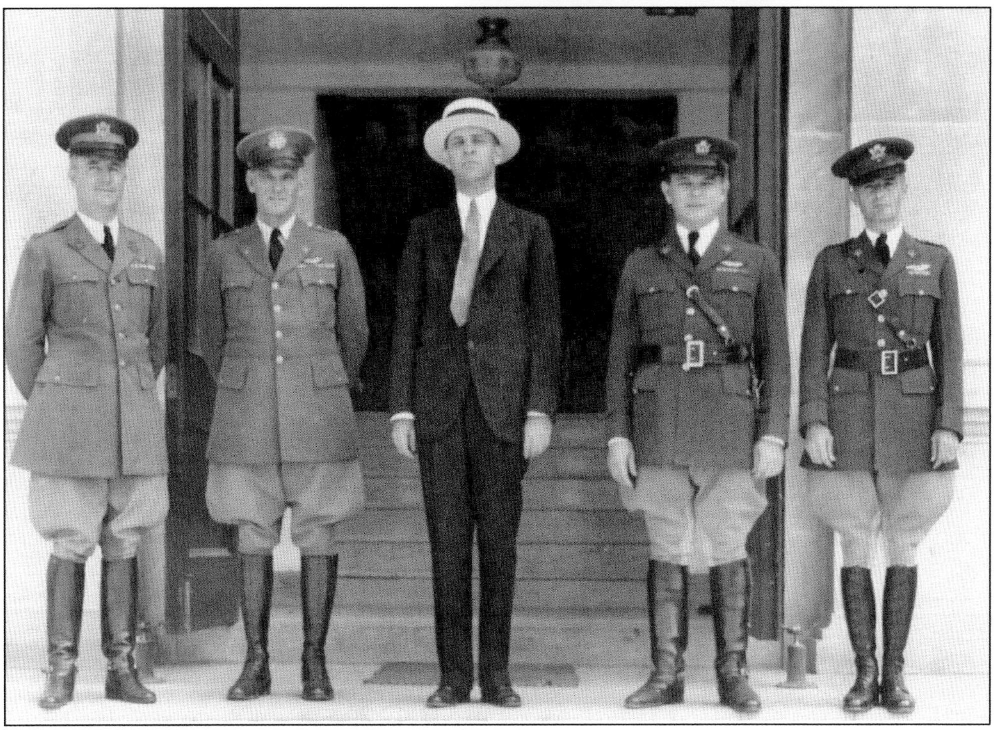

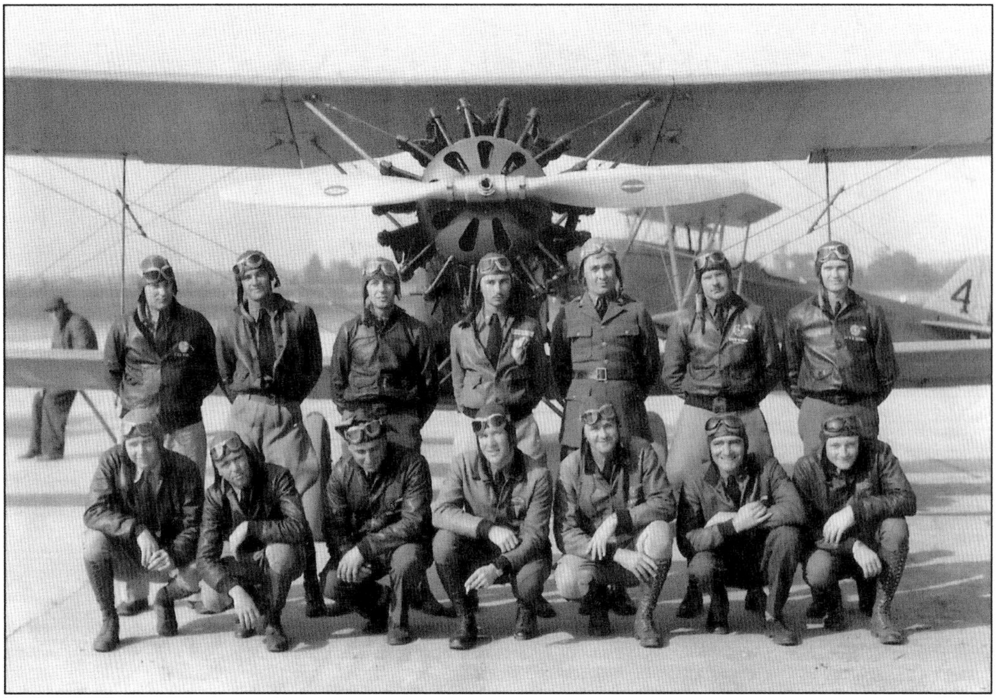

Pilots of the 22nd Observation Squadron at Maxwell Field pose in front of an O-19 reconnaissance aircraft. In May 1922, the 4th Photo Section and 22nd Observation Squadron arrived at Maxwell Field, the first expansion of personnel at the post since the end of the First World War. The 22nd Observation Squadron would remain at Maxwell Field until 1931. (Air University Office of History.)

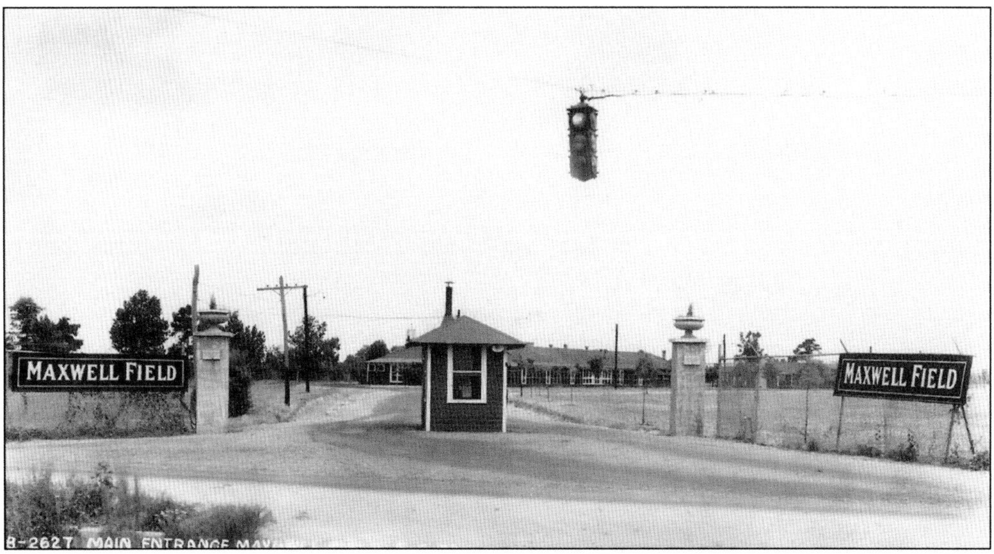

In December 1928, the War Department announced that the Air Corps Tactical School (ACTS) would be transferred to Maxwell Field from Langley Field in Virginia. The tactical school was an advanced school for officers that taught tactics, strategy, and techniques of the employment of air power. The relocation of ACTS to Maxwell Field required the construction of additional facilities for personnel, administration, and operations. (Air University Office of History.)

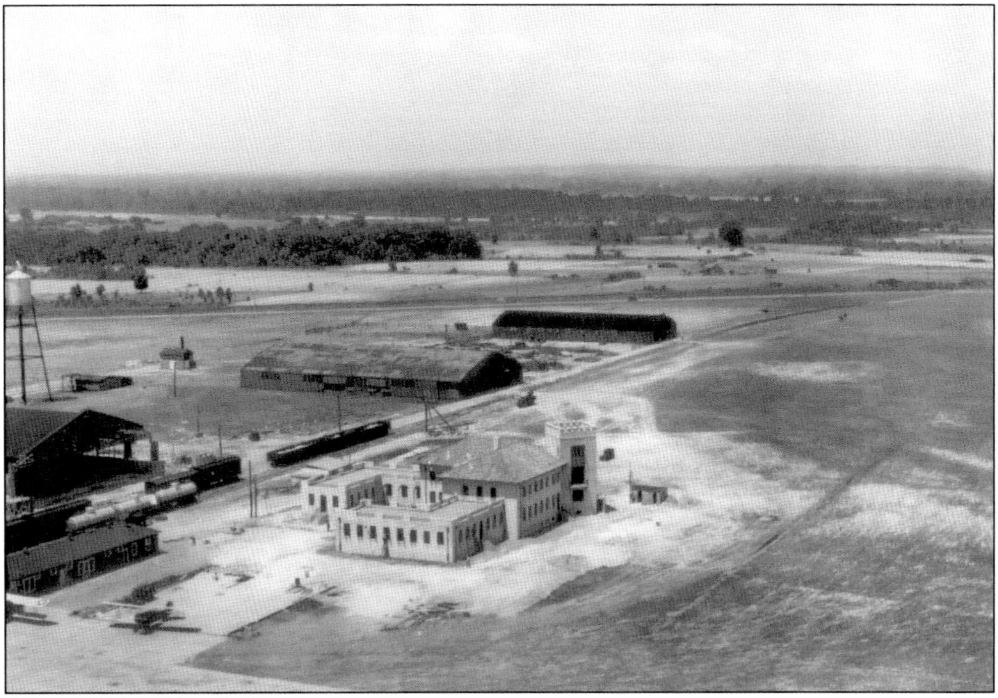

With 28 pursuit and observation aircraft assigned to ACTS, improvements to the air operations area at Maxwell became necessary. In 1931, workers began construction of a two-story operations building located adjacent to the flying field. Original hangar structures of the former depot are visible behind the operations building. (USAFHRA.)

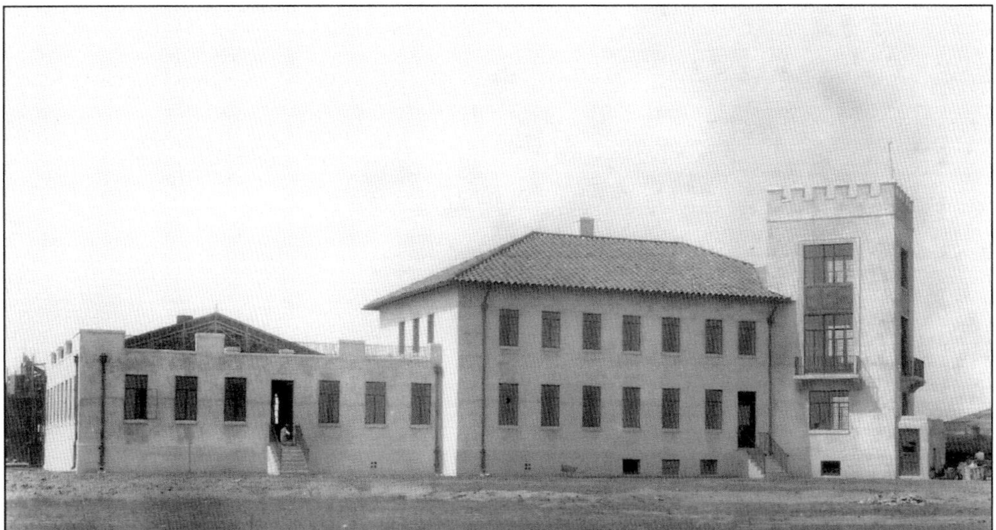

The new operations building also served as the headquarters for Maxwell Field. From his office, post commander Maj. John F. Curry had an unobstructed view of the flying field. The second story of the building included offices of the executive officer, the clerical staff, and the weather bureau. The new facility also included an area for repairing, repacking, and testing parachutes. (Air University Office of History.)

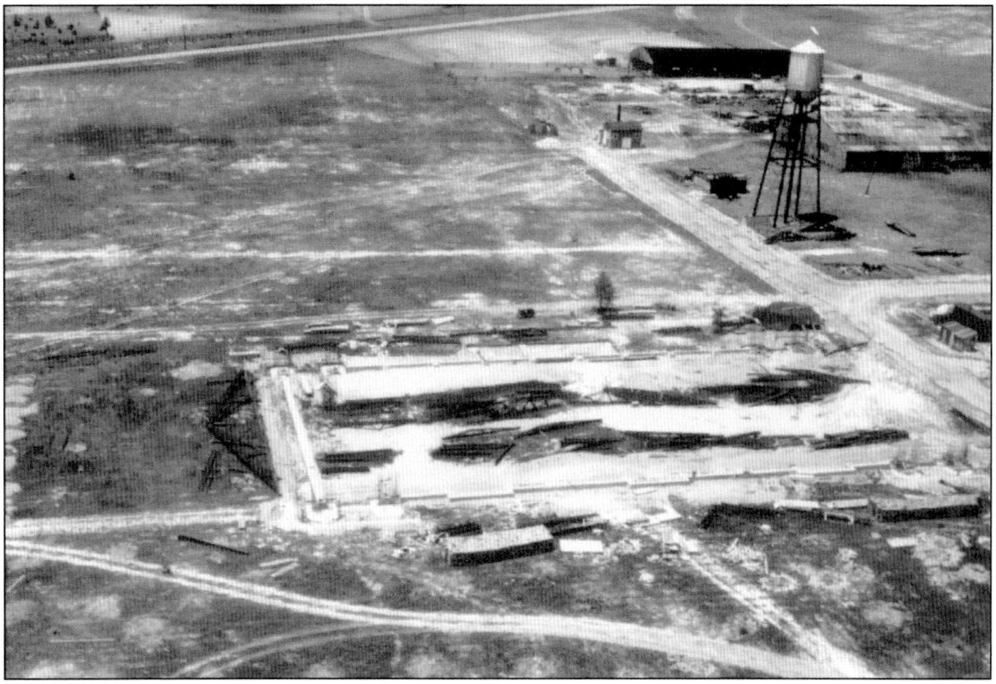

In addition to the new headquarters and operations building, workmen began construction of four large hangars adjacent to the flying field. Each hangar was designed to hold as many as 24 observation or 36 pursuit-type aircraft. In this image, materials to be used to construct Hangar D are assembled on the prepared site. (USAFHRA.)

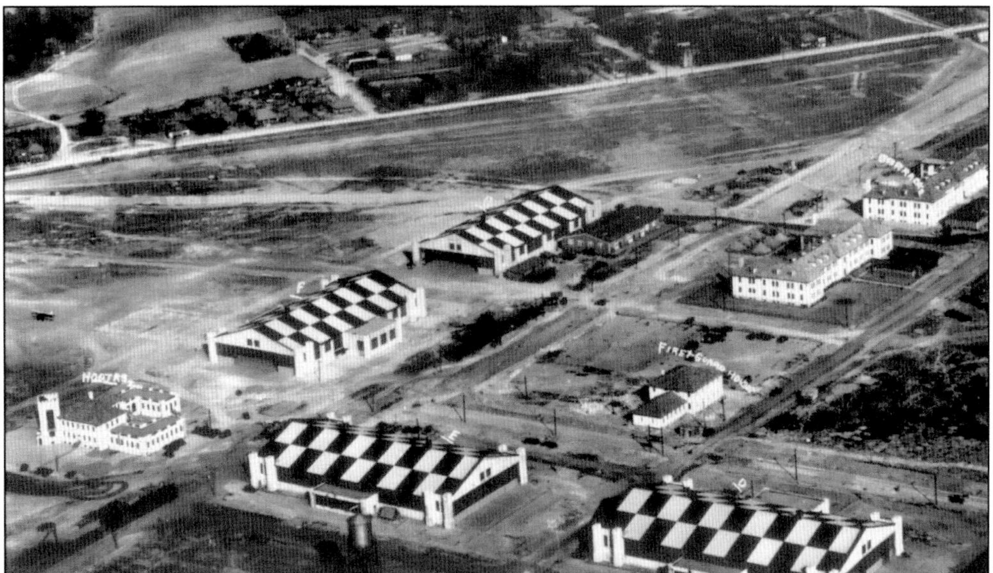

The four steel-and-concrete hangars were constructed in an *L*-shaped arrangement with the post headquarters and operations building located at the convergence of the hangar rows. The roof of each hangar was painted in a distinctive checkerboard pattern for increased visibility. Barracks buildings for enlisted men, a fire station, and a guardhouse have also been completed. (USAFHRA.)

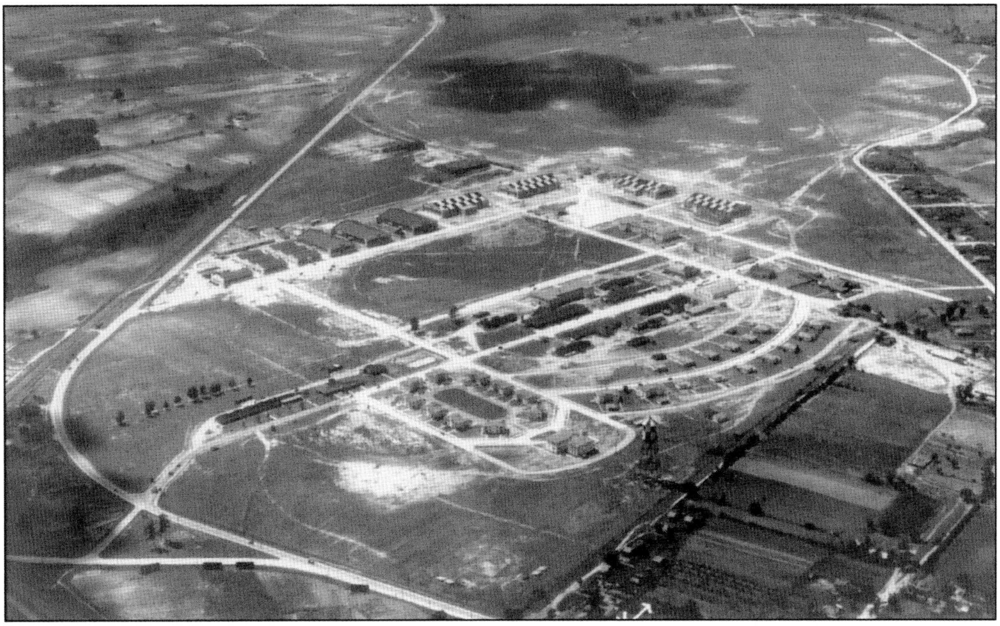

By 1932, the transition of the former aviation engine and repair depot into a modern military facility is apparent, although many of the temporary structures built during the First World War remain visible. The post is bordered by Washington Ferry Road to the east and the Birmingham Highway to the west. Washington Ferry Road would soon be closed to restrict access to the field. (USAFHRA.)

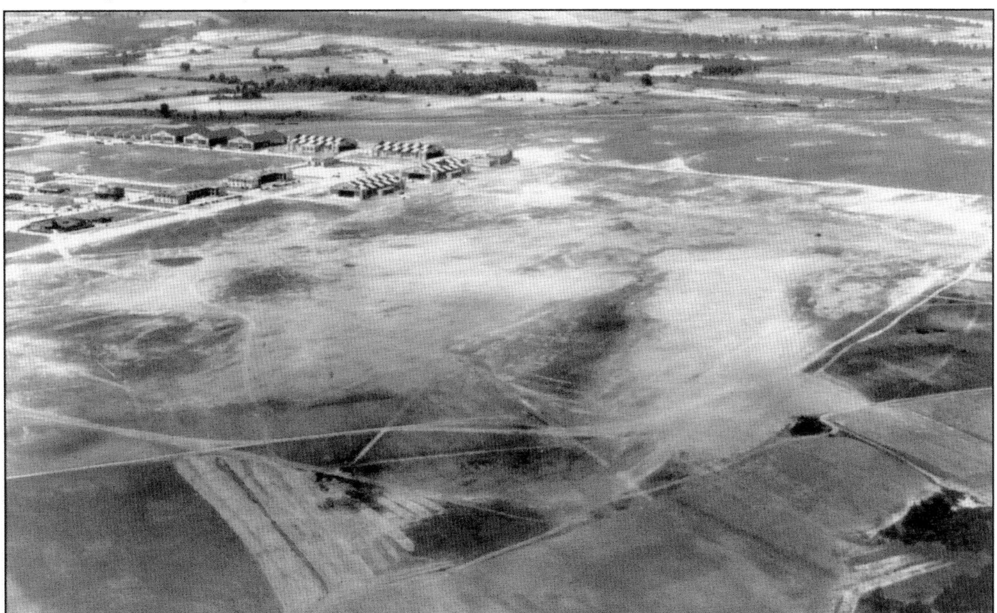

To accommodate the expansion of facilities related to the relocation of ACTS to Maxwell Field, the federal government acquired additional property that included parcels of the former Kohn plantation and adjacent lands located between the Alabama River and the Birmingham Highway. By July 1933, Maxwell Field consisted of 1,140 acres. Recent leveling and grading of the flying field give the area a more structured appearance. (USAFHRA.)

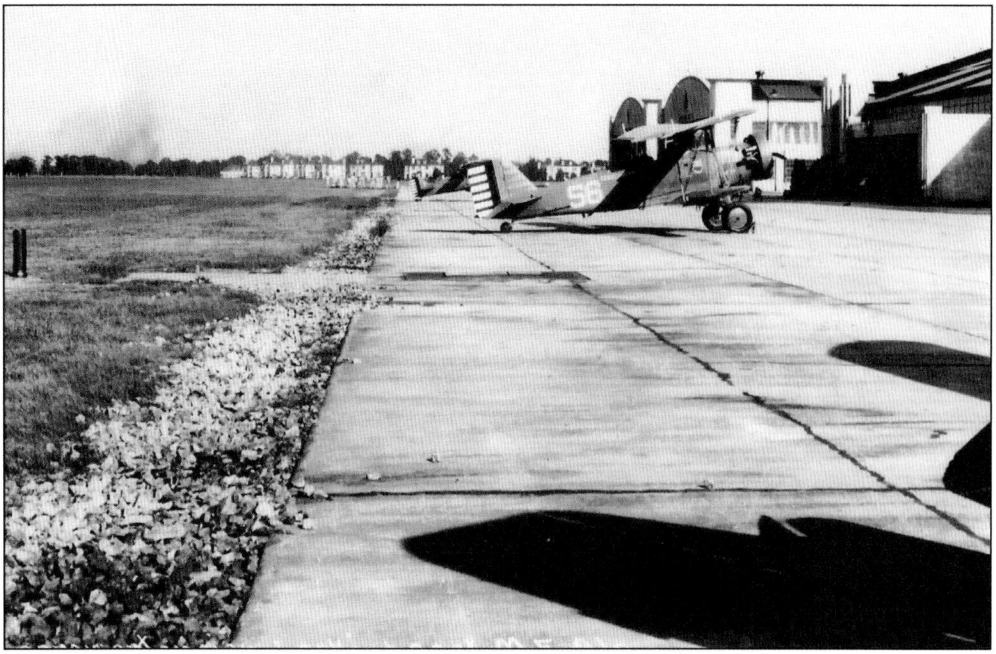

A wide concrete parking apron for aircraft was constructed on the airfield side of the hangar line. Fueling stations connected to the central storage tank by underground pipes were located at various points along the apron. This new "Aqua System" allowed aircraft to be fueled on the flight line, eliminating the need for refueling trucks. (Air University Office of History.)

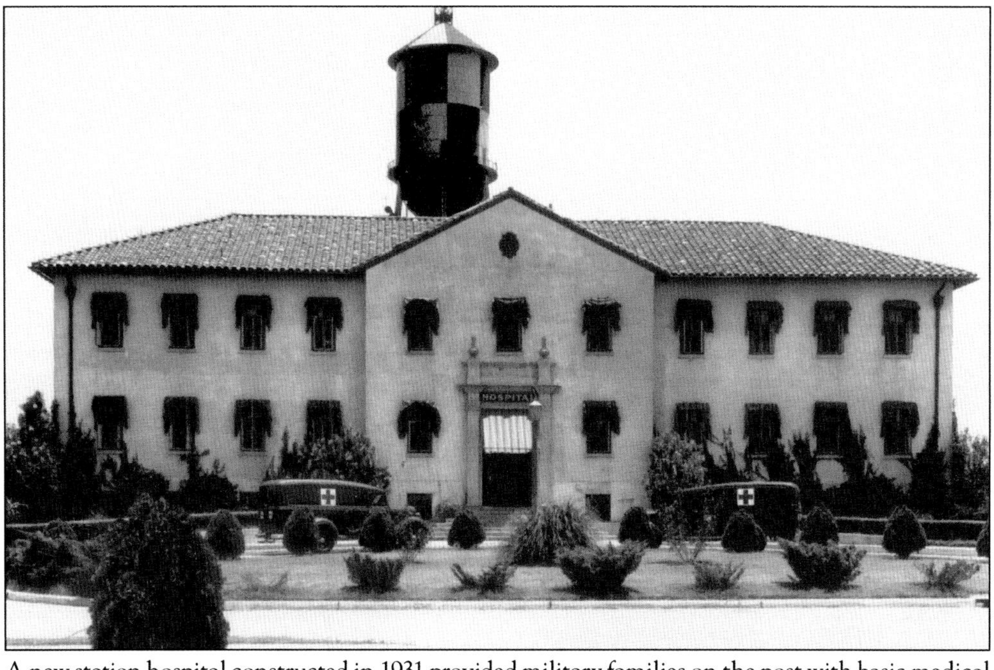

A new station hospital constructed in 1931 provided military families on the post with basic medical and dental care. The architectural design of the new building included a red ceramic tile roof and stucco-covered exterior walls. The construction of these "Weaver type" buildings created an architectural pattern that was unique among aviation fields in the Southeast. (USAFHRA.)

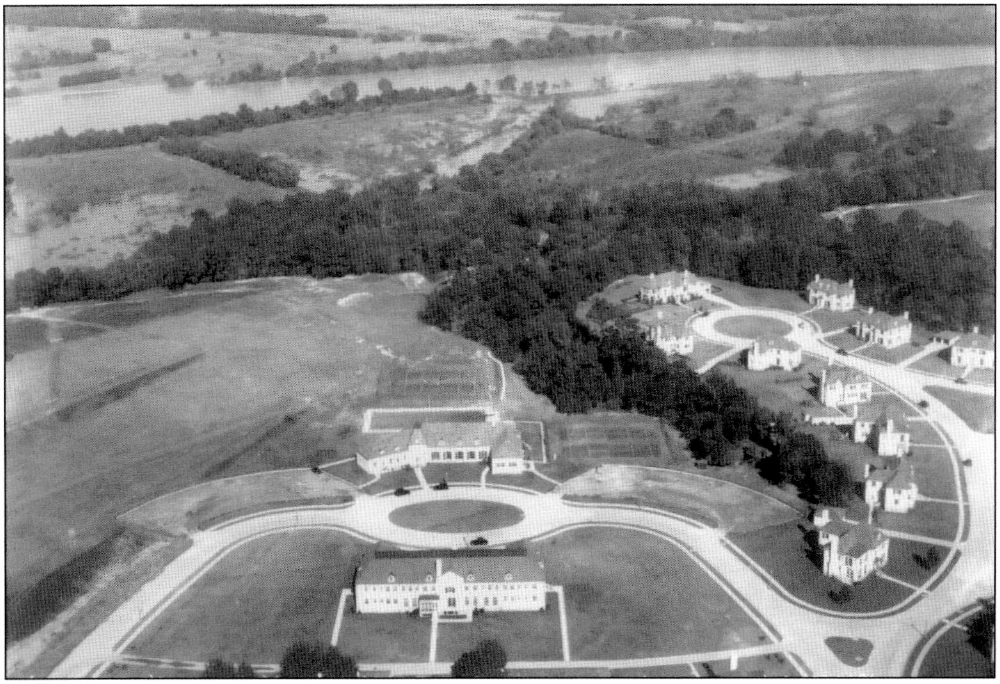

The bachelor officers' quarters had accommodations for 18 officers. A row of garages for automobiles was located to the rear of the building. The officers' club, with swimming pool, is located across the circular drive. (USAFHRA.)

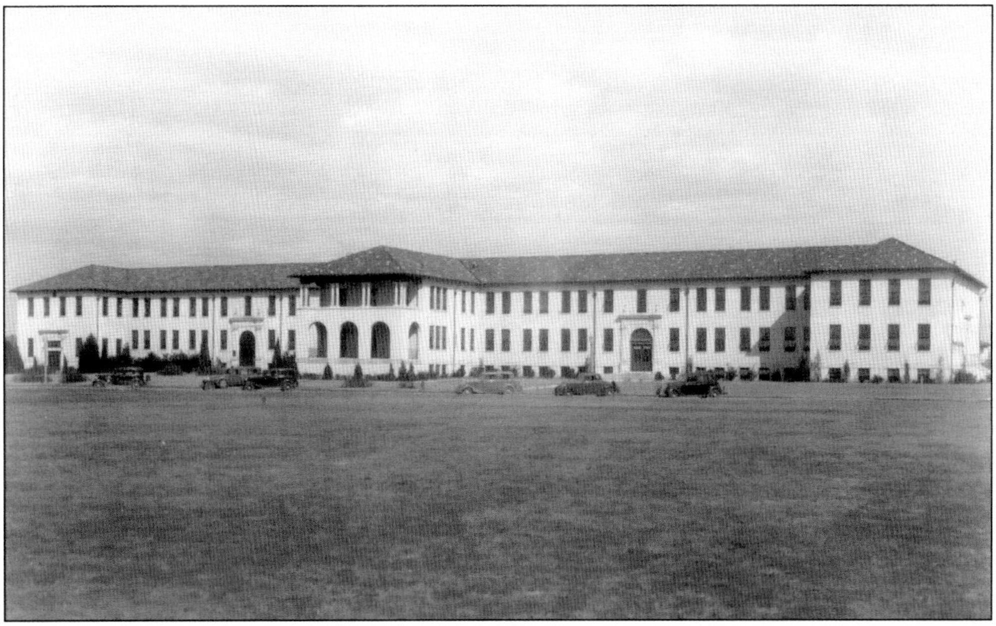

Completed in 1931, the tactical school academic facility was named Austin Hall in honor of 1st Lt. Charles B. Austin, a former ACTS instructor at Langley Field. In 1934, the structure was expanded to accommodate larger classes and to permit the tactical school headquarters to be housed in the building. During the Second World War, Austin Hall became headquarters of the Southeast Air Corps Training Center. (USAFHRA.)

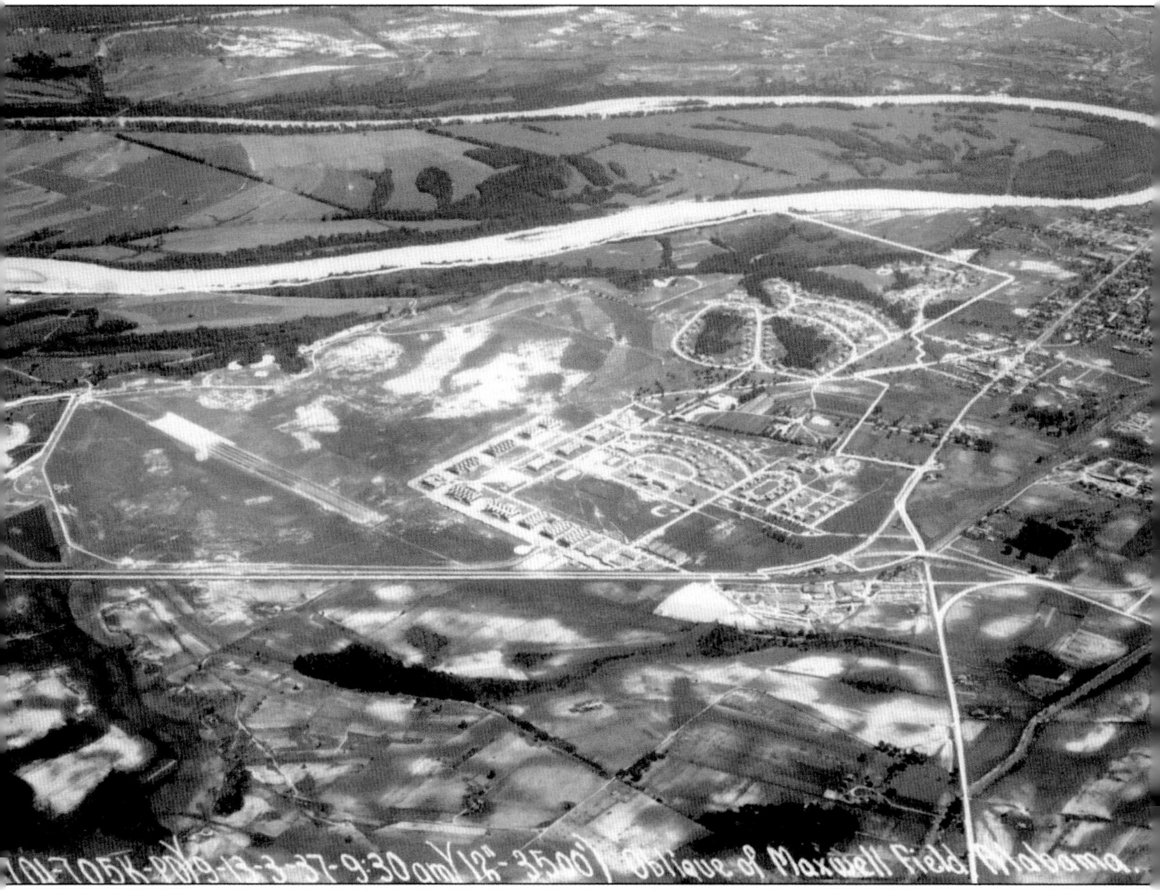

By 1937, Maxwell Field had grown into a large military aviation installation primarily as a result of the relocation of the tactical school to Montgomery. On-post housing included 99 sets of officers' quarters, 77 sets of noncommissioned officers' quarters, 3 enlisted men's barracks, and bachelor officers' quarters for 18 officers. For aircraft maintenance, the field had six hangars, an engineering building, an airplane assembly building, and an Air Corps supply building. The most evident change to the flying field is the addition of a paved runway. By 1939, the field was equipped with an airfield beacon and runway lighting system for night operations. The period from 1931 to 1940 has been called the "Pre-War Golden Age of Maxwell" because of the relocation of the tactical school and associated expansion of the post. (Air University Office of History.)

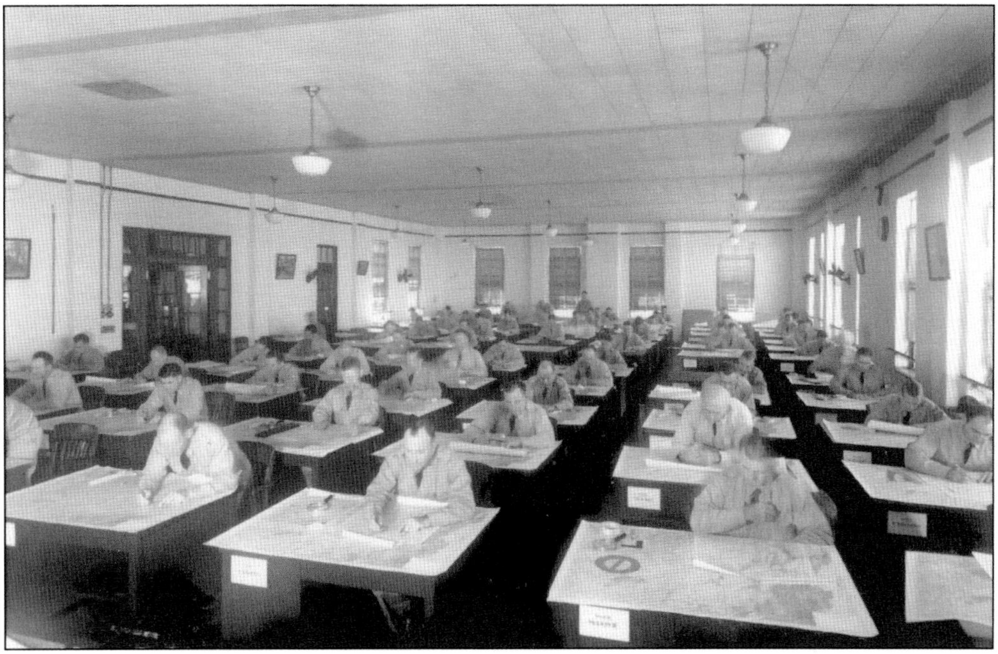

Much of the instruction of the tactical school focused on the belief that the airplane provided a new and highly effective weapon of war. During the Second World War, graduates of the tactical school assumed positions of leadership that directed American air power to achieve superiority over the Axis powers. (Air University Office of History.)

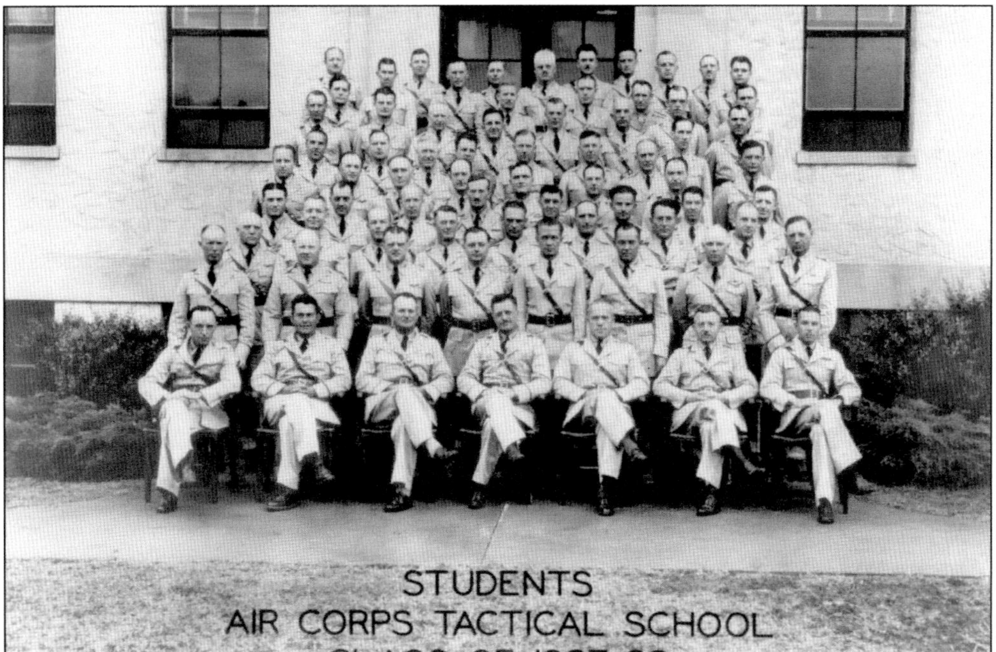

Students of the Tactical School Class of 1937–1938 included Maj. Robert D. Knapp, Lt. Haywood S. Hansell, and Capt. Lawrence S. Kuter. Of 320 Army Air Forces general officers on active duty at the end of the Second World War, 261 were graduates of the tactical school. (USAFHRA.)

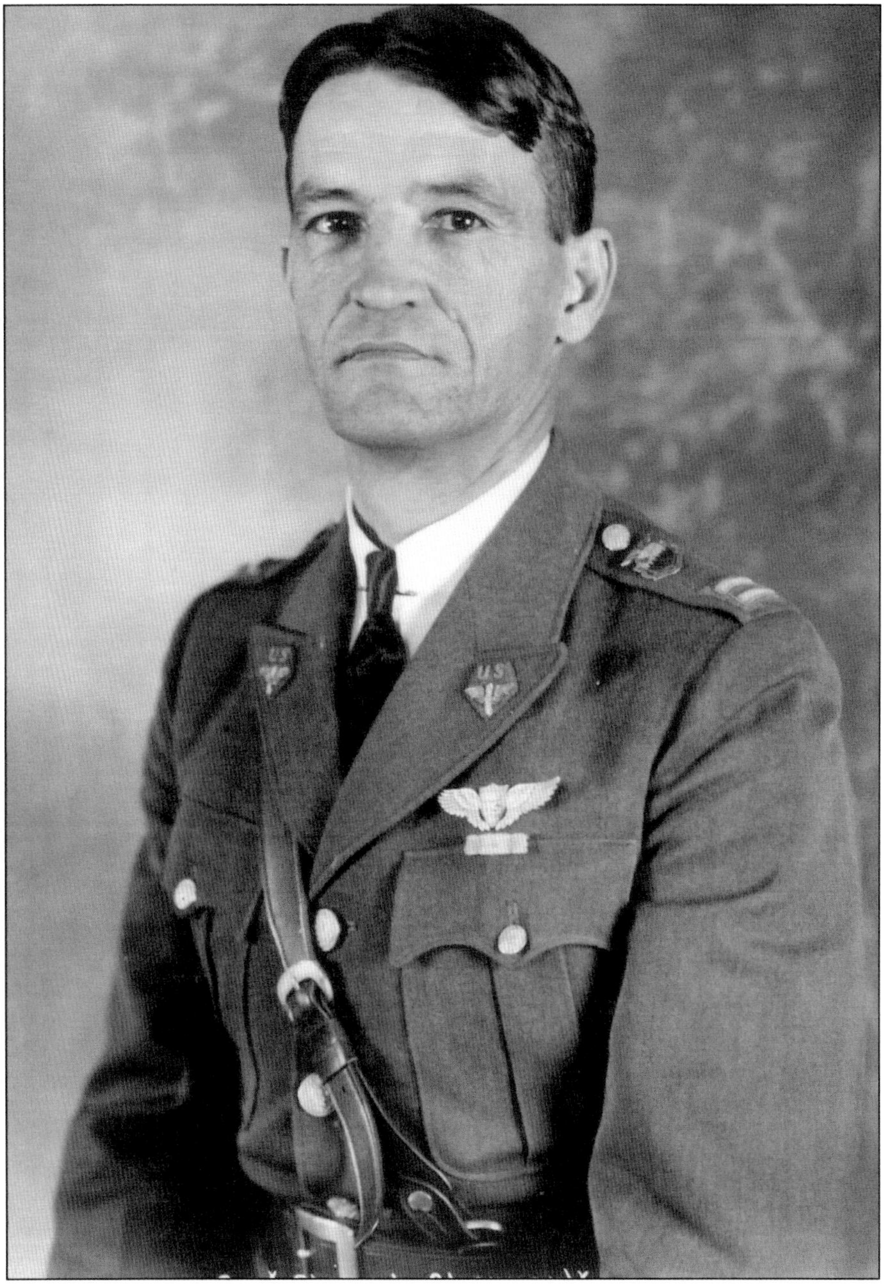

Born in Commerce, Texas, on September 6, 1893, Claire L. Chennault received a commission in the United States Army in 1917 and earned the wings of a military aviator in 1919. A graduate of the Air Corps Tactical School, Chennault served as one of the original faculty members when the school was relocated to Maxwell Field. During his tenure as an instructor at the tactical school, Chennault was a strong advocate of the role of pursuit aircraft in military airpower doctrine. In 1937, Chennault retired from the Army Air Corps. At the invitation of Madame Chiang Kai-shek, Chennault traveled to China to organize and train the Chinese air force. In August 1941, he formed the American Volunteer Group, which became known as the "Flying Tigers." (Air University Office of History.)

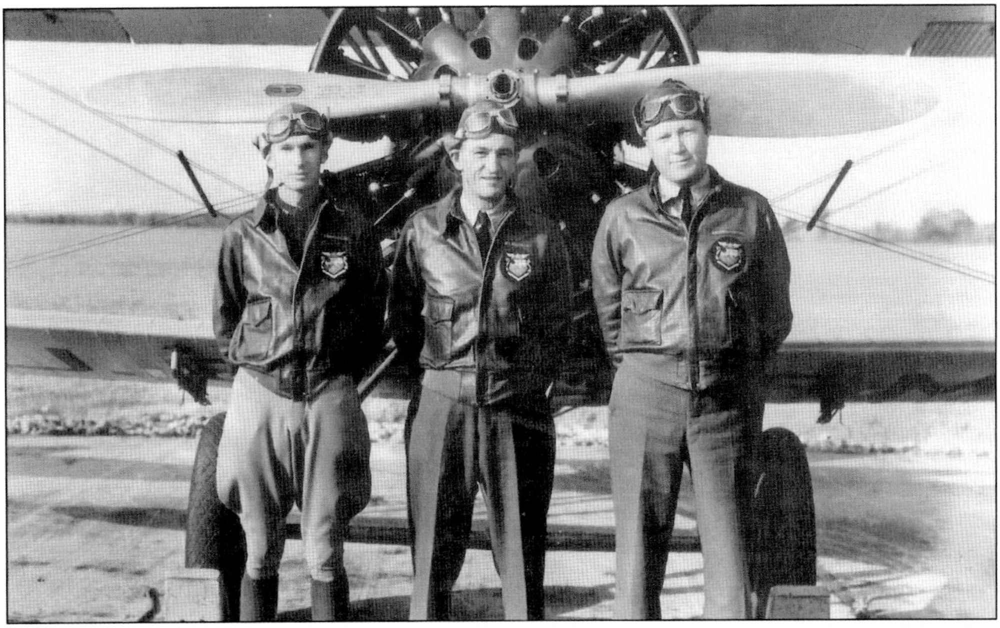

The Army Air Corps aerial demonstration team "Three Men on a Flying Trapeze" was formed in 1932 by Capt. Claire Chennault. The "Trapeze" pilots were personally selected by Chennault and represented the finest pursuit pilots available. Using Boeing P-12 aircraft, the team gained national acclaim for their daring performances. Lt. Haywood Hansell (left), Chennault (center), and Sgt. John Williamson pose at the 1934 Cleveland Air Races. (Air University Office of History.)

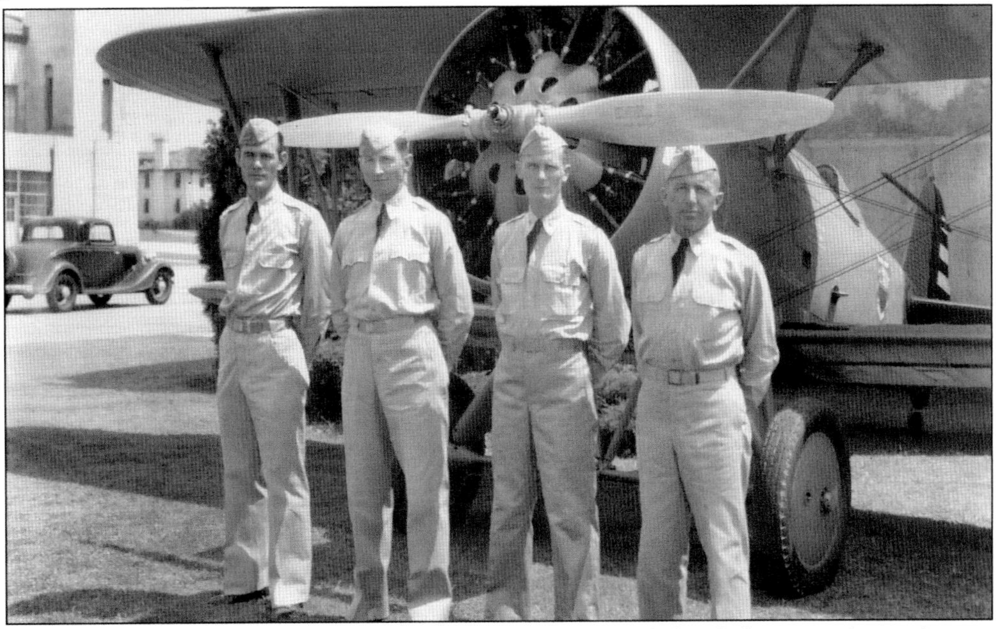

After the original Maxwell Field aerial demonstration team disbanded, a second team known as the "Skylarks" was assembled in 1937. Like their predecessors, the Skylarks excelled at close-formation aerial demonstrations. From left to right are Carl R. Storrie, Clayton E. Hughes, Wilbur W. Aring, and Capt. Charles D. McAllister, commanding officer. The Skylarks performed at the 1937 National Air Races in Cleveland, Ohio. (Author's collection.)

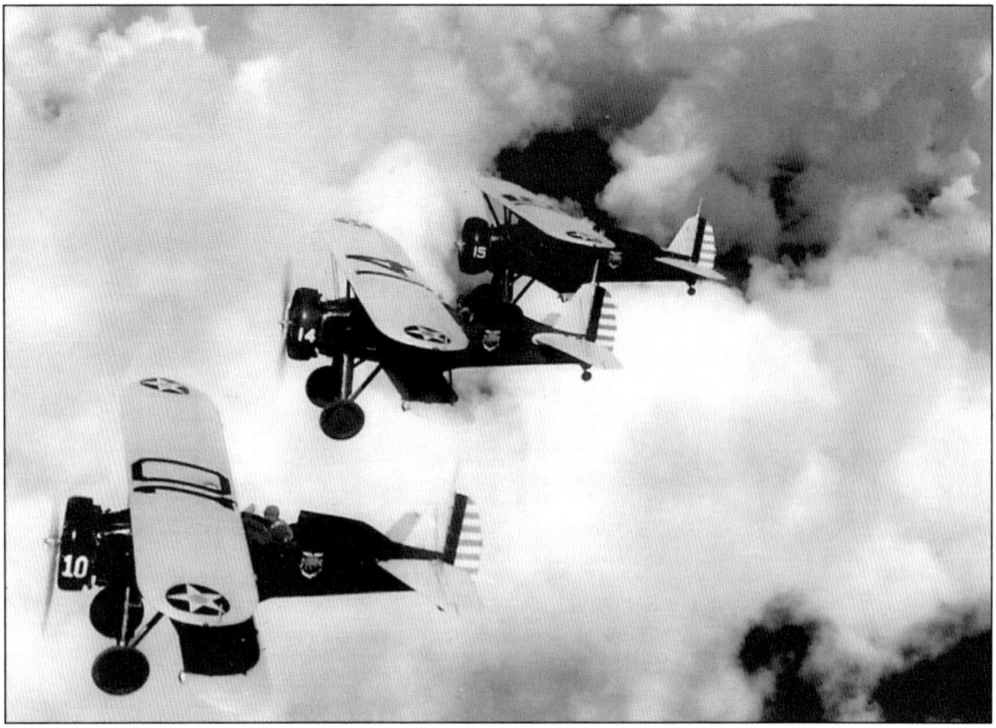

The aerial demonstration teams from Maxwell Field utilized Boeing P-12 pursuit aircraft. Powered by a 525-horsepower Pratt and Whitney R-1340 engine, the P-12 could achieve a top speed of 180 miles per hour. Three Men on a Flying Trapeze routinely flew in such close formation that they occasionally performed with the wings of their aircraft tied together by 10-foot lengths of rope. (Air University Office of History.)

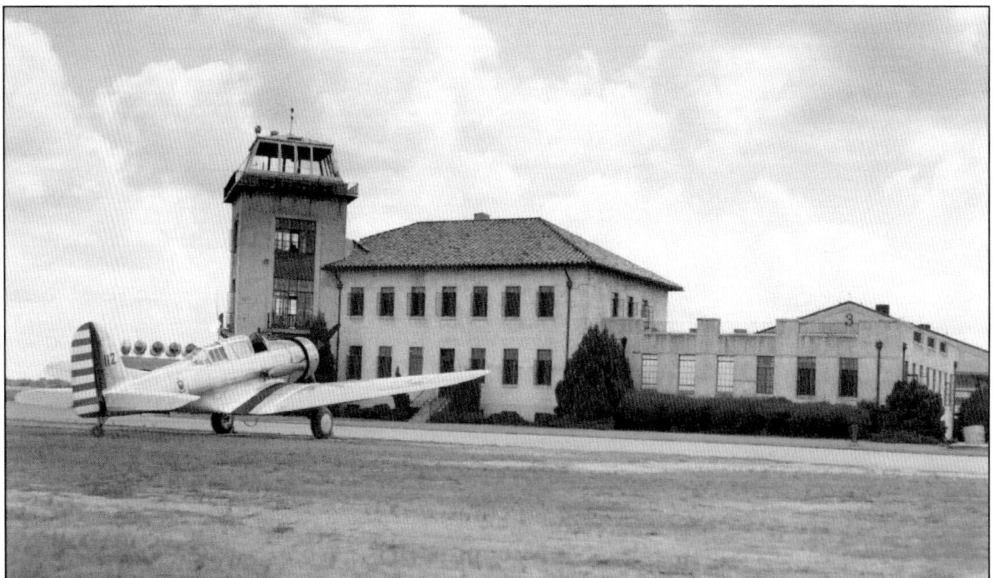

A Northrop A-17 attack/light bombardment aircraft is parked on the ramp outside of the post operations building in June 1940. (Author's collection.)

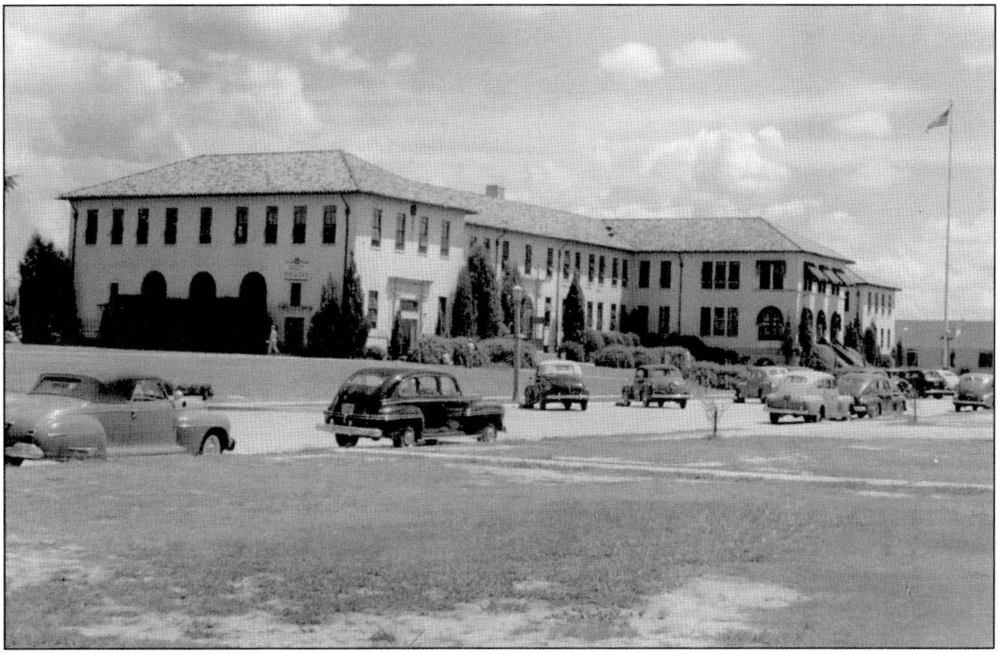

Established in July 1940, the Southeast Air Corps Training Center (SEACTC) was responsible for pilot, navigator, and bombardier training at military installations in the Southeast. Headquartered at Austin Hall, SEACTC was one of three training centers of the Army Air Corps. SEACTC was renamed Army Air Forces Southeast Training Center in May 1942 before being designated Army Air Forces Eastern Flying Training Command in 1943. (Air University Office of History.)

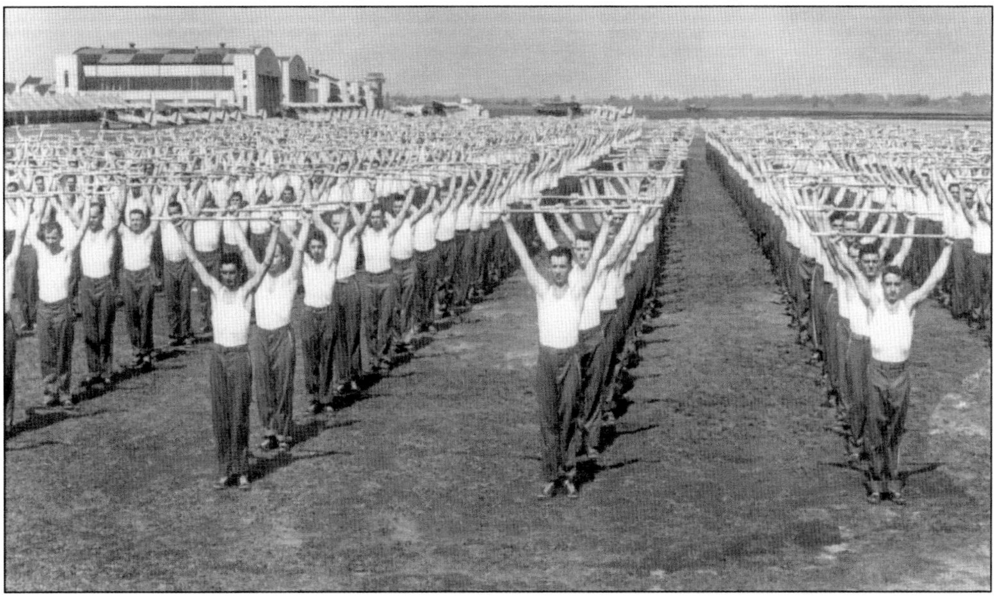

In September 1941, the Air Corps Replacement Center was established at Maxwell Field. The first facility of its kind, the center provided cadets with basic military knowledge and improved their physical conditioning prior to enrollment in flying schools. Cadets received 60 hours of intensive physical training in a series of programs designed to bring the future pilot to the peak of physical conditioning. (Air University Office of History.)

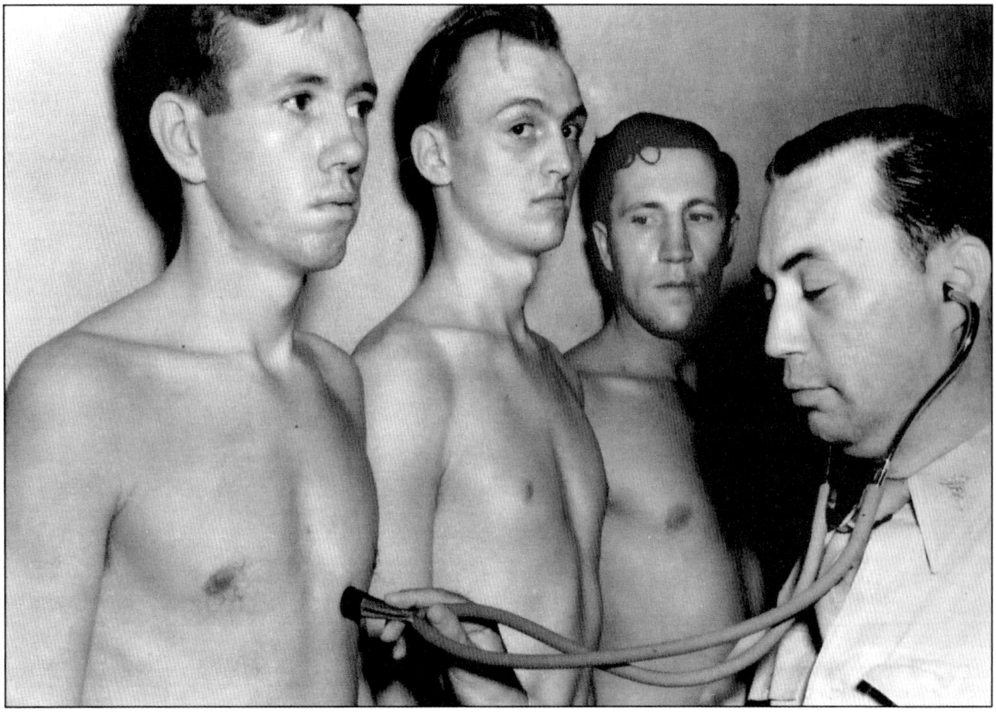

In the summer of 1942, the Replacement Center was designated the Army Air Forces Preflight School. During the peak of activity, 2,700 cadets were enrolled in the Preflight School. All cadets attended the five-week initial phase. A second three-week phase consisted of cadets who failed to qualify as pilots but elected to remain in the service as bombardiers or navigators. (Air University Office of History.)

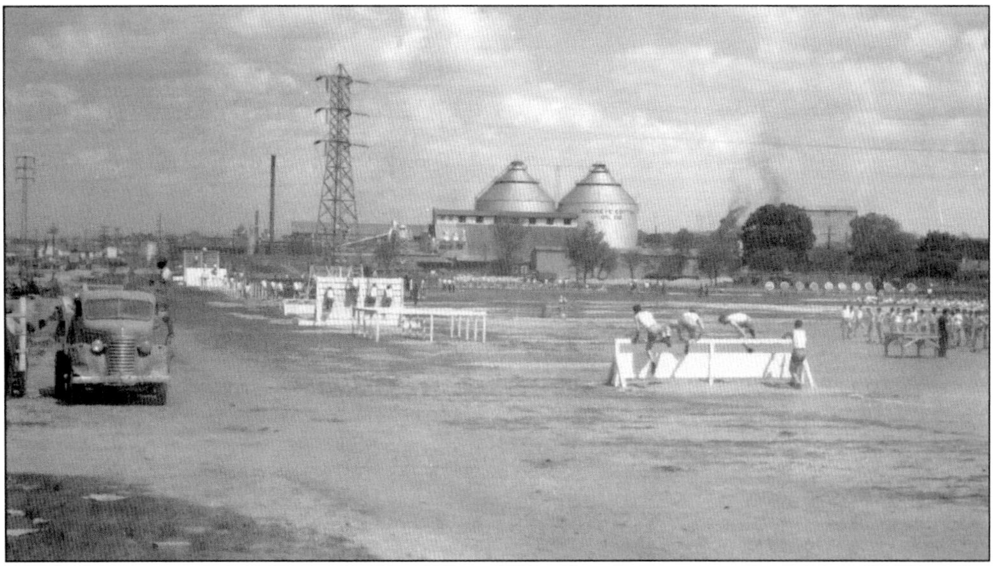

Aviation cadets of the Preflight School at Maxwell Field transverse the obstacle course during physical training exercises. The storage silos of the Buckeye Cotton Oil Company are visible in the background. These silos were located near the entrance of the present-day Bell Street Gate. (USAFHRA.)

Aviation cadets in the Preflight School received instruction in basic military and officer training. Subjects included customs and courtesies of military service, inspections, leadership, and close order drill. (USAFHRA.)

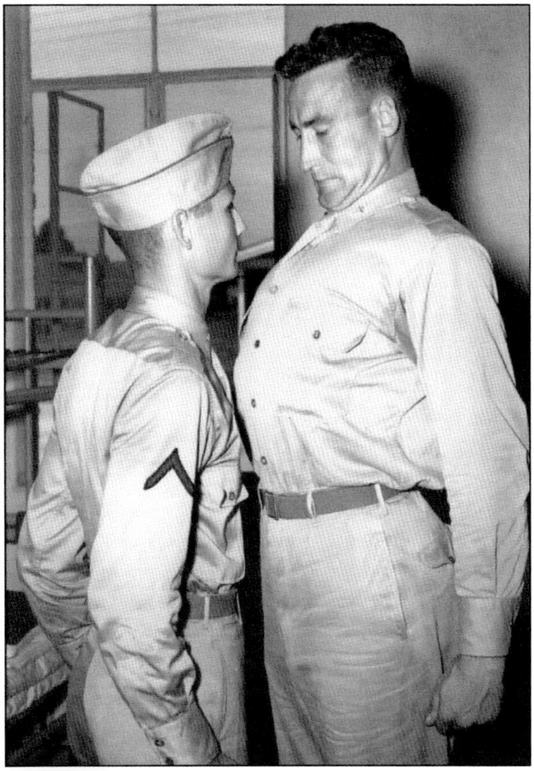

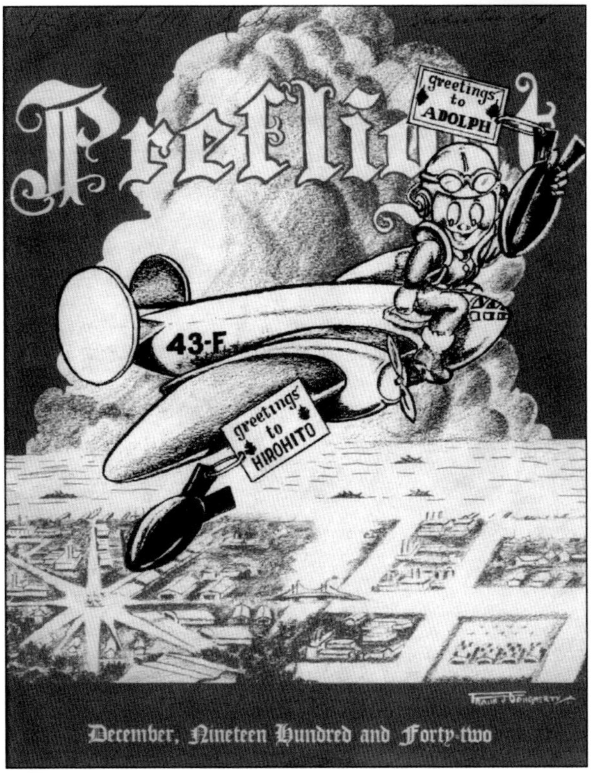

Preflight was published by the Aviation Cadet Social Fund as a guide for the new cadet. The booklet explained the daily routine at Maxwell Field, the cadet command structure, sick-call procedures, required reading, and budgeting of the $75-a-month base pay. (Author's collection.)

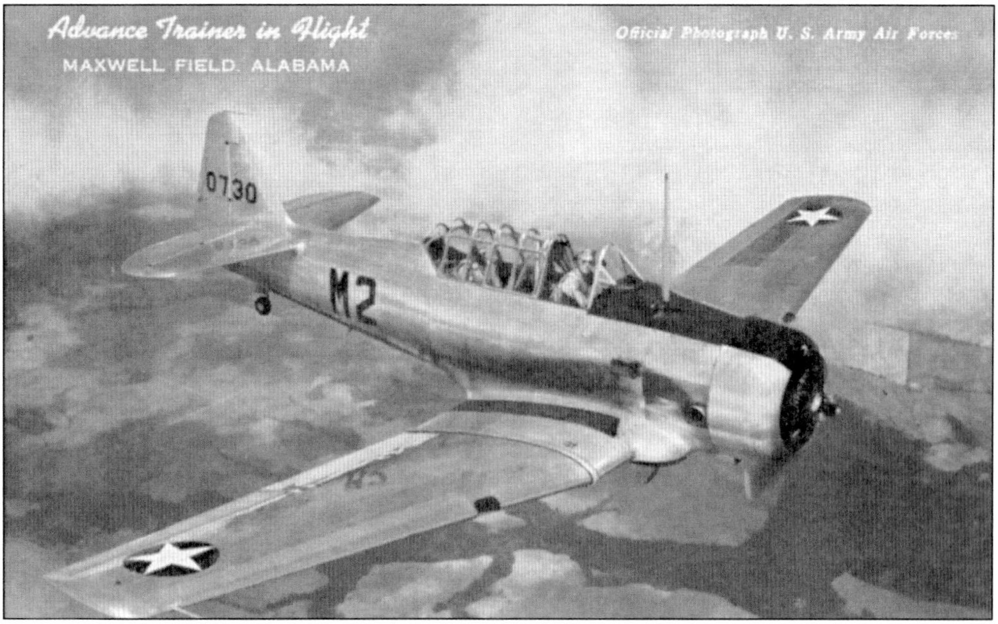

In August 1940, an advanced single-engine flying school was activated at Maxwell Field. The 10-week program consisted of 70 hours of flight training and included instruction in formation flying, advanced aerobatics, cross-country and night operations, instrument flying, and gunnery practice. The advanced program also included 56 hours of ground instruction in advanced aviation subjects such as military organizations and traditions and fighter and bombardment operations in aerial warfare. Graduates of Basic Flying School Class SE (Southeast) 41A became the first advanced class at Maxwell Field. In addition to Air Corps cadets, members of the Royal Air Force from Great Britain received training at the advanced school. The first contingent of 750 British cadets arrived in the fall of 1941. In the summer of 1942, the Advanced School was relocated to Albany, Georgia. (Above, author's collection; below, USAFHRA.)

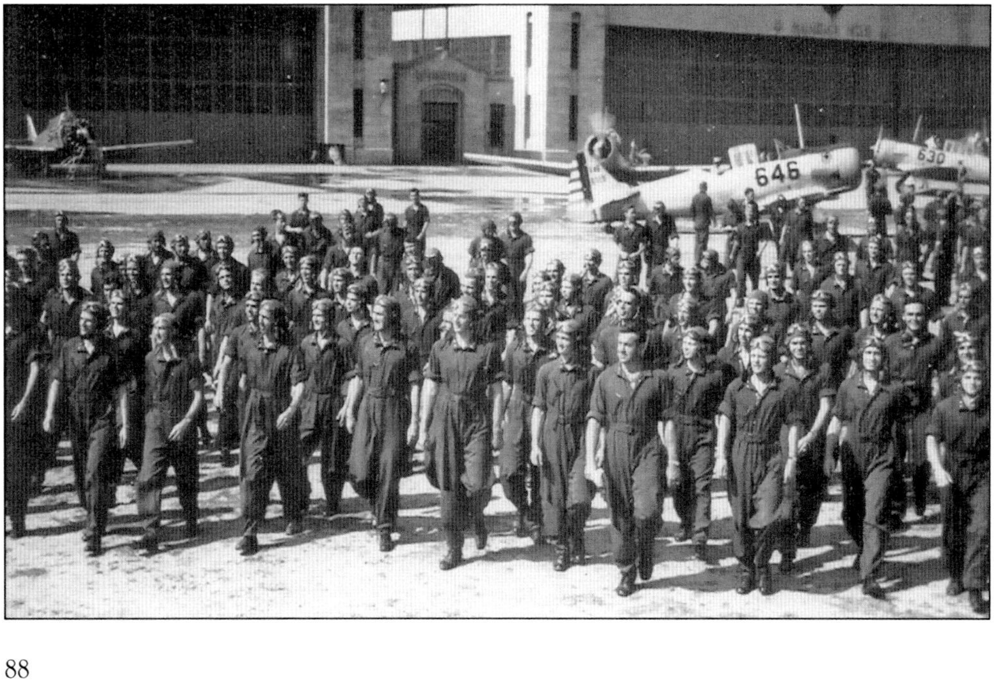

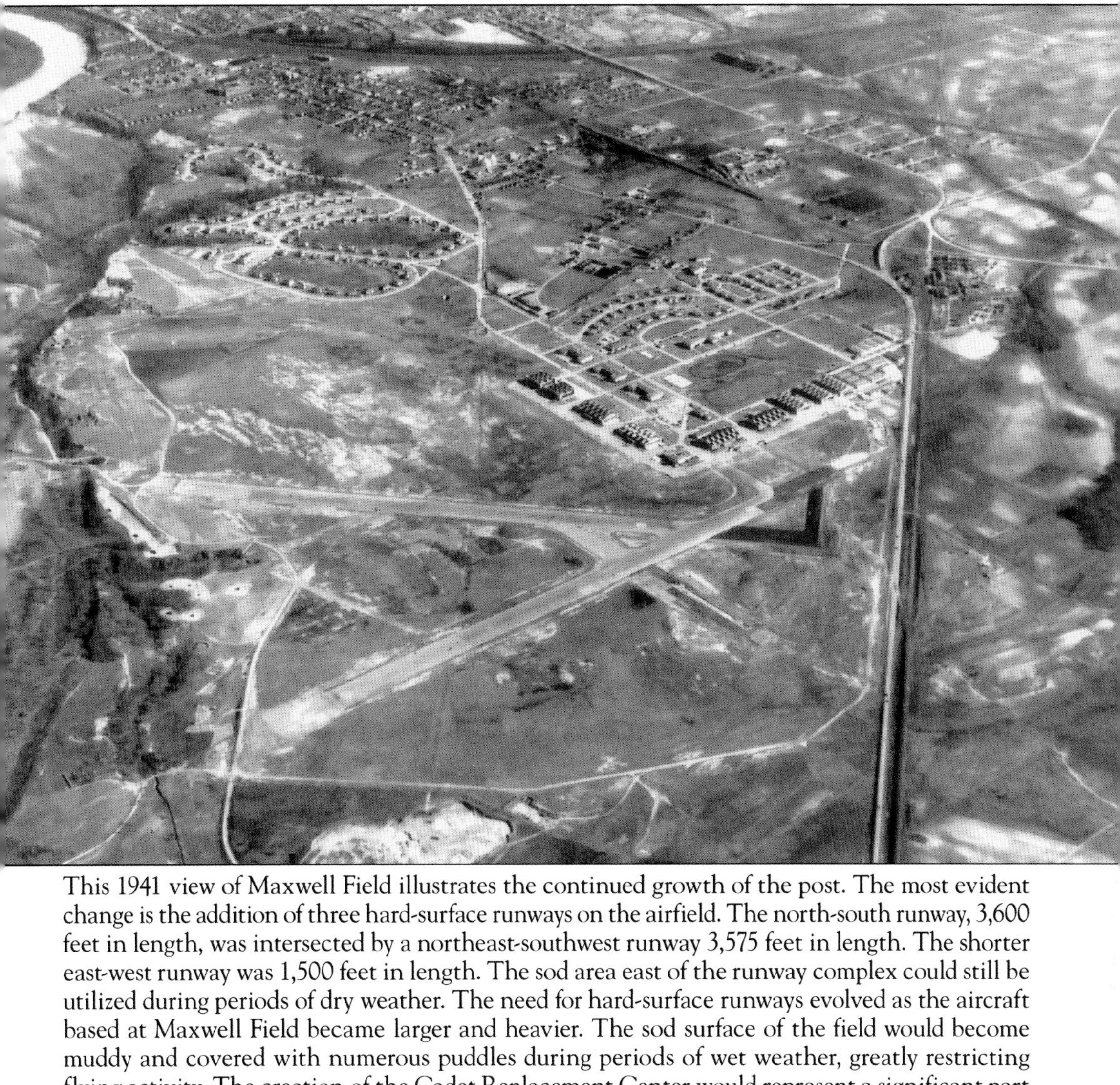

This 1941 view of Maxwell Field illustrates the continued growth of the post. The most evident change is the addition of three hard-surface runways on the airfield. The north-south runway, 3,600 feet in length, was intersected by a northeast-southwest runway 3,575 feet in length. The shorter east-west runway was 1,500 feet in length. The sod area east of the runway complex could still be utilized during periods of dry weather. The need for hard-surface runways evolved as the aircraft based at Maxwell Field became larger and heavier. The sod surface of the field would become muddy and covered with numerous puddles during periods of wet weather, greatly restricting flying activity. The creation of the Cadet Replacement Center would represent a significant part of the future expansion of the field. (Air University Office of History.)

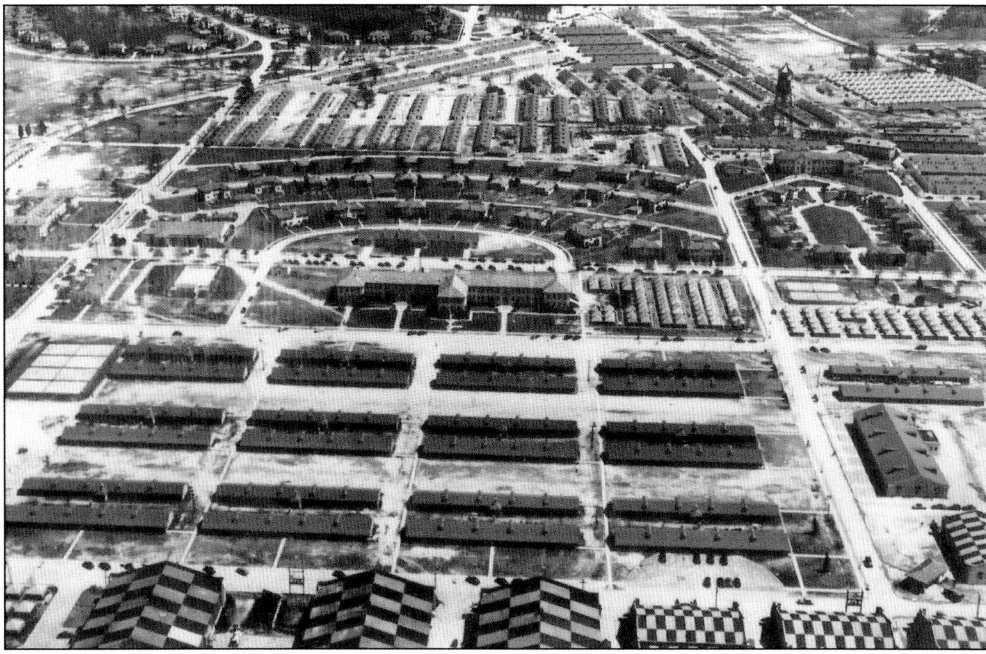

The massive and immediate increases in personnel at Maxwell Field created significant problems relating to housing. The arrival of 2,000 additional enlisted men in September 1940 resulted in a total of more than 6,400 enlisted personnel on the post. Temporary two-story wooden barracks structures were built on the old parade ground in front of Austin Hall. (USAFHRA.)

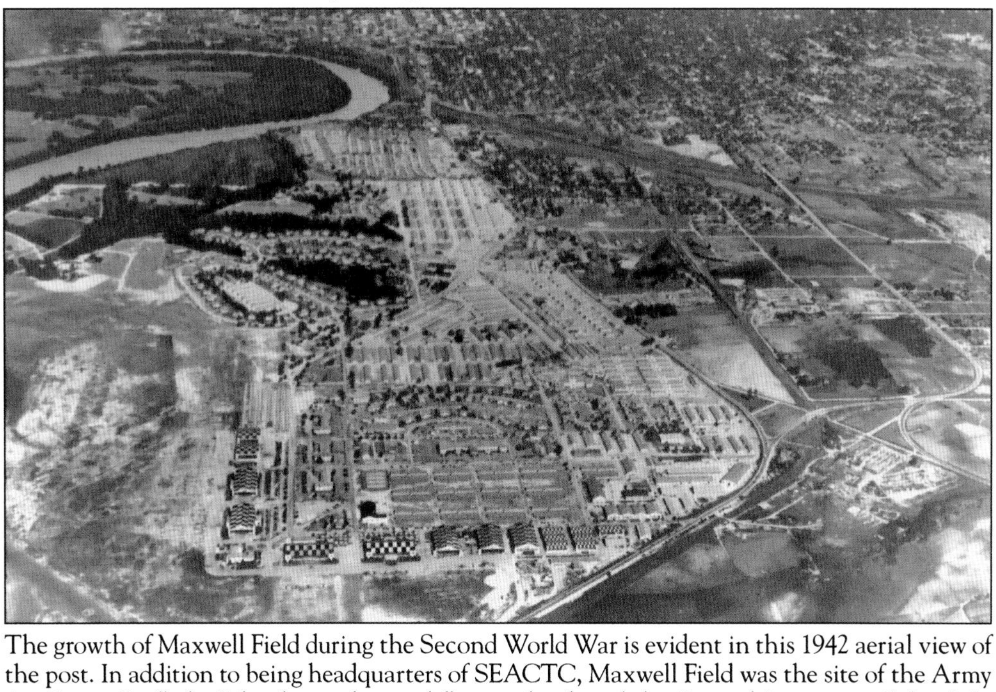

The growth of Maxwell Field during the Second World War is evident in this 1942 aerial view of the post. In addition to being headquarters of SEACTC, Maxwell Field was the site of the Army Air Forces Preflight School, an advanced flying school, and the Central Instructors School. In 1943, the post would be further enlarged to accommodate the integration of specialized four-engine aircraft training. (Air University Office of History.)

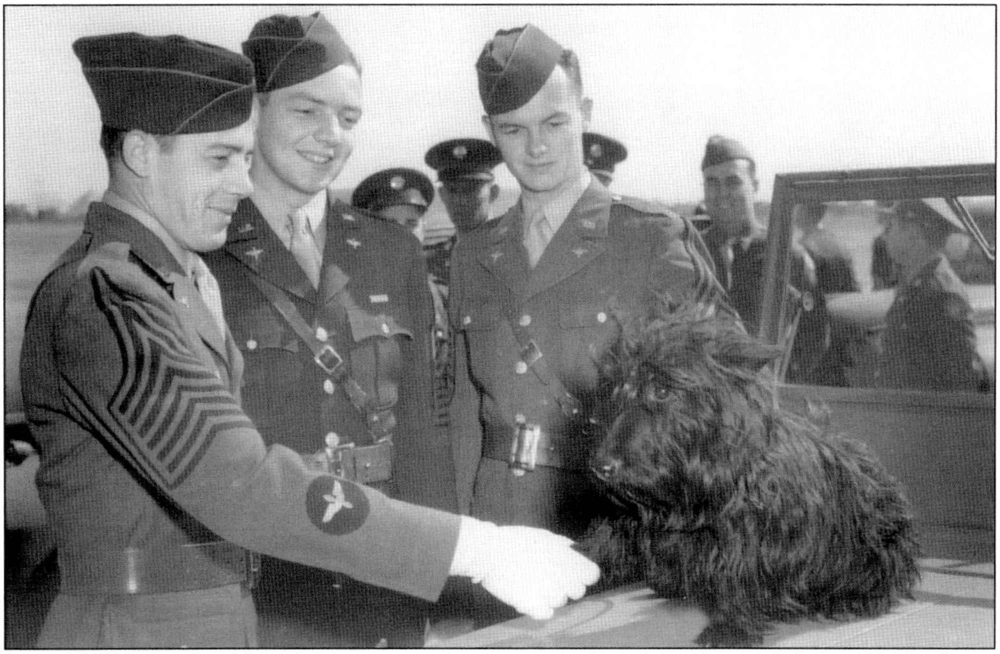

Officers of the Aviation Cadet Corps greet Pres. Franklin Roosevelt's Scottish terrier Fala, the world's most famous dog. A constant companion of the president, Fala accompanied Roosevelt during a 1943 visit to Maxwell Field. (USAFHRA.)

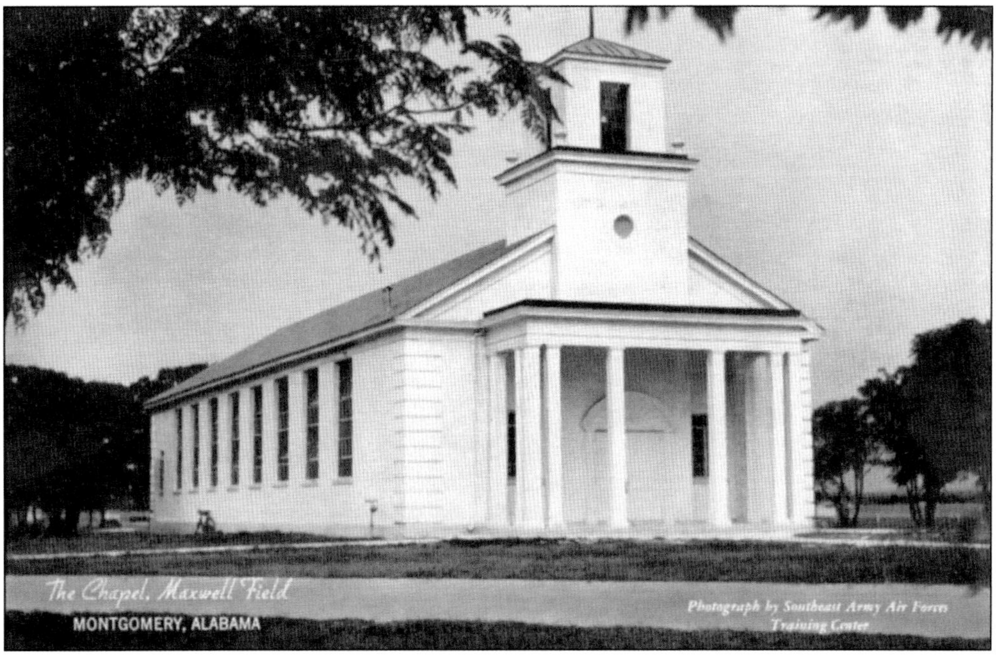

According to the Maxwell Field *Key to Preflight* booklet, "There are no atheists in the Army." The guide states that attendance at church is compulsory for underclassmen and recommended for upperclassmen in the hope that each cadet would become a better officer and eventually a better citizen. Before chapels were constructed on the post in 1942, Protestant, Catholic and Jewish chaplains ministered to personnel in hangars and post theaters. (Author's collection.)

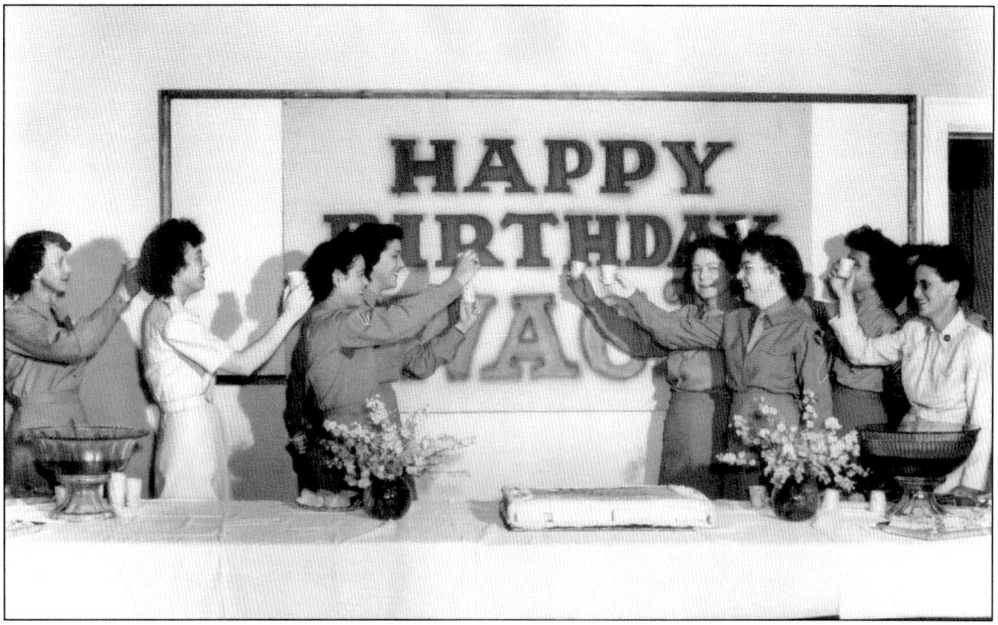

Established in 1942, the Women's Army Auxiliary Corps (WAAC) consisted of women trained to serve in noncombatant positions to relieve male soldiers for duty overseas. In July 1943, a bill transforming the WAAC into the Women's Army Corps (WAC) was signed into law by President Roosevelt. The first contingent of 156 female soldiers arrived at Maxwell Field in April 1943 to serve as clerks, stenographers, and technicians. (USAFHRA.)

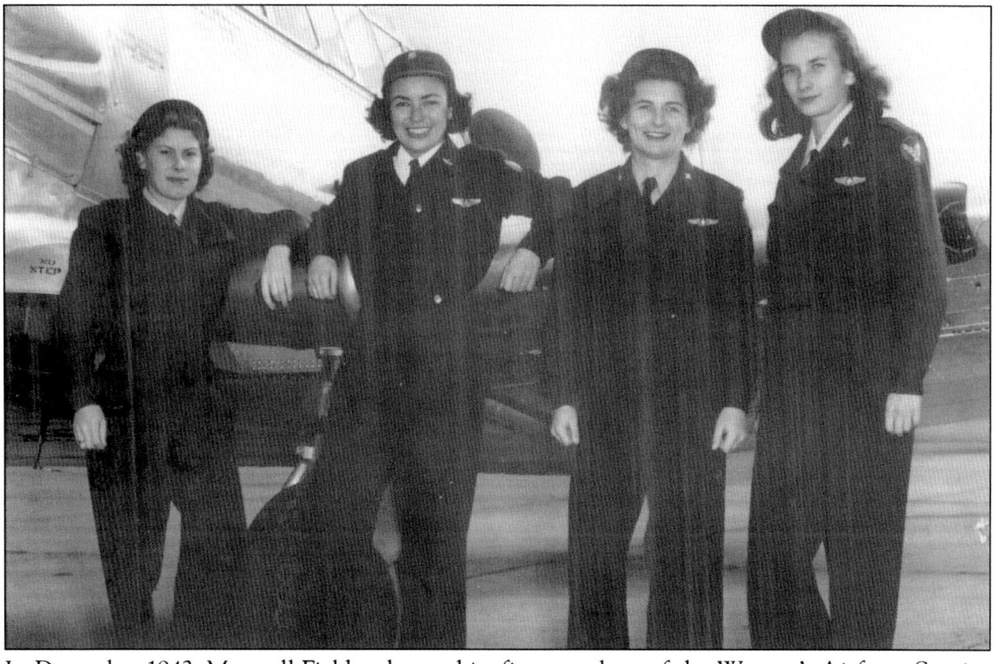

In December 1943, Maxwell Field welcomed its first members of the Women's Airforce Service Pilots (WASP). At Maxwell, female pilots served as copilots in the B-24 heavy bombardment transition training. WASP detachments were also based at other basic and advanced schools in Alabama, including Gunter Field and Craig Field in Selma. (USAFHRA.)

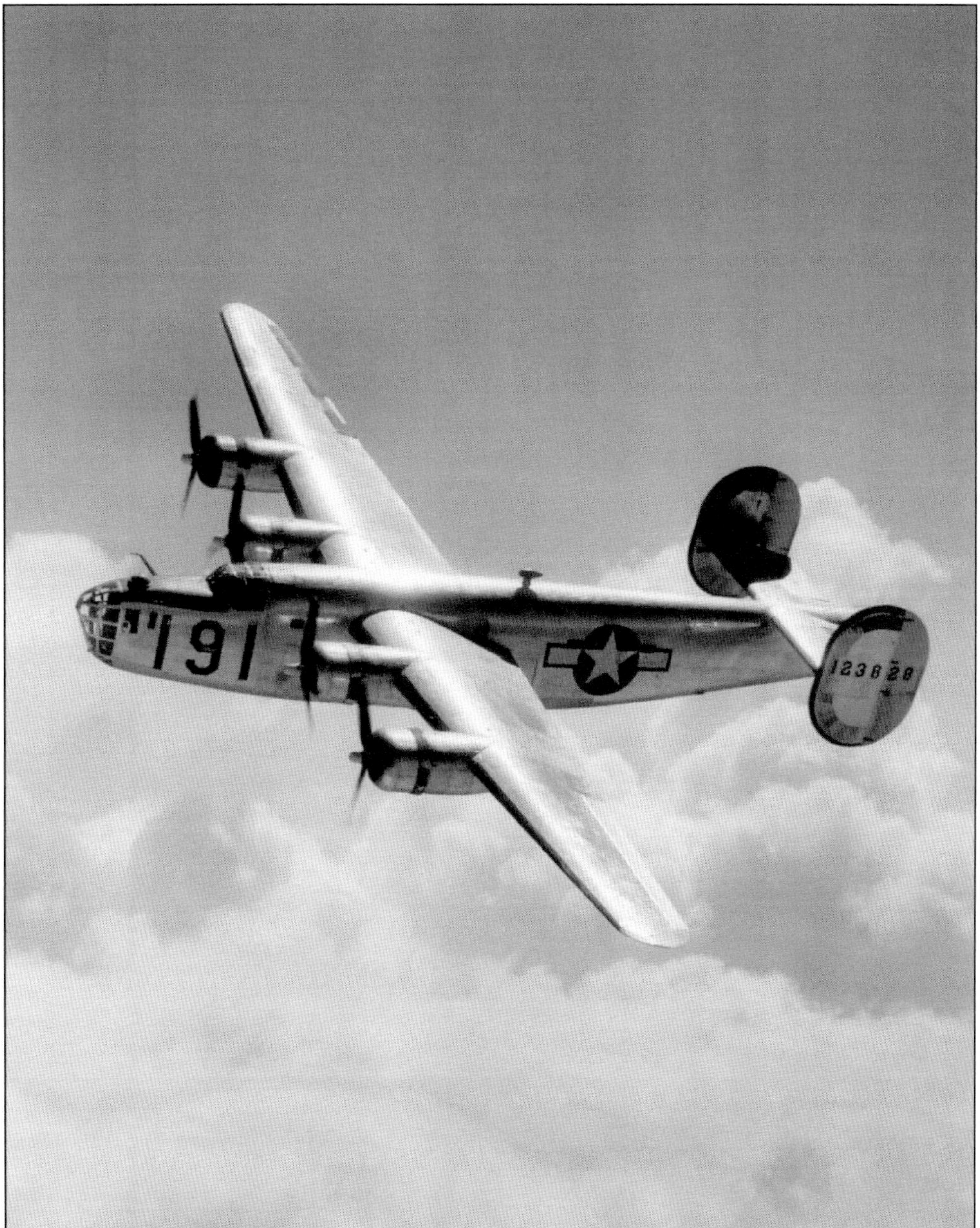

In July 1943, an Army Air Forces pilot school (specialized four-engine) was established at Maxwell Field to provide transition training in Consolidated B-24 heavy bombardment aircraft. The nine-week course included extensive ground training in the operation of aircraft systems. In flight, students received instruction in basic flight maneuvers, navigation and formation flying, high-altitude operations, and use of oxygen equipment. Graduates of advanced twin-engine schools were selected for the transition course because of their potential ability to pilot the larger four-engine aircraft. Pilots were evaluated on both flying skill and leadership ability. Training began on August 5, 1943, when a B-24 departed Maxwell Field with four students, a crew chief, and a flight instructor. (USAFHRA.)

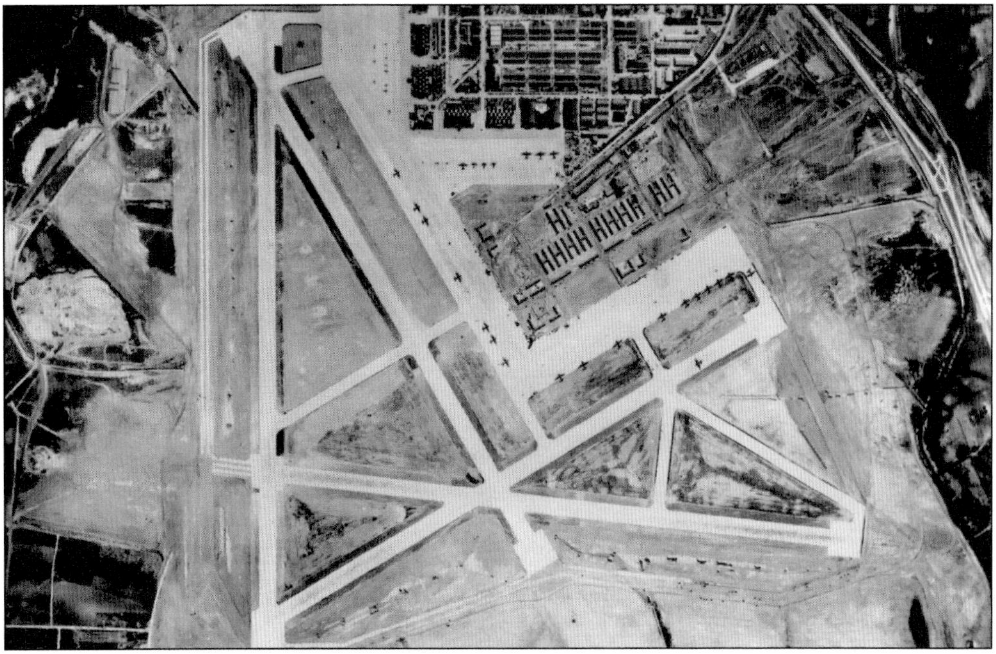

In preparation for the operation and support of heavy bombardment training, an additional 1,000 acres of land was acquired for the construction of four new runways, 300 feet in width and 5,500 feet in length. In addition to the new runways, a modern control tower and related facilities were included in the improvements to the airfield. (Air University Office of History.)

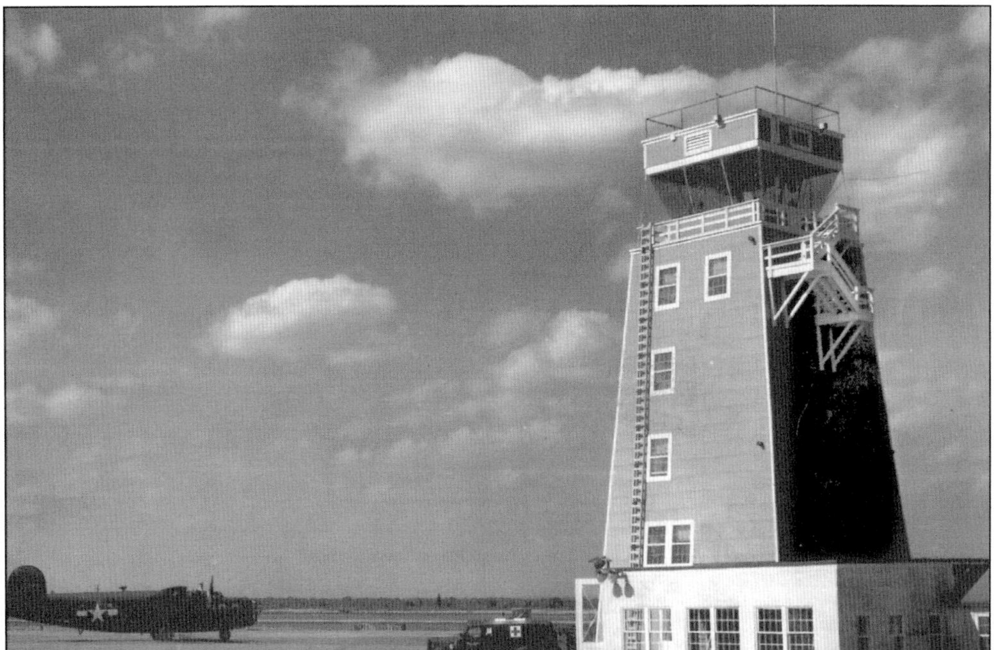

A Consolidated B-24 taxis past the control tower at Maxwell Field. The Specialized Four-Engine School produced 2,653 B-24 pilots. These student pilots amassed 165,544 flying hours and 230,720 landings in the aircraft at Maxwell Field. (Southern Museum of Flight.)

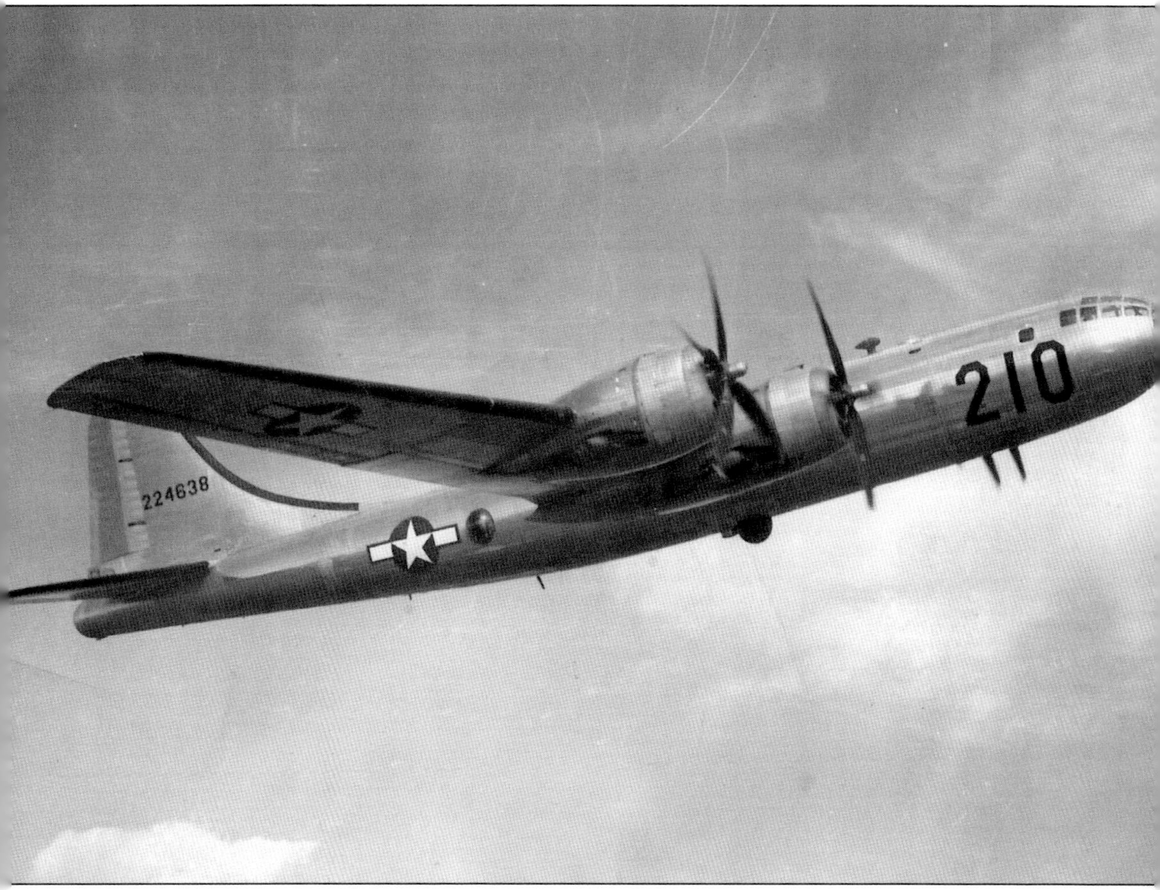

In 1945, the Specialized Four-Engine School at Maxwell Field was moved to the Courtland Army Air Field at Courtland, Alabama. The program was replaced by a pilot transition school for the Boeing B-29 Superfortress. The B-29 was one of the most advanced aircraft of the Second World War, featuring innovations such as a pressurized cabin, a central fire-control system, and remote-controlled machine gun turrets. With a wingspan of 141 feet and a maximum takeoff weight of 133,000 pounds, the integration of the B-29 into the training program at Maxwell Field required the runways to be lengthened from 5,500 feet to 7,000 feet. To conduct maintenance on the aircraft, the War Department authorized construction of the largest hangar built on the field through the end of the Second World War. (Southern Museum of Flight.)

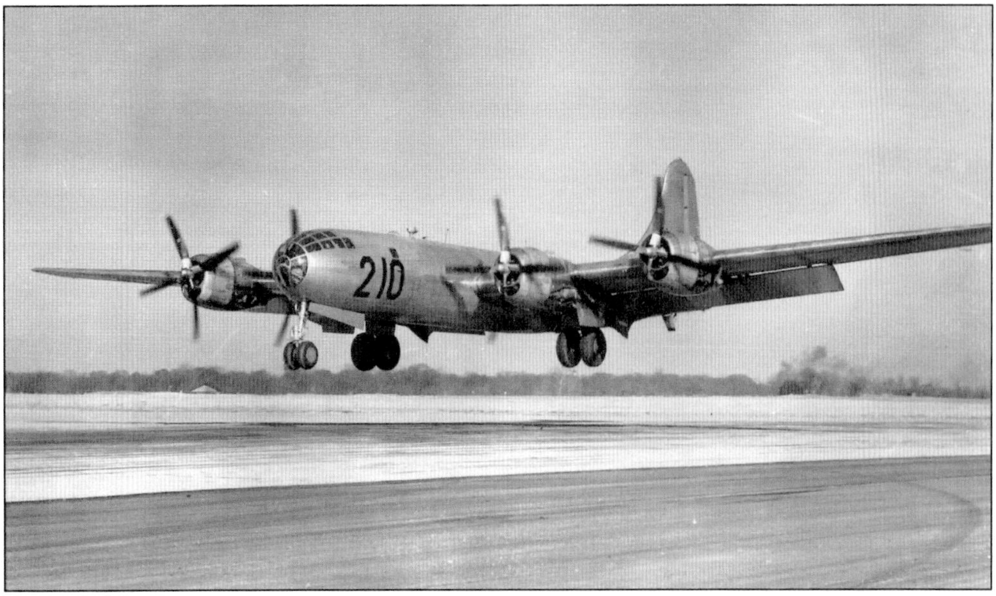

The B-29 transition course at Maxwell Field lasted five weeks. Flight crews trained in groups of three: the two pilots and a flight engineer. By April 1945, the B-29 training program was at peak production, with a class graduating every two and one-half weeks. The B-29 program would be the last new training school at Maxwell Field before the end of the Second World War. (Southern Museum of Flight.)

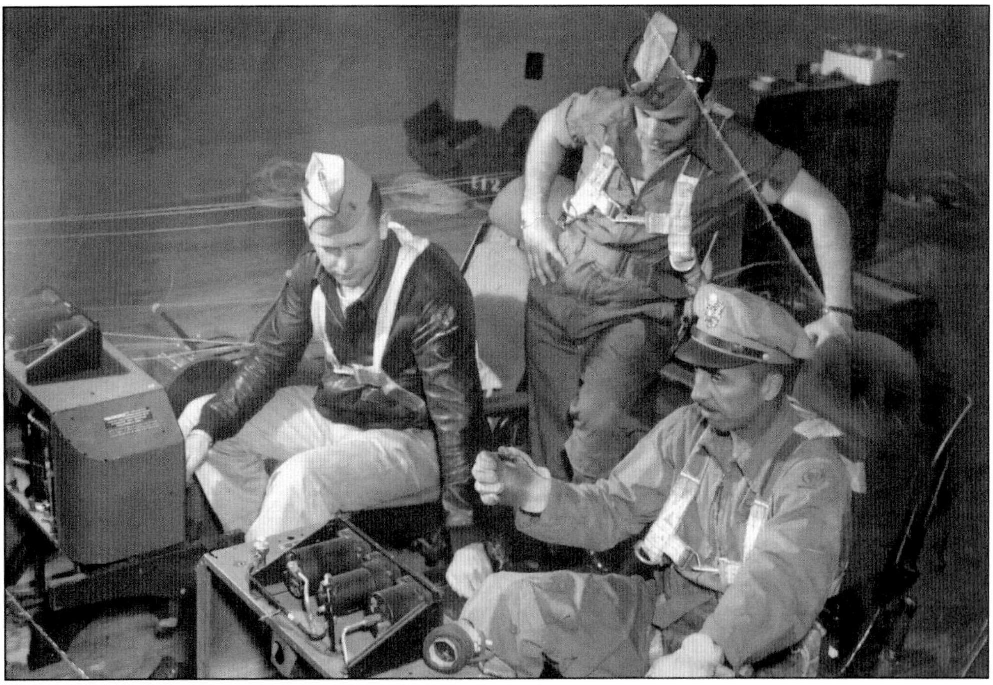

The flight crew of a Boeing B-29 Superfortress practices procedures in a mock-up of the aircraft cockpit. In addition to intensive ground-school training, each crew received 40 to 50 hours of flight training. The B-29 Transition School at Maxwell produced 728 flight crews who flew 46,554 hours in the aircraft, including 112,809 landings. (Southern Museum of Flight.)

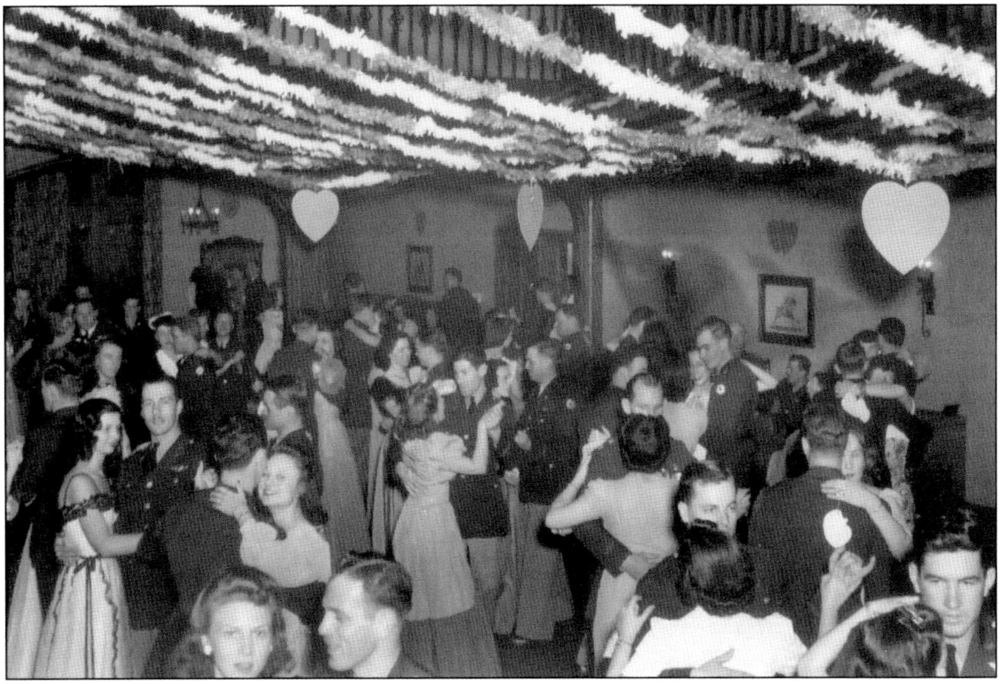

The intensive training programs at Maxwell Field did allow time for recreation. Cadet dances and graduation balls were among the most popular social events on the post. Dances were held at the officers' club and individual wing recreation halls. For the larger graduation balls, cadets used Hangar No. 6 or the city auditorium in Montgomery. In this image, aviation cadets enjoy a Valentine's Day dance with their sweethearts. (USAFHRA.)

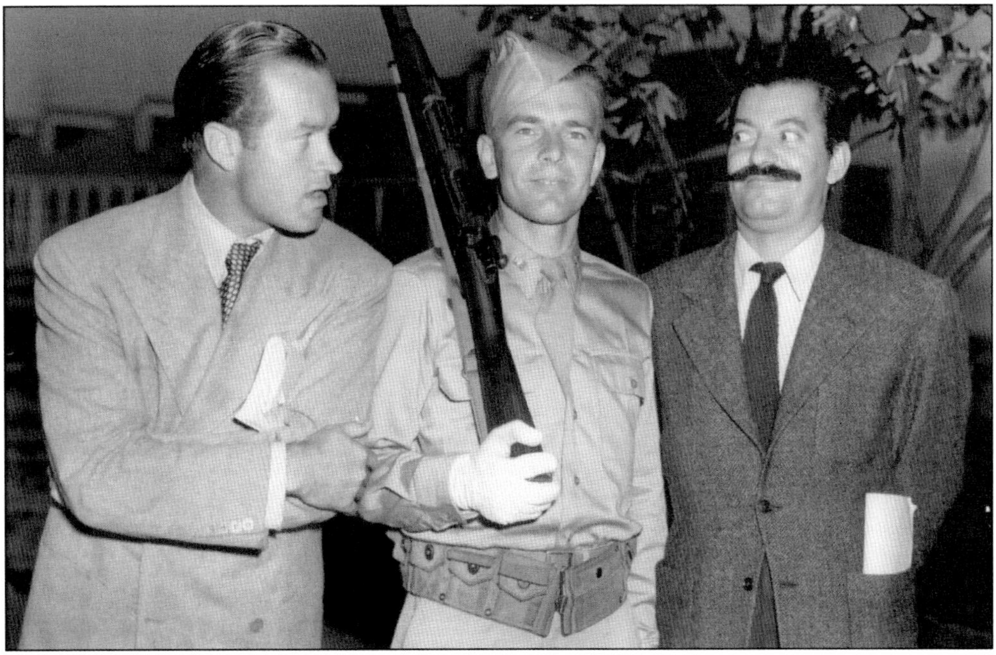

Comedians Bob Hope and Jerry Colonna were among the celebrity performers who visited Maxwell Field as part of USO shows. (USAFHRA.)

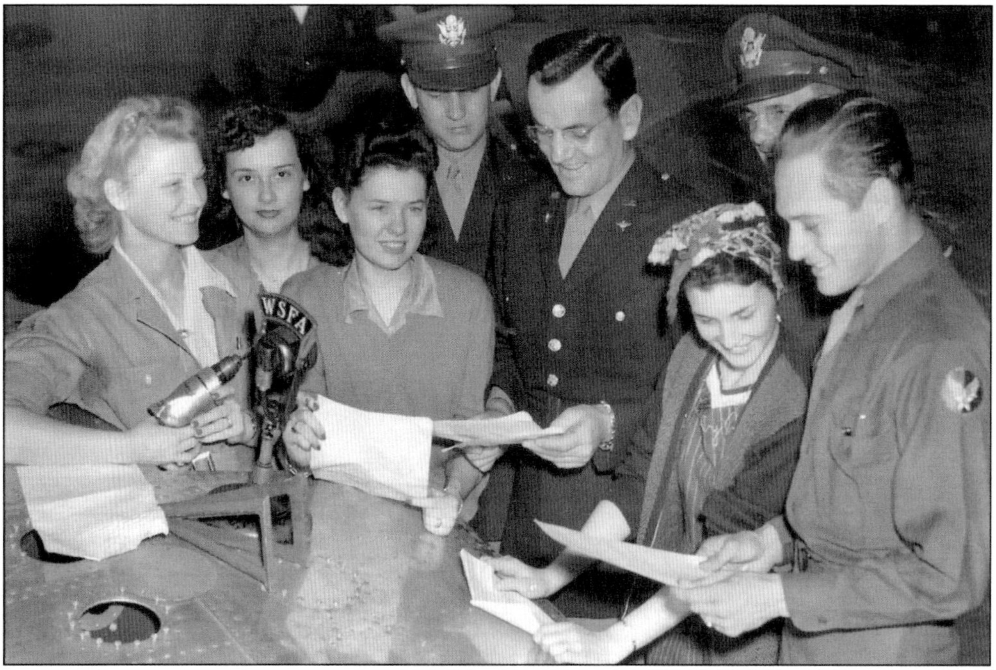

Capt. Glenn Miller visits women working as riveters in one of the aircraft repair shops at Maxwell Field. Miller volunteered for the Army Air Forces in 1942 to bring big band music to members of the armed forces. In December 1942, Captain Miller was assigned to Maxwell Field as assistant special services officer. (Air University Office of History.)

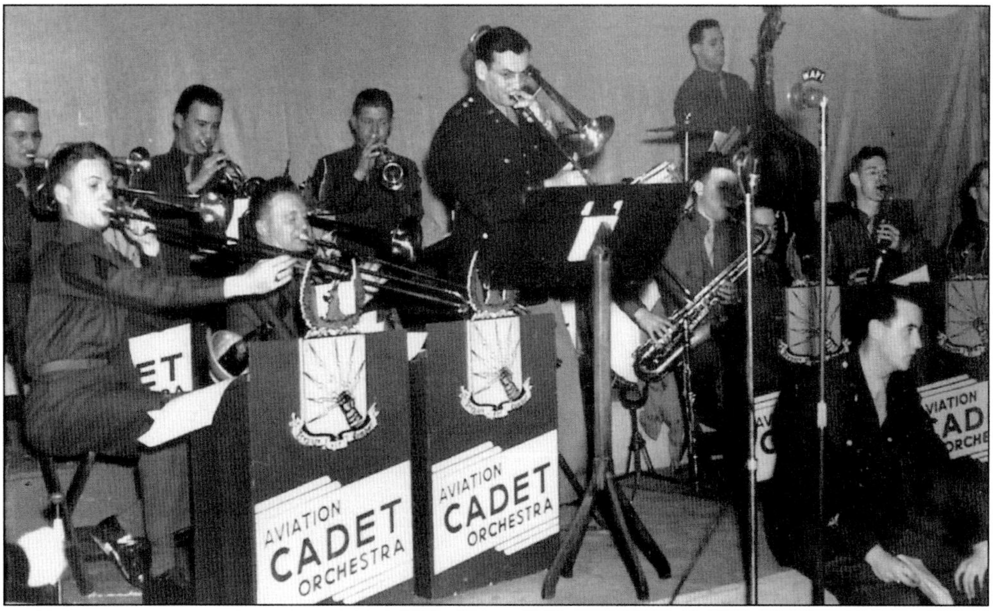

During his stay in Montgomery, Miller performed with members of the Rhythmaires, a dance band consisting of musicians from the Maxwell Field marching and concert bands. The founder of the Rhythmaires was S.Sgt. Jerry Yelverton (middle front row), a native of Montgomery and graduate of Alabama Polytechnic Institute. Yelverton had been a member of the Glenn Miller band before the war. (Air University Office of History.)

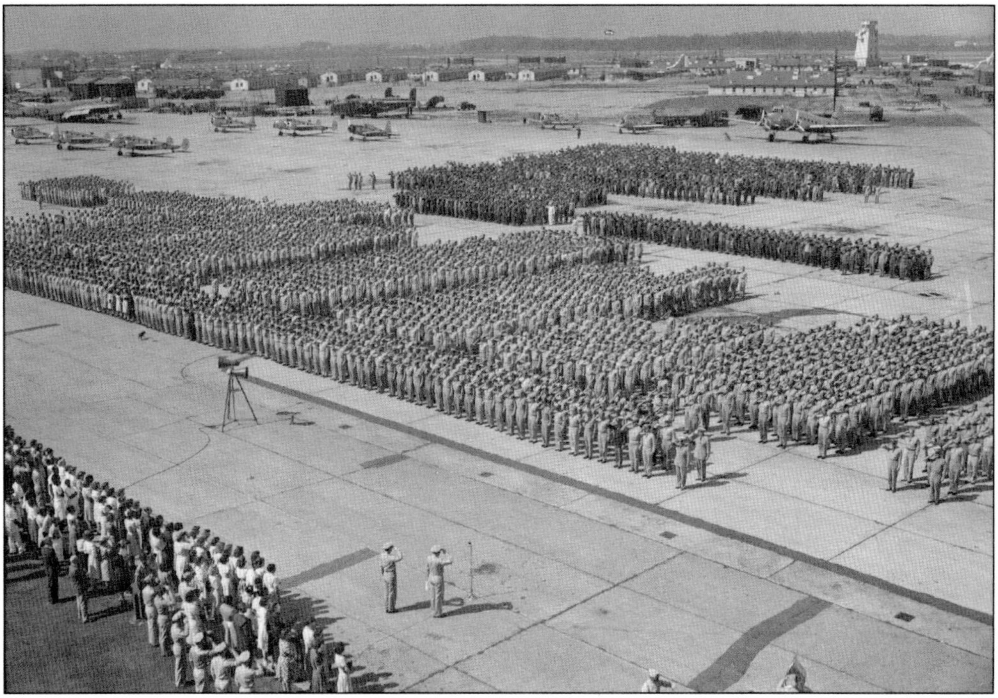

In April 1945, Post Commander R. E. L. Choate announces the death of Pres. Franklin Delano Roosevelt to assembled military and civilian personnel of Maxwell Field. (Author's collection.)

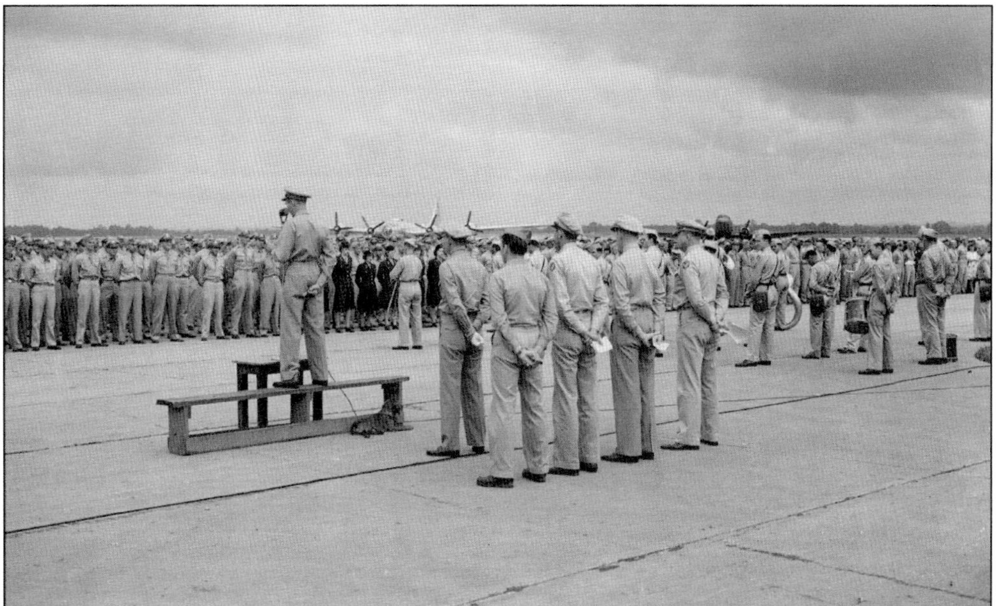

In May 1945, Commander Choate assembled military and civilian personnel of Maxwell Field to announce the formal surrender of the German armies and the Allied victory in Europe. In September, a separation center was established at Maxwell Field to facilitate the release of Army Air Forces personnel within a 300-mile radius of Montgomery. In November, the War Department announced that the Eastern Flying Training Command would be closed. (Author's collection.)

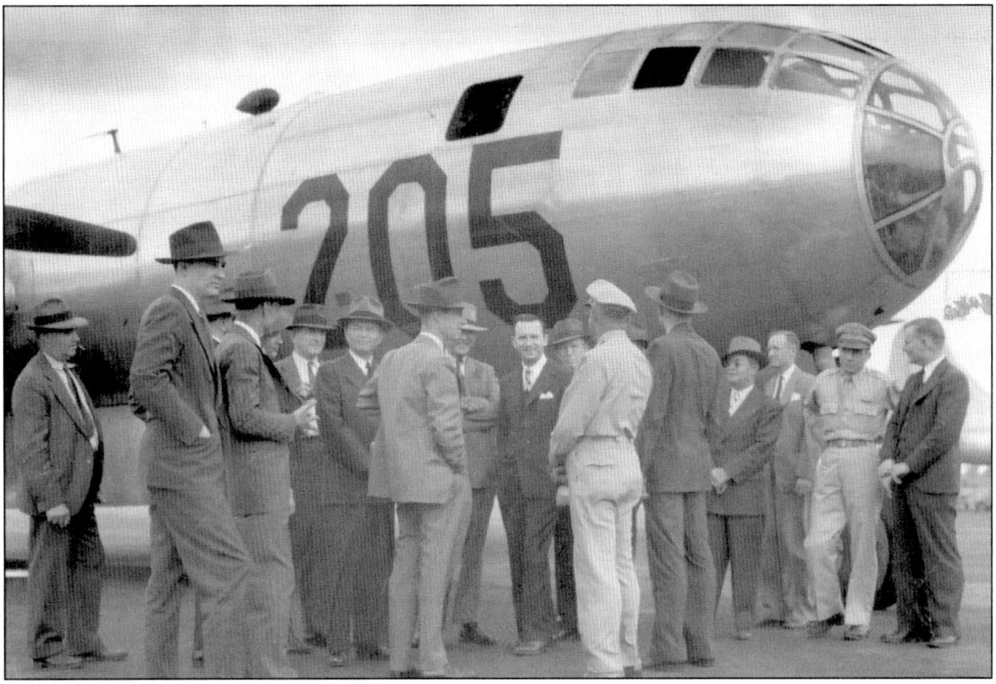

Members of the Montgomery Lions Club are given a tour of the post during a 1945 visit to Maxwell Field. (USAFHRA.)

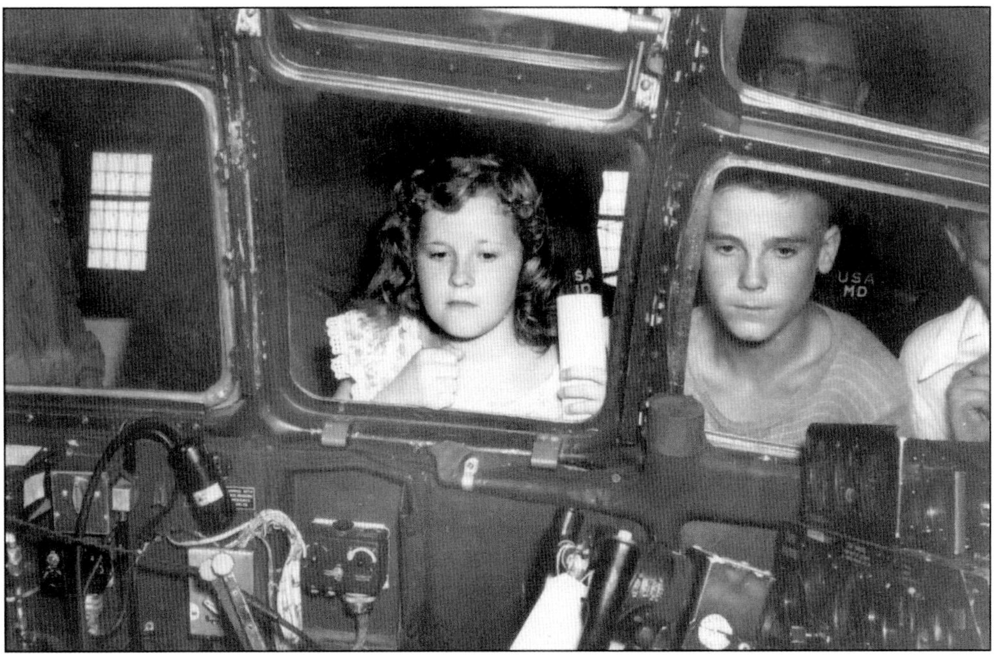

Young people stare intently into the cockpit of a Boeing B-29 Superfortress at an open house held at Maxwell Field in August 1946 to celebrate the 39th anniversary of the army's air arm. A platform had been placed beside the nose of the aircraft so the visitors could view the pilot and flight engineer stations. The last aircraft of the B-29 Transition School left Maxwell Field in November 1945. (USAFHRA.)

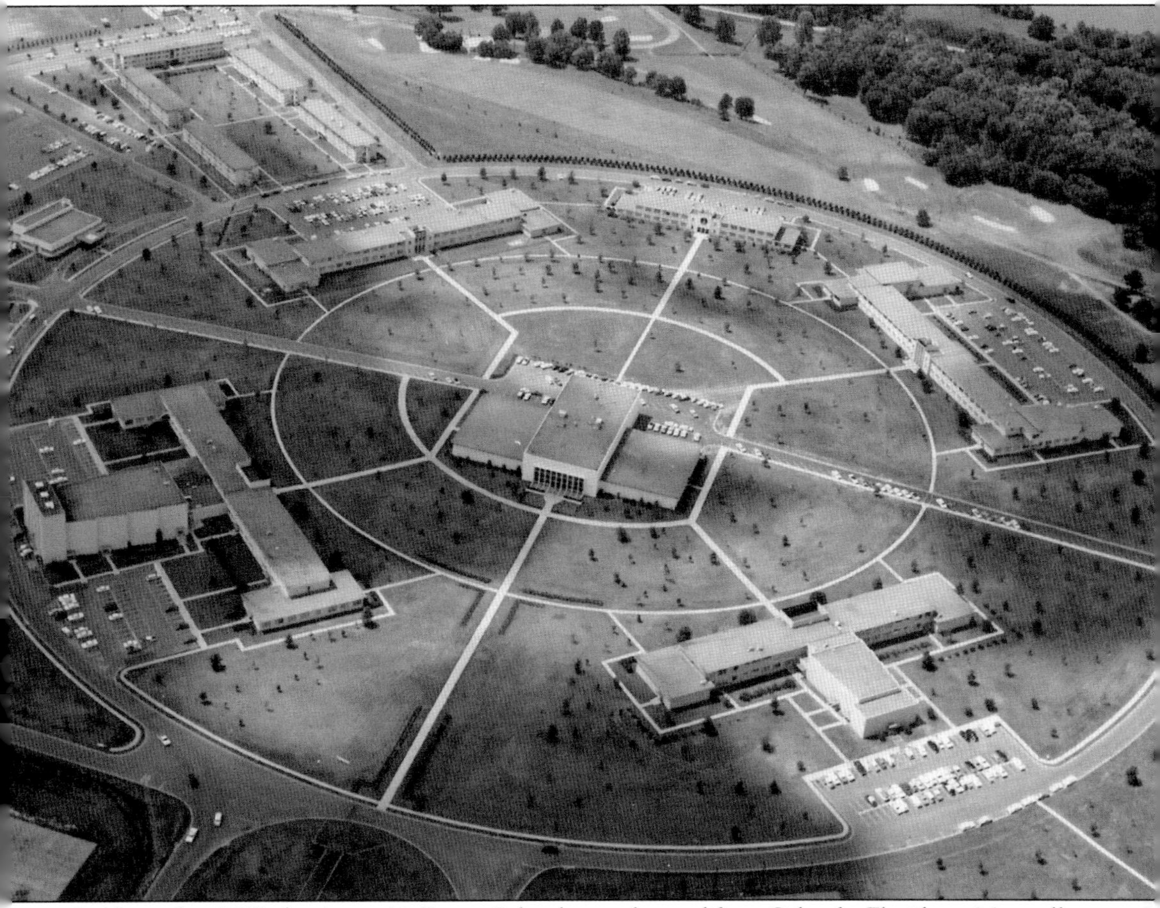

In November 1945, the Army Air Forces School was relocated from Orlando, Florida, to Maxwell Field, where better facilities existed. In March 1946, the school was designated Air University. A separate command of the Army Air Forces, Air University was created for the study, formulation, and teaching of the theories and methods of aerial warfare. The Air War College, the Air Command and Staff School, and the Air Tactical School initially served as the nucleus of the continuing education curriculum of Air University. Gen. Muir S. Fairchild was the first commander of Air University. In 1975, the academic circle complex was named in honor of Maj. Claire Chennault. (Air University Office of History.)

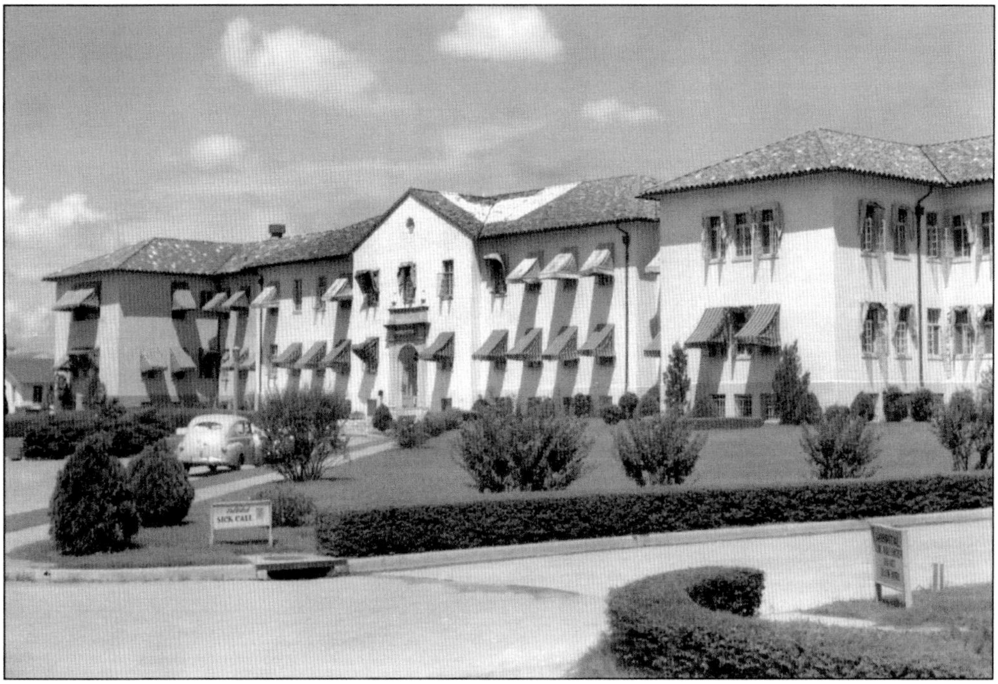

In 1940, plans for the expansion of the post hospital had been completed. The addition to the building included a mess for the preparation of meals and a morgue. The base hospital would remain in this building until 1968, when a new facility was completed. (USAFHRA.)

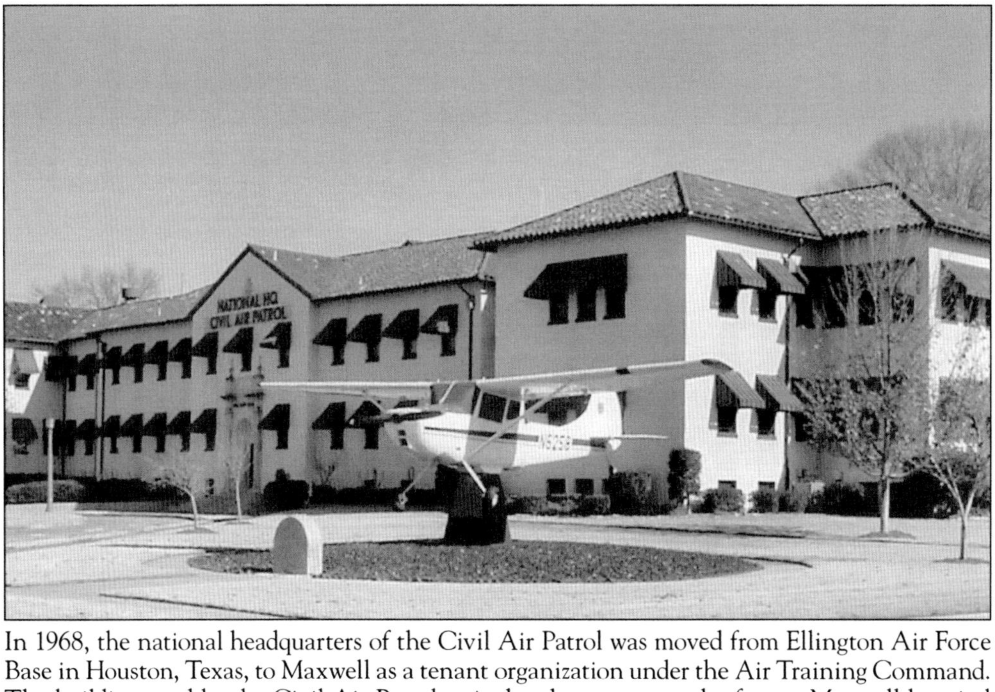

In 1968, the national headquarters of the Civil Air Patrol was moved from Ellington Air Force Base in Houston, Texas, to Maxwell as a tenant organization under the Air Training Command. The building used by the Civil Air Patrol as its headquarters was the former Maxwell hospital facility. The headquarters building of the Civil Air Patrol was dedicated to Gill Robb Wilson. (Headquarters Civil Air Patrol.)

Five

Dannelly Field

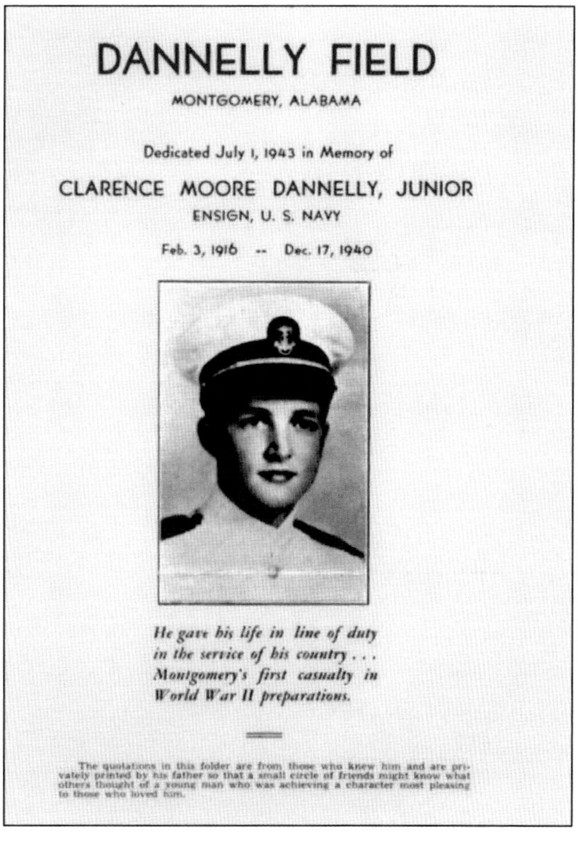
DANNELLY FIELD

MONTGOMERY, ALABAMA

Dedicated July 1, 1943 in Memory of

CLARENCE MOORE DANNELLY, JUNIOR

ENSIGN, U. S. NAVY

Feb. 3, 1916 -- Dec. 17, 1940

He gave his life in line of duty in the service of his country . . . Montgomery's first casualty in World War II preparations.

The quotations in this folder are from those who knew him and are privately printed by his father so that a small circle of friends might know what others thought of a young man who was achieving a character most pleasing to those who loved him.

Montgomery Regional Airport, named Dannelly Field, was dedicated on July 1, 1943, and named in honor of Montgomery native Clarence Moore Dannelly Jr. An ensign in the U.S. Navy, Dannelly lost his life in an aircraft training accident at the Pensacola Naval Air Station. Dannelly was the first resident of Montgomery to lose his life in preparation for war. (Montgomery Regional Airport Authority.)

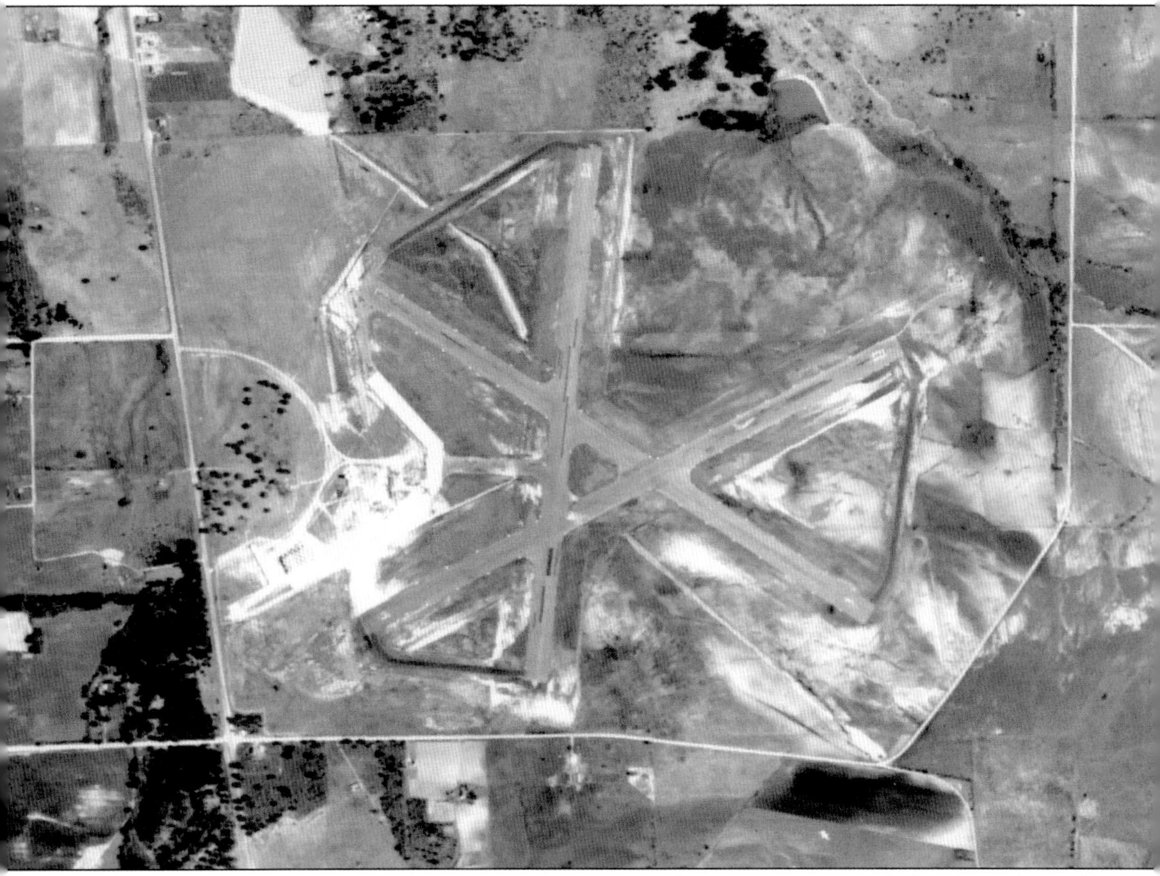

The new Montgomery Municipal Airport was constructed on a 508-acre parcel of property located seven miles west of the city on the Selma highway. Three asphalt runways were constructed on the site; the northwest-southeast and northeast-southwest runways were 4,000 feet in length. The remaining east-west runway was 3,500 feet in length. The field was served by an air traffic control tower and had the most modern runway, boundary, and beacon lighting available. In November 1942, the new municipal airport was leased by the War Department as an auxiliary landing field for aircraft operating from the basic flying school at Gunter Field. During this period, Eastern Air Lines was allowed joint use of the field to provide passenger and airmail service to Montgomery. (University of Alabama Map Library.)

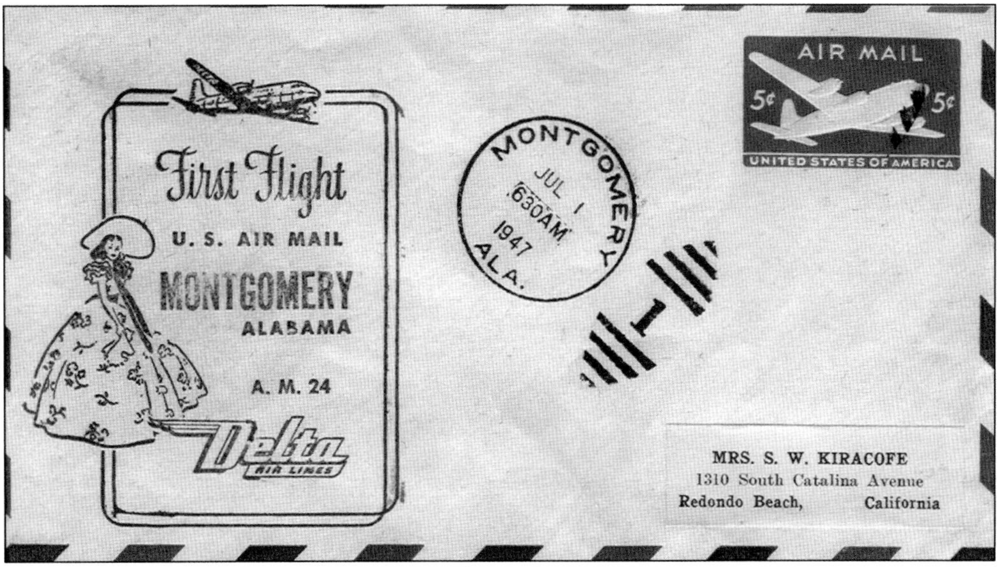

On July 1, 1947, Delta Air Lines inaugurated Douglas DC-3 service into Montgomery as part of Air Mail Route 24 connecting Atlanta and Dallas, Texas. The route included intermediate stops in Columbus, Montgomery, and seven other cities before arriving in Dallas. The new service provided Montgomery passengers with nonstop flights to Atlanta as well as connecting service to Cincinnati and New Orleans. (Author's collection.)

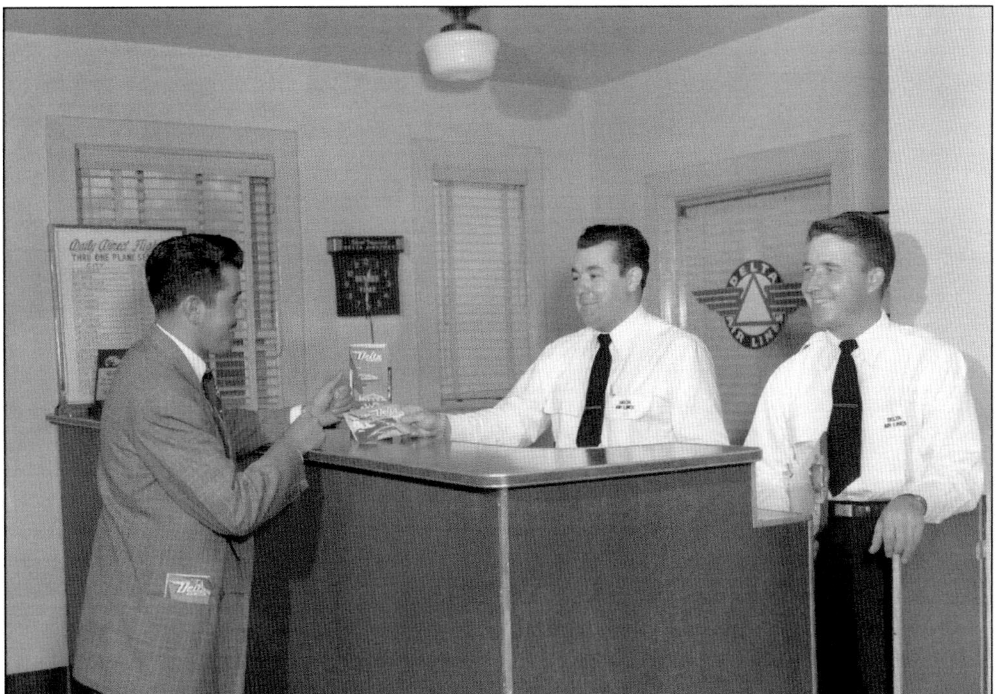

The Delta Air Lines ticket counter at Dannelly Field is pictured in 1947. (Delta Air Transport Heritage Museum.)

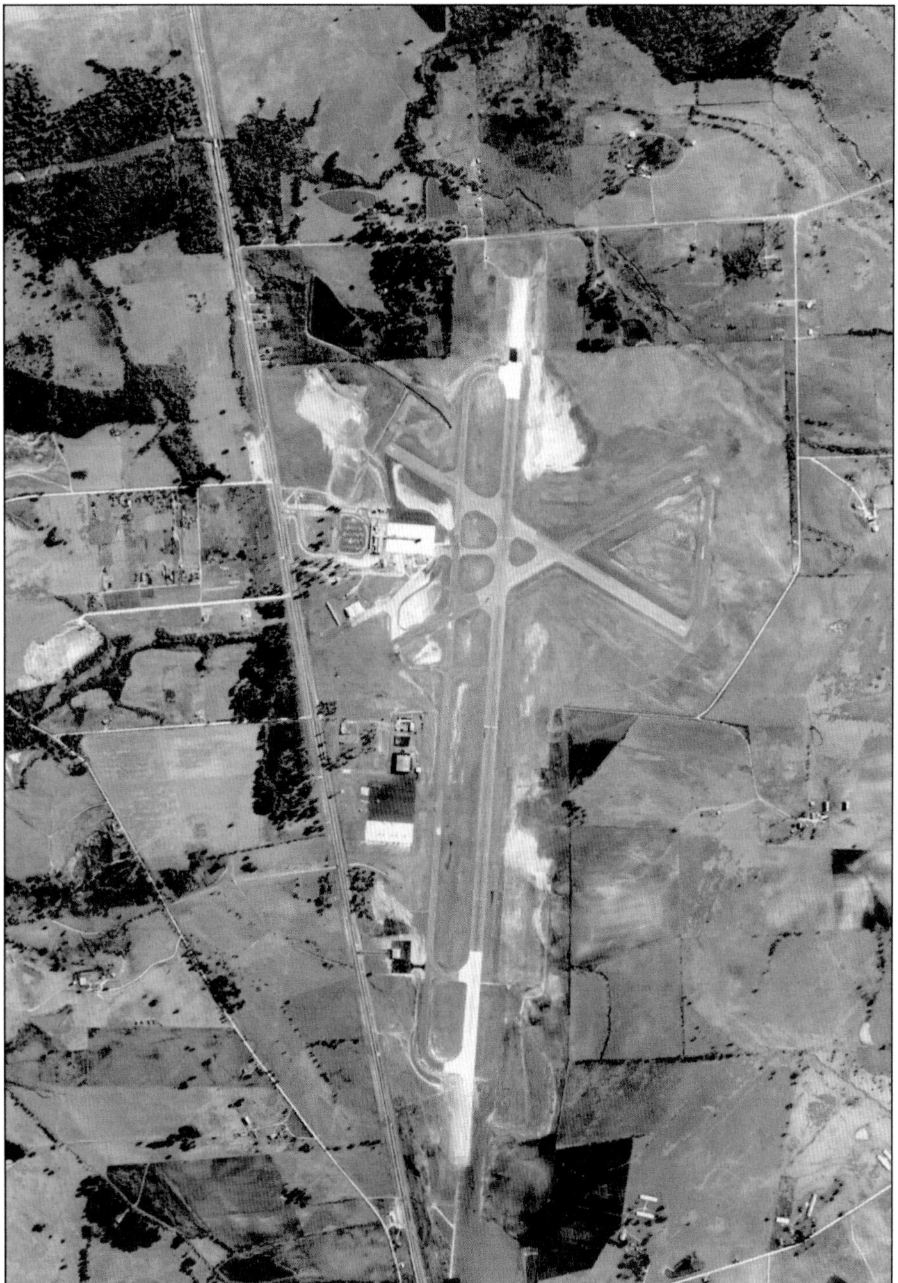

At the conclusion of the Second World War, city officials attempted to reacquire the original municipal airport site. The decision by the federal government to continue the lease of Gunter Field forced city officials to establish and execute plans to make Dannelly Field the new municipal airport. Returned to the city in 1946, an expansion program was initiated at the airport to meet the needs of a developing aviation industry. In 1952, the east-west runway was extended to a length of 7,000 feet. In 1956, the runway was lengthened an additional 1,000 feet. With the exception of the Miami International Airport, the runway at Montgomery was the longest paved civilian runway in the Southeast. (University of Alabama Map Library.)

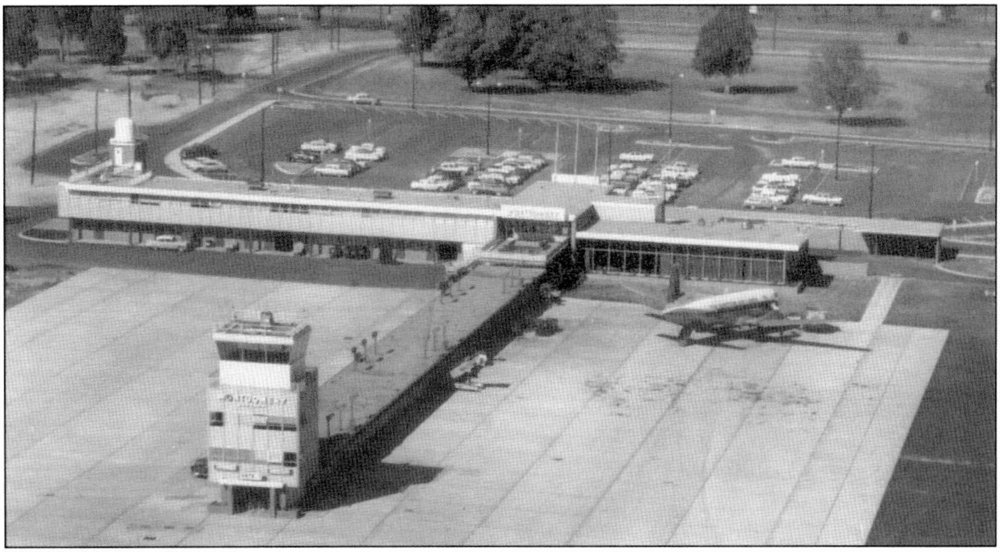

Dedicated in 1958, the terminal building at Dannelly Field included the Sky Ranch Restaurant, a gift shop, a barbershop, and two car rental agencies. Eastern and Delta Air Lines maintained ticket counters and gates at the terminal building. Accommodations were available for two additional airlines. The Civil Aeronautics Administration, U.S. Weather Bureau, and Montgomery Radio also maintained offices in the new terminal building. (Montgomery Regional Airport Authority.)

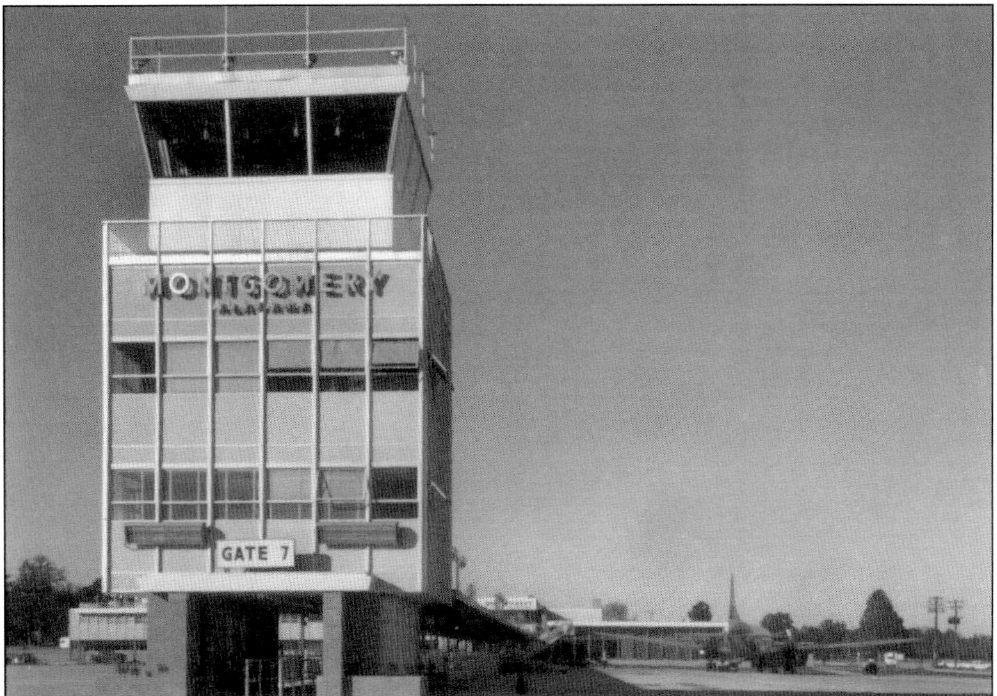

The air traffic control tower, located at the end of the 450-foot concourse, was named in honor of Frank and Gayle Harvey. The brothers lost their lives in combat during the Second World War. The control tower housed Civil Aeronautics Administration personnel responsible for controlling air traffic at Dannelly Field. (Montgomery Regional Airport Authority.)

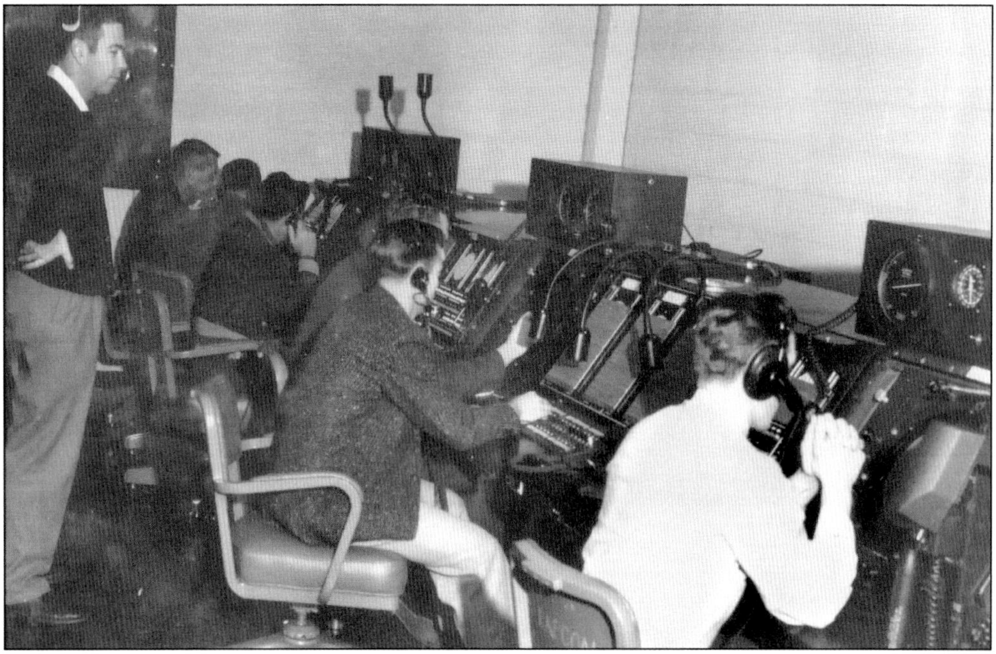

Fred D. Jones, facility chief of the Montgomery Radar Approach Control, supervises air traffic control personnel directing aircraft in the Montgomery area. The facility was operated by the Civil Aeronautics Administration and could detect airborne aircraft within a 40-mile radius of Dannelly Field. (Jacqueline Jones Sheldon.)

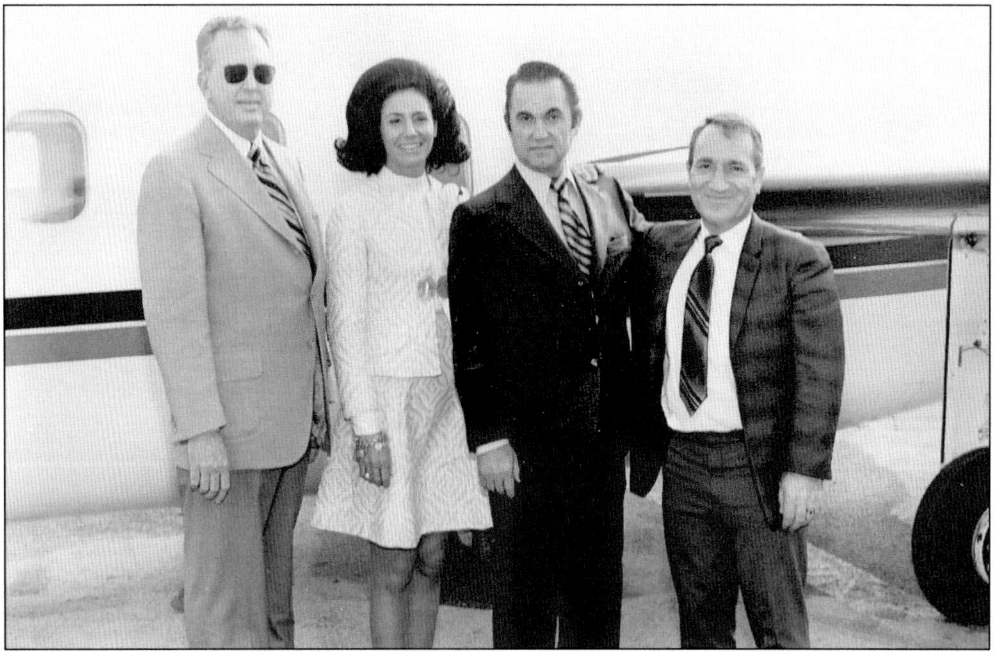

Shown from left to right are Alabama Air Transportation Division pilot Jimmy Baswell, First Lady Cornelia Wallace, Gov. George C. Wallace, and pilot Jack Gibbons before departing Montgomery on a flight in the State of Alabama Air Transportation Division Jet Commander aircraft. (Author's collection.)

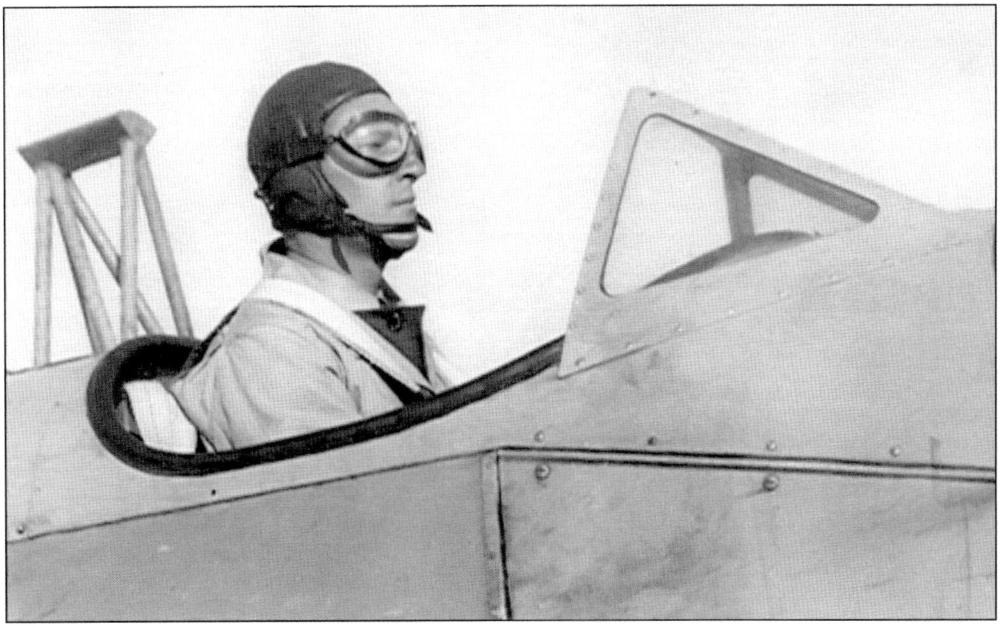

A former military pilot, Robert P. Hudgens and four partners formed the Montgomery Aviation Corporation in 1945 at the Norman Bridge Airport. The company relocated to Dannelly Field in October 1947, when restrictions limiting activities at the field to military and airline operations were lifted. A small, wood-frame building located at the base of the original air traffic control tower was converted into an office and service area. (Hudgens family.)

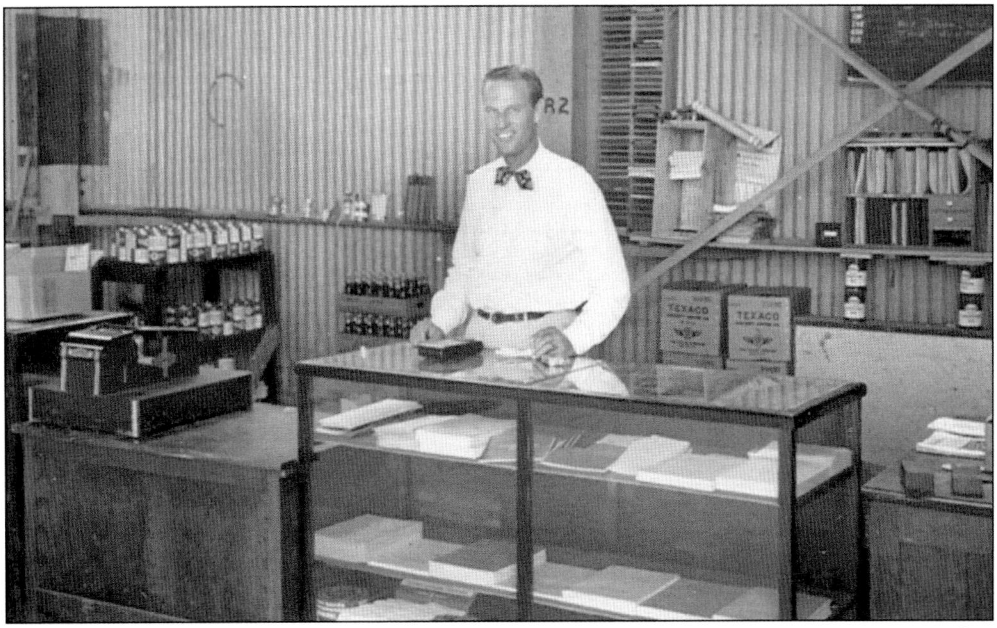

After relocating to Dannelly Field in 1947, the Montgomery Aviation Corporation continued to expand, making a move to a larger facility necessary. Hudgens set up shop in a former military hangar that had been moved to Dannelly Field from the Tuskegee Army Air Field. This historic hangar has been a cornerstone of the Montgomery Aviation Corporation for more than 50 years. (Hudgens family.)

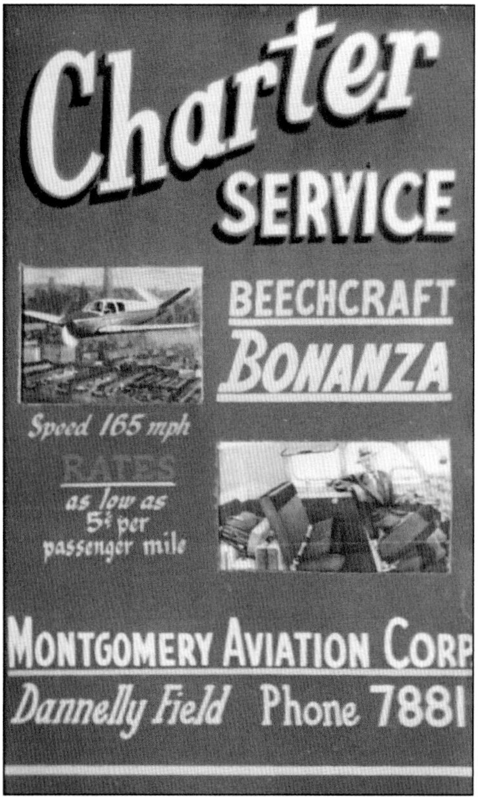

Beginning with a fleet of five surplus aircraft, Robert Hudgens continued to expand the services offered by Montgomery Aviation to include aircraft sales and service, flight instruction, air charter, aerial photography, aircraft maintenance, and power line patrol. The Montgomery Aviation Charter Service provided transportation for passengers and air cargo. Montgomery Aviation operated airmail service between the cities of Dothan and Memphis with intermediate stops in Montgomery and Birmingham. One of the most unique services provided by the company was transportation of medical patients by airplane. (Hudgens family.)

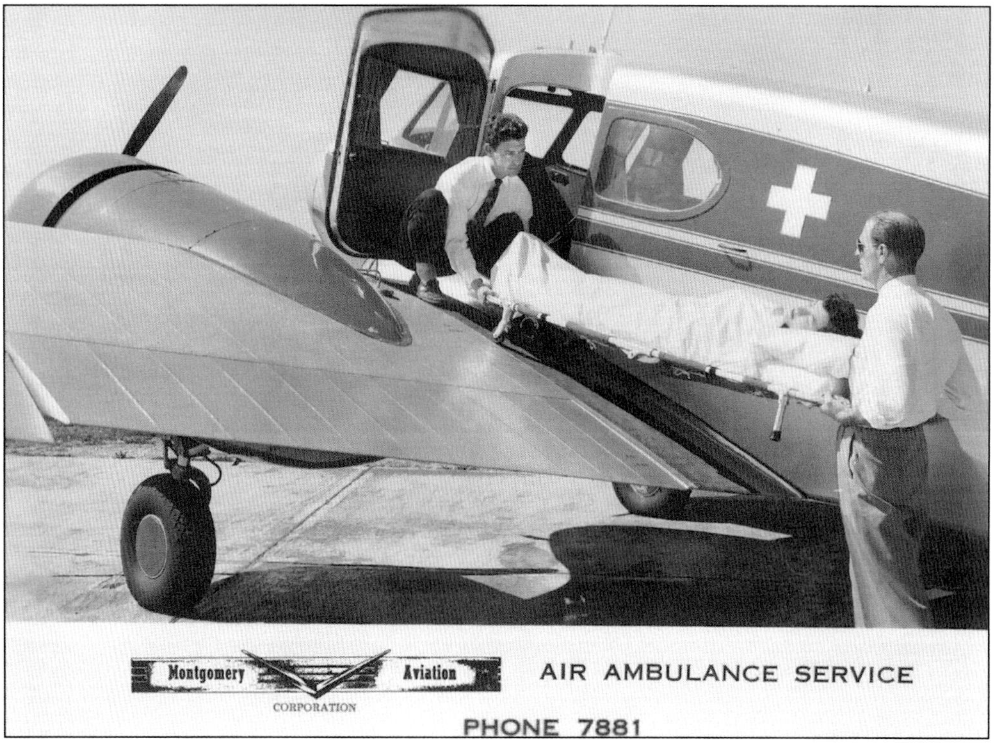

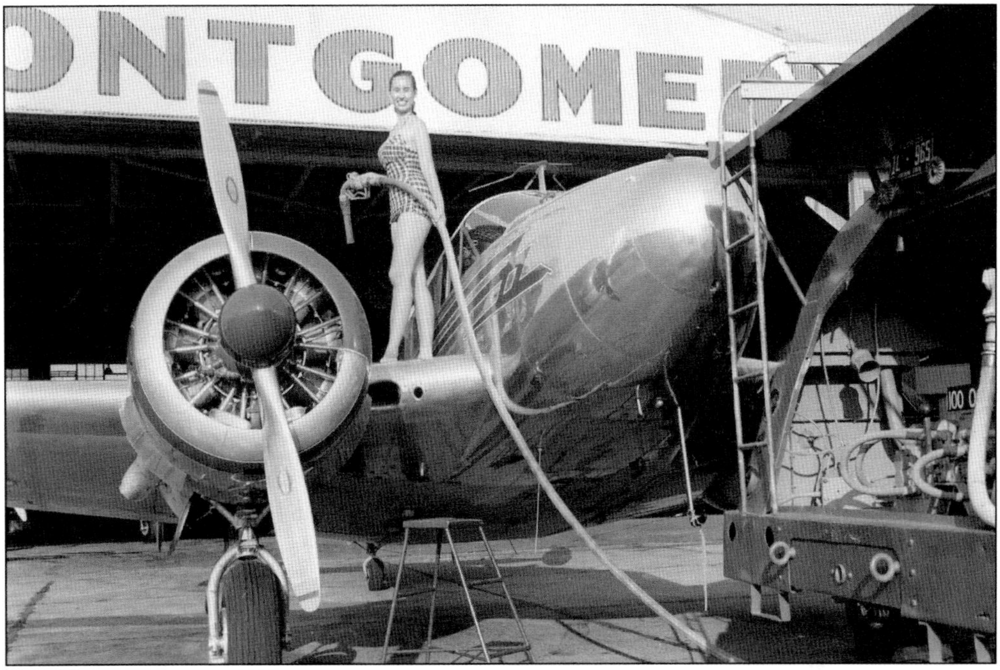

This early publicity photograph promotes the excellent customer service at Montgomery Aviation. (Scott Photographic Services via Montgomery Aviation Corporation.)

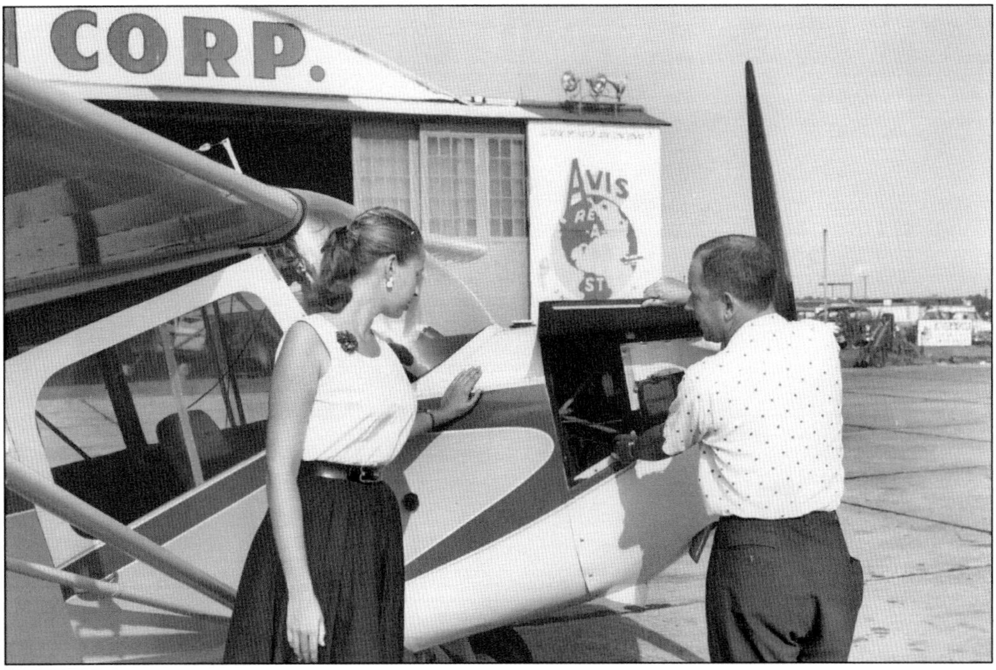

The growth of general aviation in the years following the Second World War produced a constant supply of student pilots. During the early years of Montgomery Aviation, flight training represented a significant percentage of the revenue generated by the company. A Montgomery Aviation flight instructor demonstrates a proper preflight inspection of an Aeronca 7AC Champ to a prospective student. (Scott Photographic Services via Montgomery Aviation.)

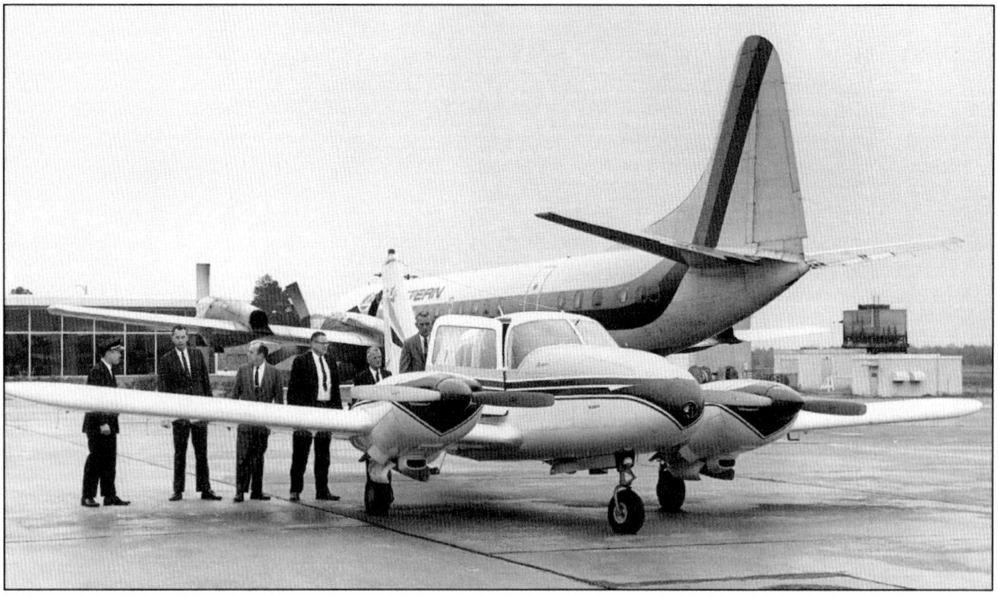

In March 1966, Montgomery Aviation inaugurated "The Executive Commuter" air taxi service between the cities of Montgomery and Huntsville. Utilizing five-passenger Piper Aztec aircraft, the service provided two round-trip flights each Monday, Wednesday, and Friday. The one-way fare was $25, with the round-trip priced at an affordable $49. Reservations were available through Montgomery Aviation, travel agents, and airline ticket offices. (Paul Robertson via Montgomery Aviation.)

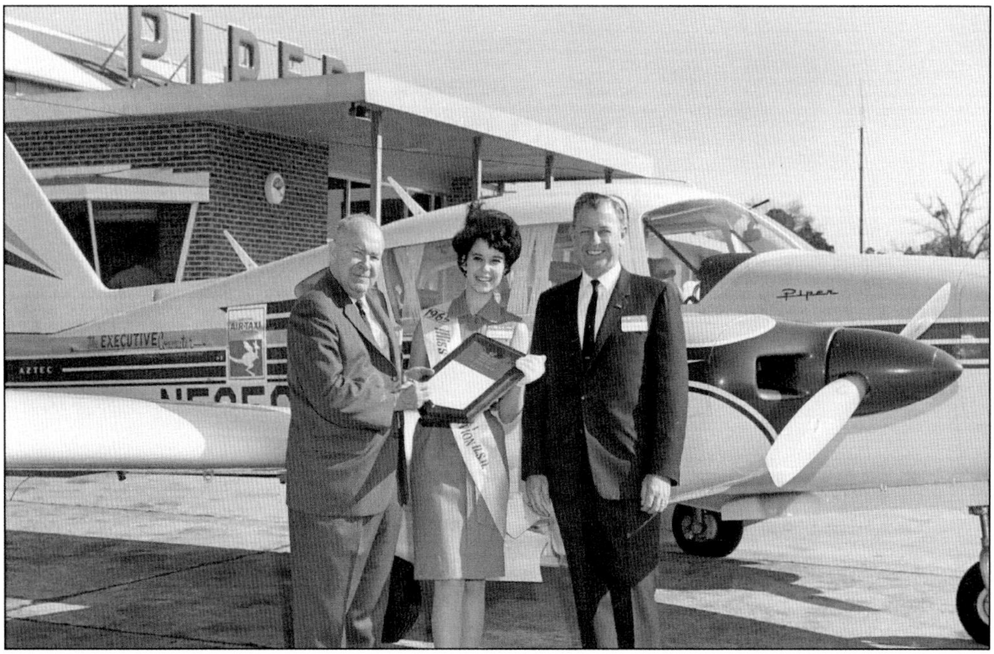

State director of aeronautics Asa Rountree Jr. (left) signs a proclamation commemorating the inaugural service of the Executive Commuter. Rountree was a passenger on the first flight from Montgomery to Huntsville. Participating in the ceremony are "Miss Transportation" Donna Martin and pilot Kenneth Snyders. (Paul Robertson via Montgomery Aviation.)

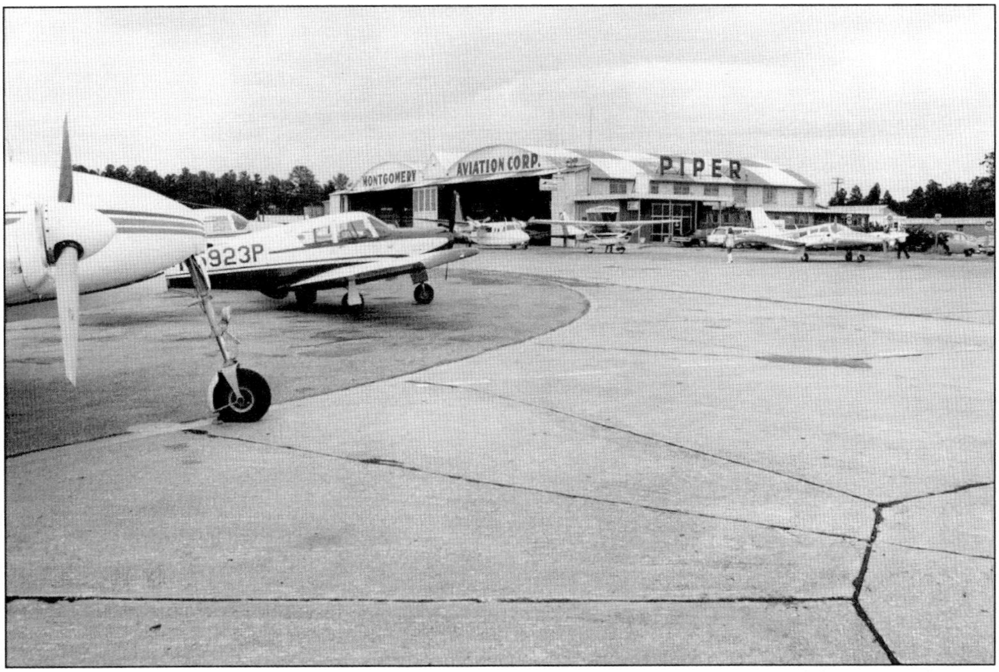

The Montgomery Aviation Corporation is the oldest fixed-base operation in Alabama. With more than 60 airplanes based at three locations in Alabama, Montgomery Aviation once operated the largest nongovernment fleet of airplanes in the state of Alabama. In 1961, Montgomery Aviation was named the outstanding member of the national Air Taxi Conference for the United States. (Paul Robertson via Montgomery Aviation.)

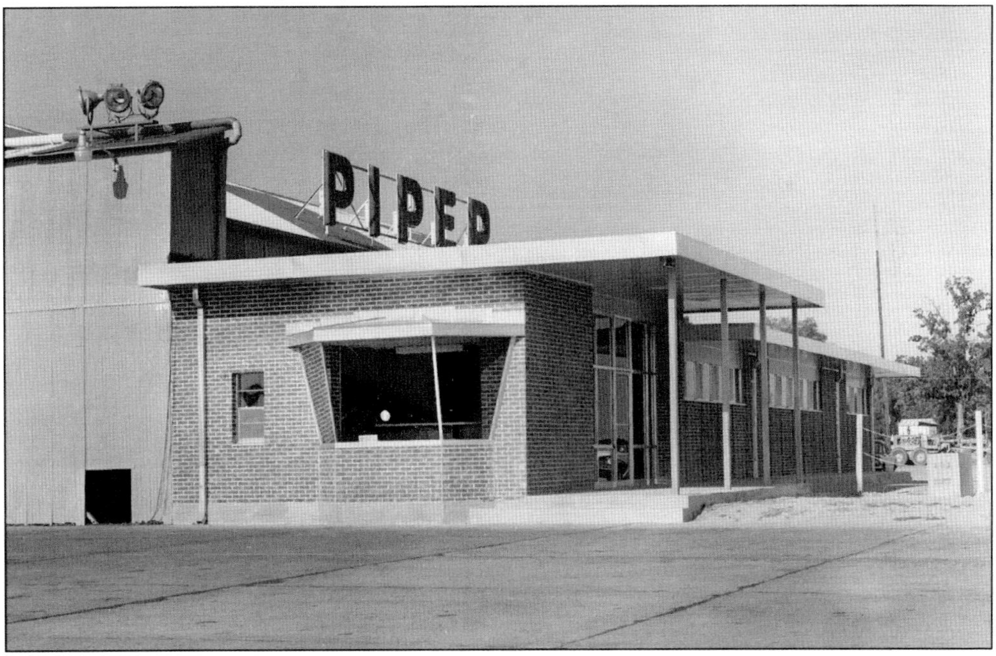

In 1961, Montgomery Aviation became a Piper Aircraft distributor for Alabama and West Florida. For the next 21 years, visitors to the Montgomery Aviation ramp were greeted by a large illuminated Piper sign located above the new building addition that served as a passenger lounge and customer service area. (Paul Robertson via Montgomery Aviation.)

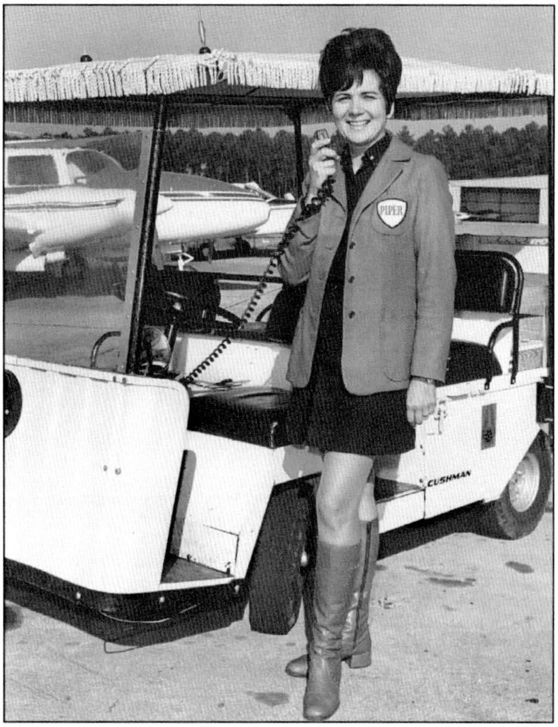

A Montgomery Aviation hostess provides a warm welcome to pilots and passengers of arriving aircraft. (Paul Robertson via Montgomery Aviation.)

Customer service representatives of Montgomery Aviation invite customers to discover flying in a Piper aircraft. As the exclusive Piper distributor for Alabama and West Florida, Montgomery Aviation not only sold Piper products, but also provided maintenance and support for owners of all models of Piper aircraft. Montgomery Aviation also used the Piper brand in their air charter, flight training, and power line patrol operations. (Paul Robertson via Montgomery Aviation.)

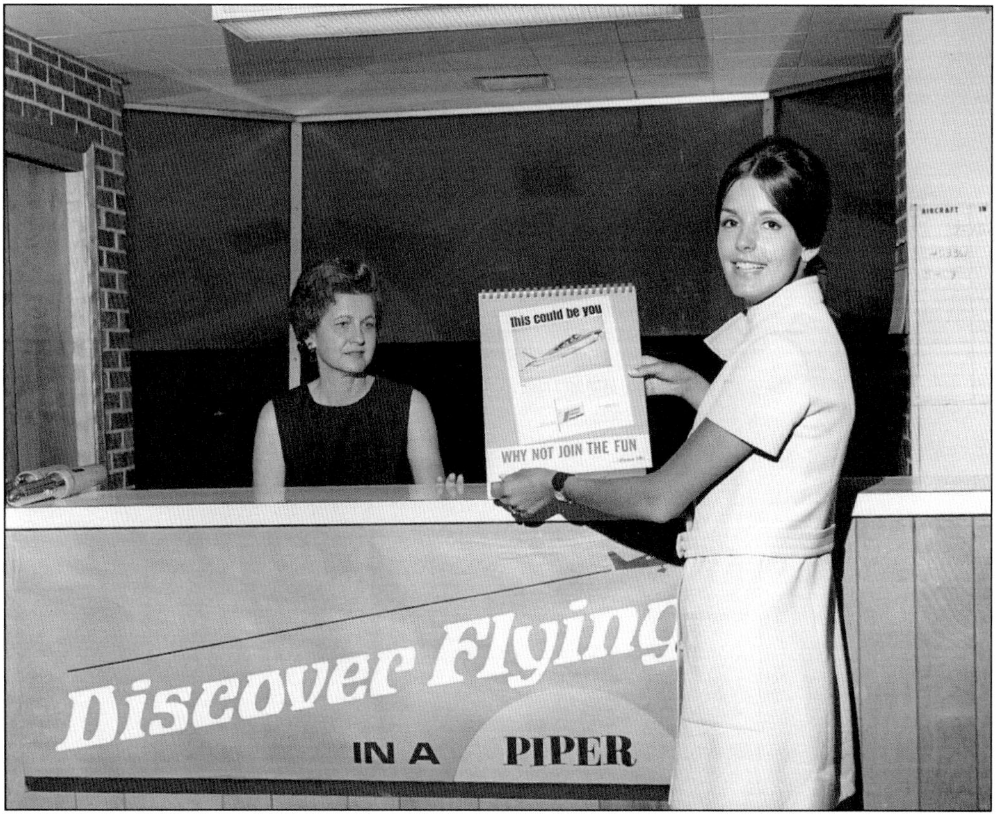

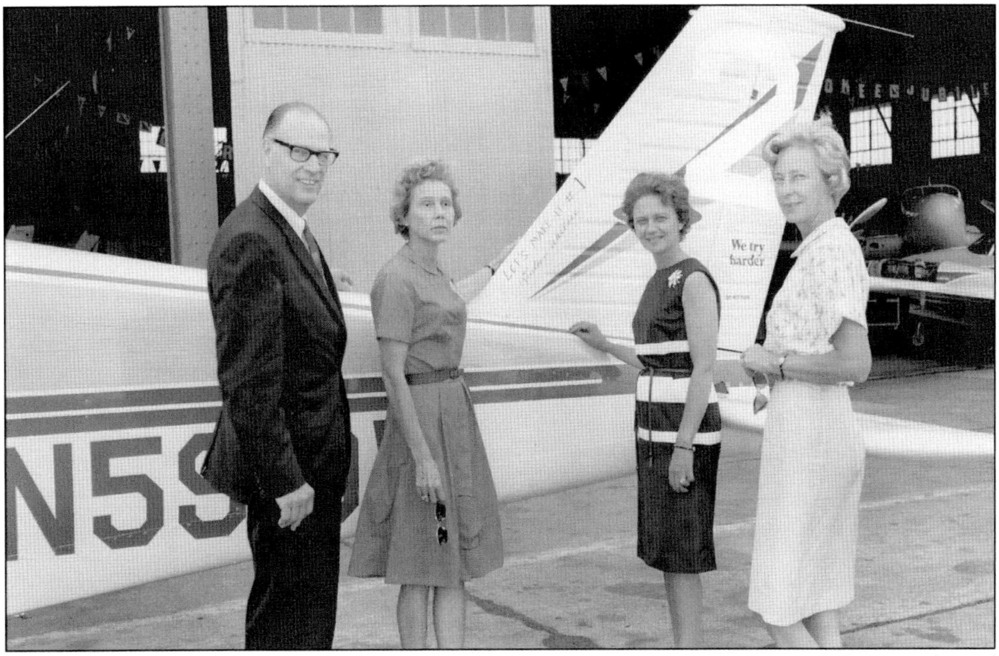

For more than 60 years, the Montgomery Aviation Corporation has supported the growth and development of general aviation. First Lady and future governor of Alabama Lurleen Wallace (third from left) and Robert Hudgens join Montgomery pilots Nancy Beeland (second from left) and Juanita Halstead (right) as they prepare for the All Woman Transcontinental Air Race sponsored by the Ninety-Nines Organization. (Montgomery Aviation.)

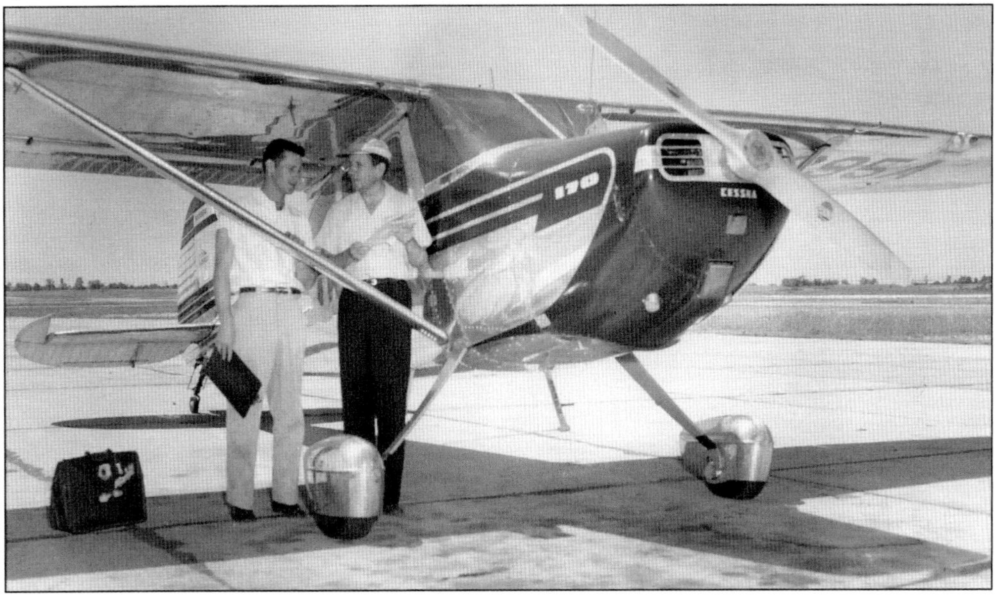

Montgomery Aviation chief pilot and flight instructor John Edward Long Jr. (right) briefs a pilot prior to a flight in a new Cessna 170B aircraft. In addition to being the chief pilot for Montgomery Aviation, Long served as a pilot examiner for the Federal Aviation Administration with authority to conduct examinations for private and commercial pilot certificates. (Horace Perry via Montgomery Aviation.)

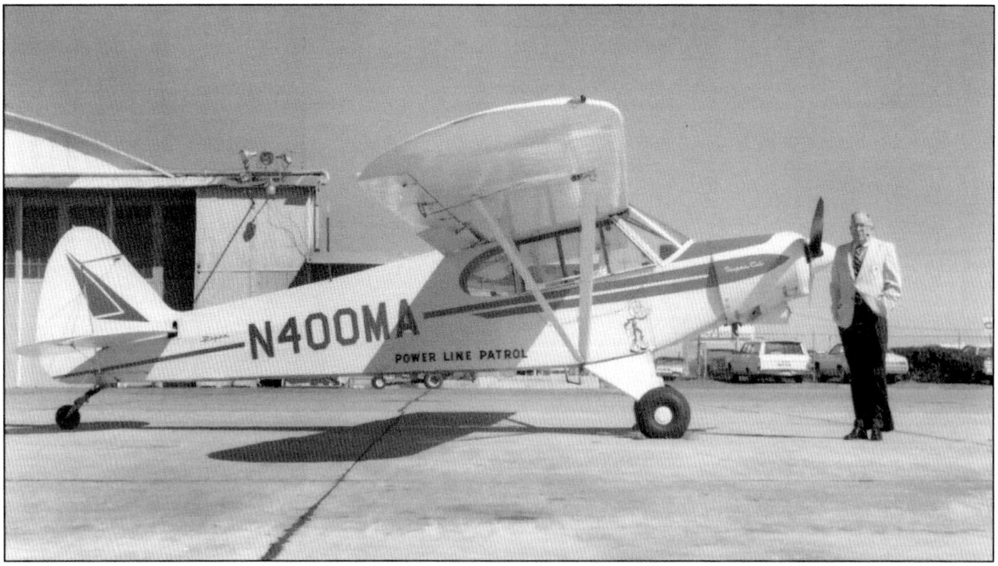

John Edward Long Jr. began flying power line patrol in 1952 and continued in this capacity for more than 45 years. A native of Montgomery, Long was an employee and part owner of the Montgomery Aviation Corporation for more than 50 years. Long took his first flying lesson in May 1933 and first flew solo after only 1 hour and 40 minutes of flight instruction. (Scott Photographic Services via Montgomery Aviation.)

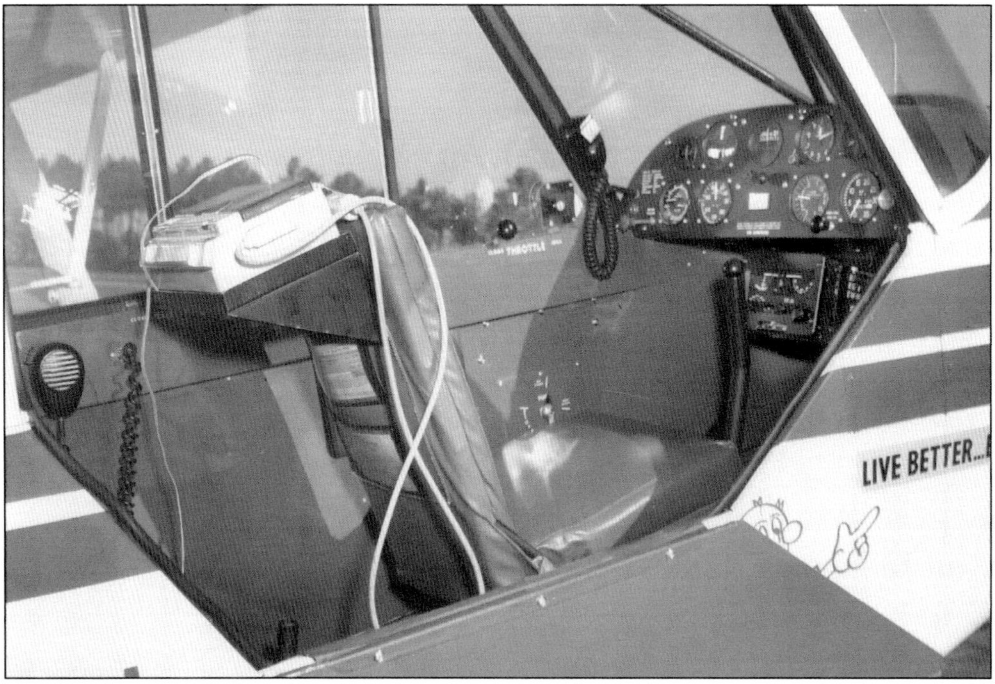

The Piper Super Cub flown by John Edward Long Jr. had a tandem seating arrangement with the pilot operating the flight controls from the front seat and observer occupying the rear seat. From an altitude of 200 feet, the pilot and observer searched for damaged power transmission lines. Problems were reported to Alabama Power Company maintenance teams utilizing the radio in front of the observer seat. (Scott Photographic Services via Montgomery Aviation.)

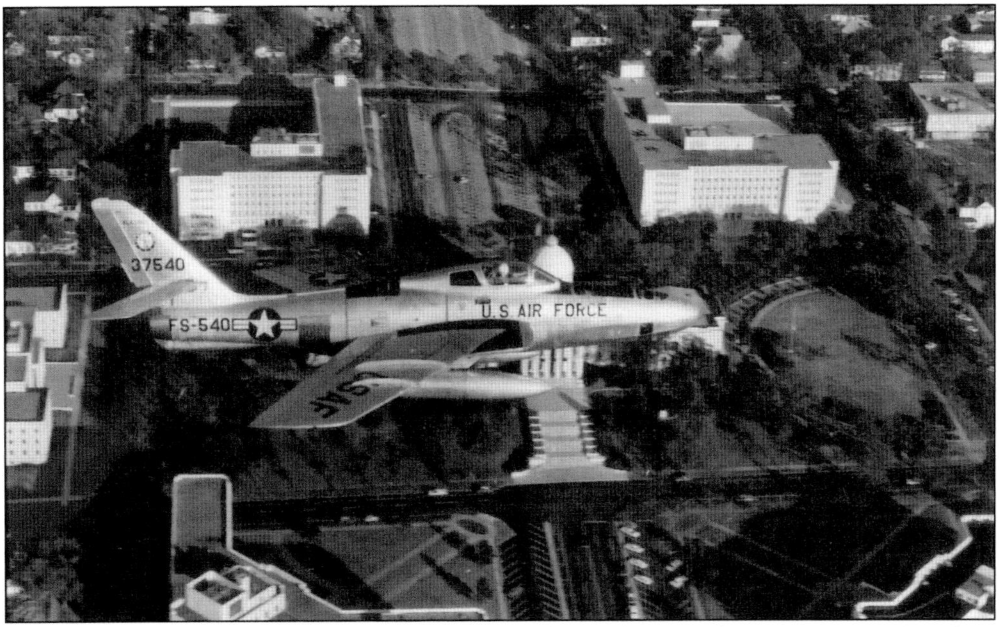

In 1952, the Alabama Air National Guard organized the 160th Tactical Reconnaissance Squadron in Birmingham utilizing RF-51 Mustang aircraft. The squadron was relocated to Dannelly Field in January 1953 and entered the jet age two years later with the integration of the Republic RF-80 reconnaissance aircraft. In 1956, the squadron transitioned to the Republic RF-84 Thunderflash. (187th Fighter Wing.)

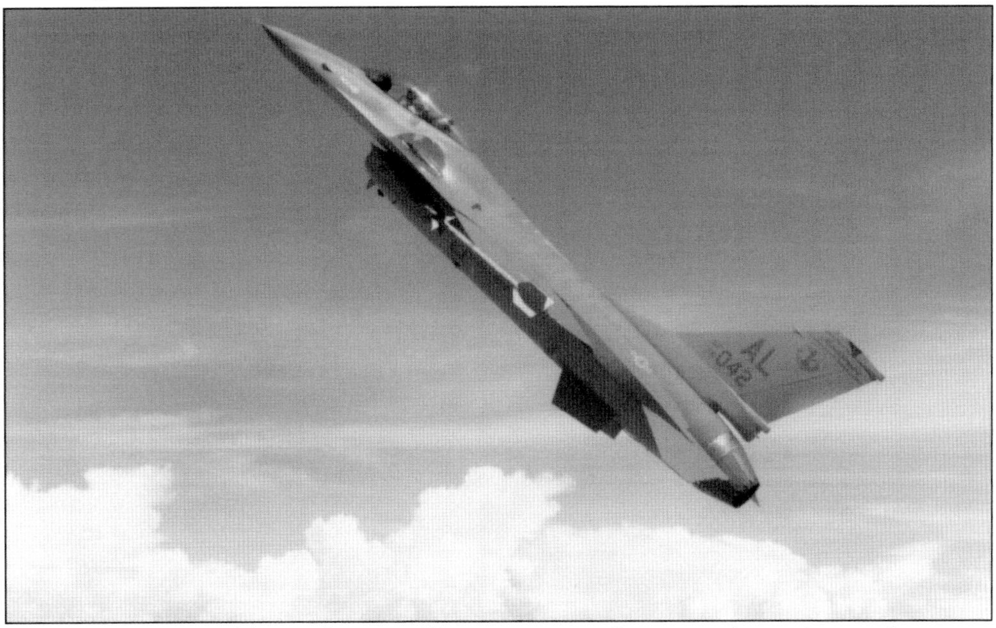

In 1982, the mission of the 187th Tactical Reconnaissance Group was changed to a multipurpose fighter role. In 1987, the unit transitioned from the F-4D to F-16 fighter aircraft and became a premier tactical fighter unit, achieving top honors in Air National Guard competition. In October 1995, the 187th Group was designated the 187th Fighter Wing during a reorganization of the U.S. Air Force. (187th Fighter Wing.)

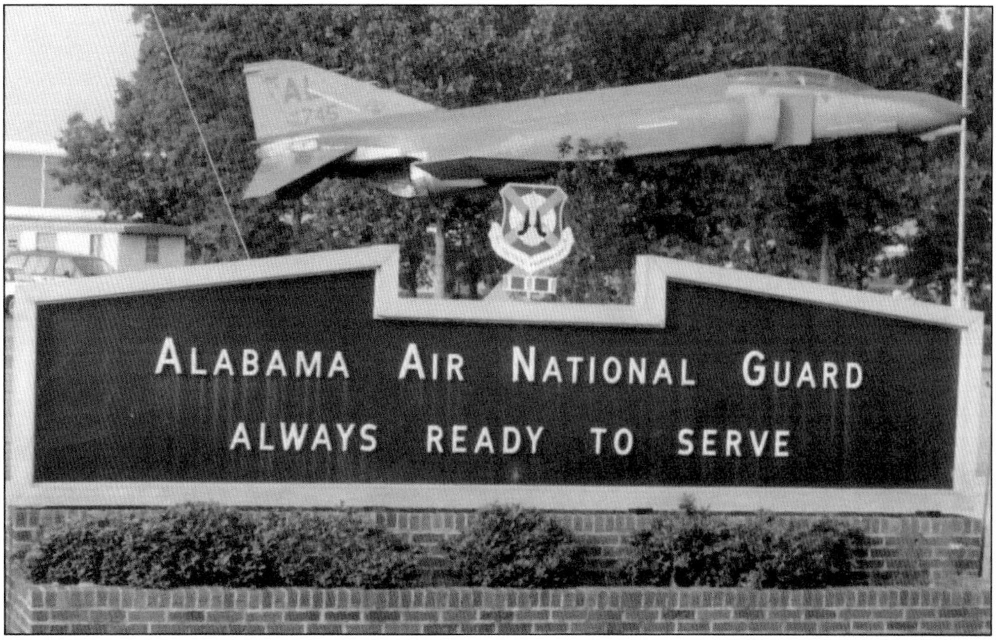

Within hours of the 2001 terrorist attacks on the United States, pilots of the 187th Fighter Wing were flying Combat Air Patrol missions over the largest cities in the Southeast. In 2003, the wing was called to active duty during Operation Iraqi Freedom, the largest military mobilization since the 1991 Gulf War. Since 2003, the 187th Fighter Wing has flown numerous missions in support of Operation Iraqi Freedom. (187th Fighter Wing.)

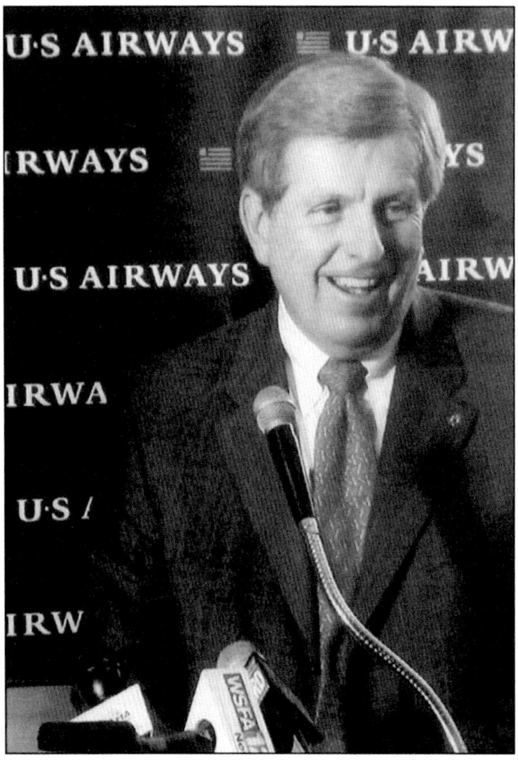

In 2003, Montgomery-based Retirement Systems of Alabama became the majority stockholder in US Airways, the nation's seventh-largest airline. Dr. David G. Bronner, chief executive officer of Retirement Systems of Alabama, was elected chairman of the 15-member US Airways Board of Directors. At the time, the airline employed 28,000 workers and served destinations in the United States, Canada, Latin America, Mexico, and Europe. (Retirement Systems of Alabama.)

Six

MONTGOMERY AVIATORS

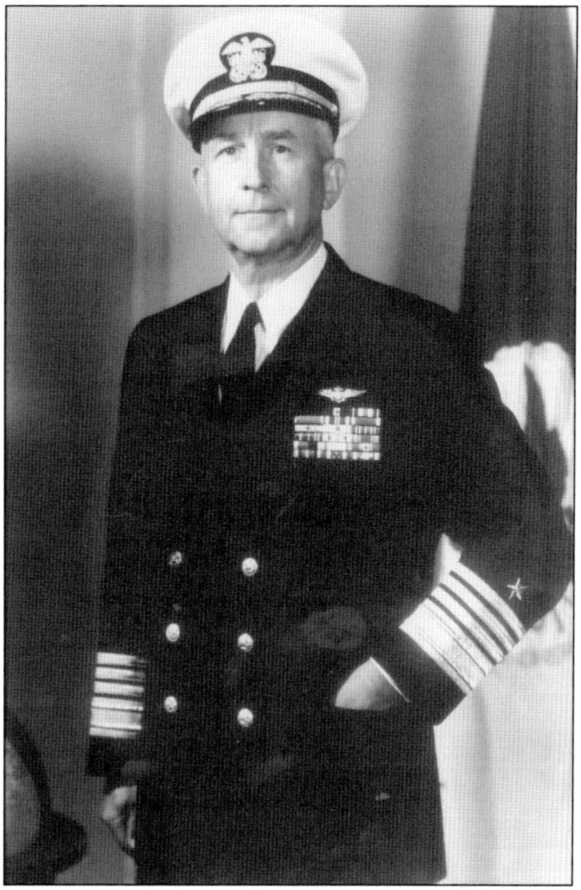

Thomas H. Moorer was born in Mount Willing and graduated from Cloverdale High School in Montgomery. A graduate of the U.S. Naval Academy and a naval aviator, Admiral Moorer was named chief of naval operations before being appointed chairman of the joint chiefs. Admiral Moorer is a member of the National Aviation Hall of Fame and was inducted into the Alabama Aviation Hall of Fame in 1995. (National Museum of Naval Aviation.)

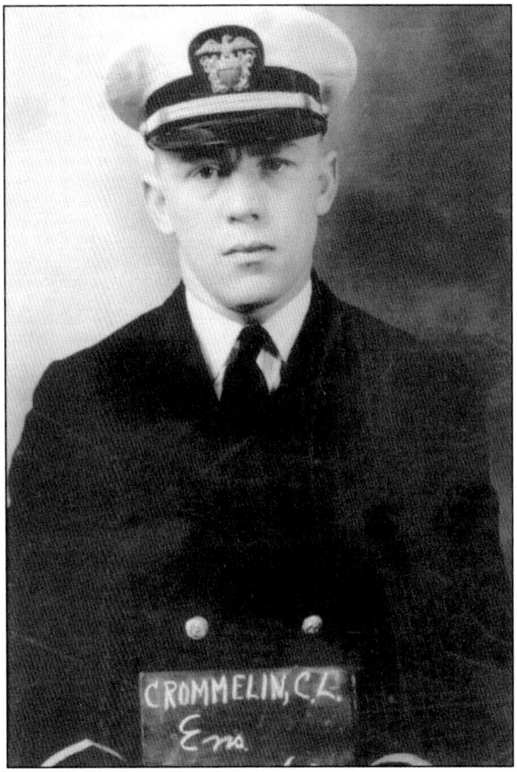

One of five brothers to graduate from the U.S. Naval Academy, Comdr. Charles L. Crommelin served as a fighter pilot in the Pacific theater, where he was twice awarded the Distinguished Flying Cross. Three days before the invasion of Okinawa, Crommelin volunteered for a pre-invasion mission but never returned. The Crommelin brothers were inducted into the Alabama Aviation Hall of Fame in 1999. (National Museum of Naval Aviation.)

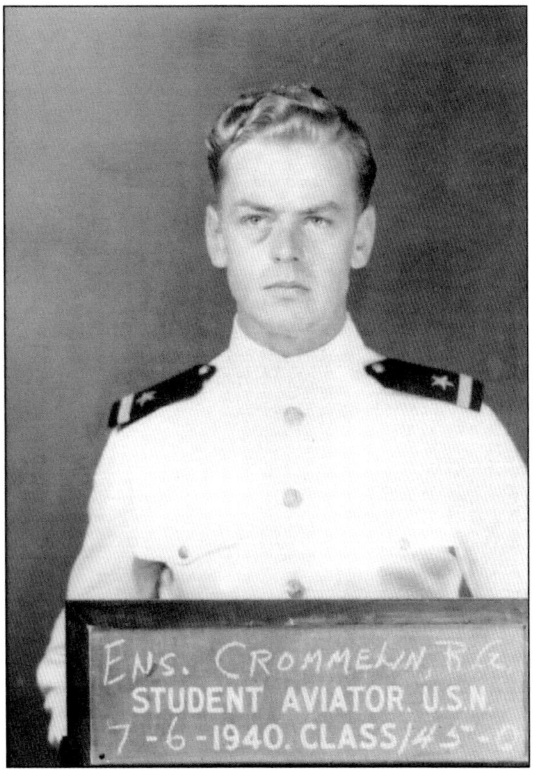

Comdr. Richard G. Crommelin graduated from the U.S. Naval Academy in 1938. A fighter pilot in the Pacific theater, Crommelin earned two Navy Crosses during the Battle of Coral Sea and the Battle of Midway. In July 1945, Crommelin was killed in action as a result of a midair collision during a mission he led against the Japanese island of Hokkaido. (National Museum of Naval Aviation.)

Rear Adm. John G. Crommelin graduated from the U.S. Naval Academy in 1923. A flight instructor at Naval Air Station Pensacola, Crommelin became a member of one of the early naval flight demonstration teams. Crommelin served in naval command positions during the Second World War. Assigned to the staff of the joint chiefs after the war, Crommelin achieved the rank of rear admiral in retirement. (National Museum of Naval Aviation.)

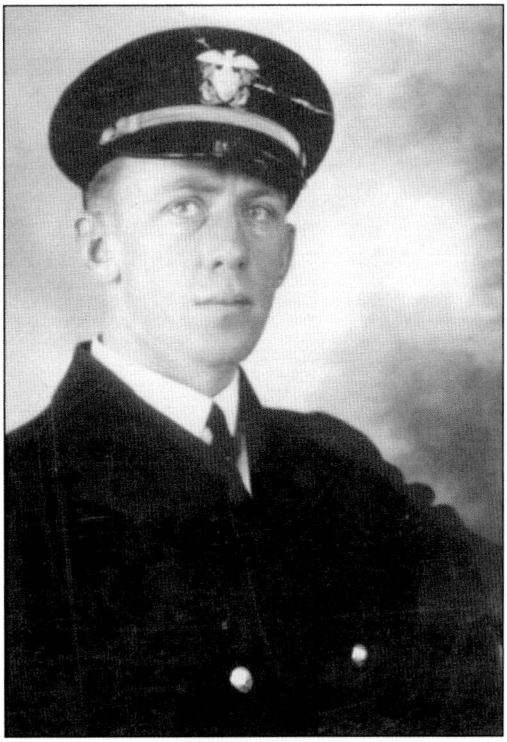

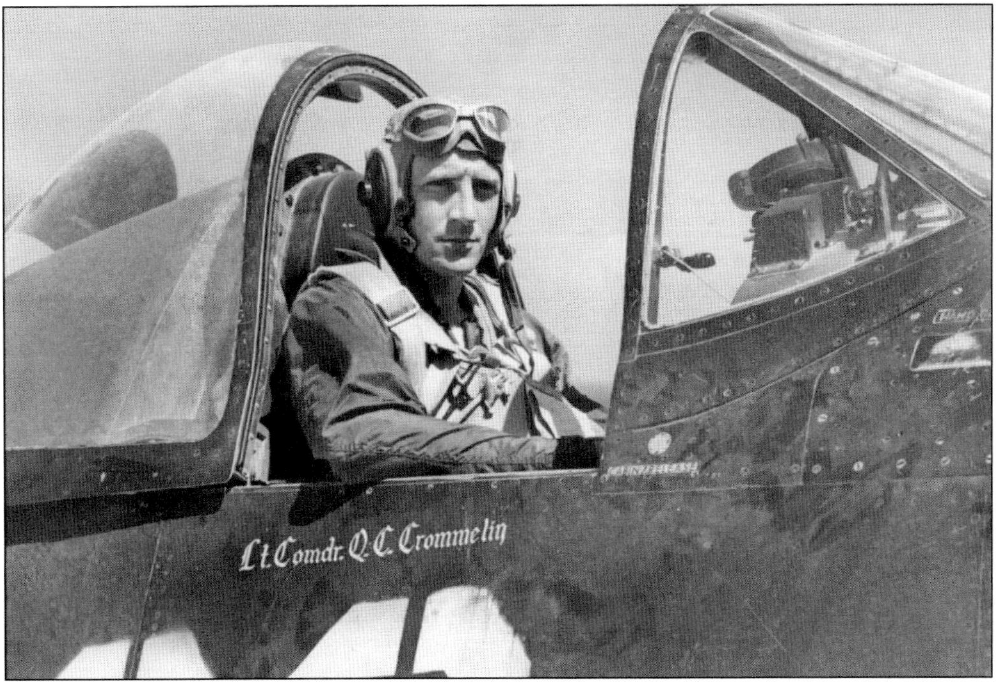

Capt. Quentin C. Crommelin graduated from the U.S. Naval Academy in 1941. A naval aviator, Crommelin flew the Grumman F6F Hellcat and the Vought F4U Corsair. The war ended as his squadron embarked on the USS *Antietam* for the Pacific theater. After the war, Crommelin remained in the navy, commanding an air group and the aircraft carrier USS *Lexington*. (Priscilla Ball.)

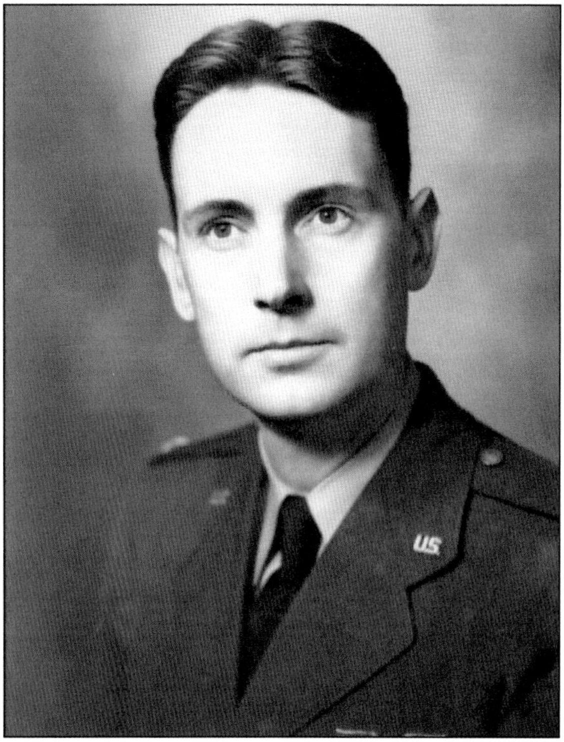

William R. Lawley Jr. served as an aircraft commander on Boeing B-17 bombardment aircraft during the Second World War. The 20-year-old Lawley was awarded the Congressional Medal of Honor for heroism and exceptional flying skill demonstrated during a February 1944 mission. In 1997, Lawley was inducted into the Alabama Aviation Hall of Fame. (Alabama Aviation Hall of Fame.)

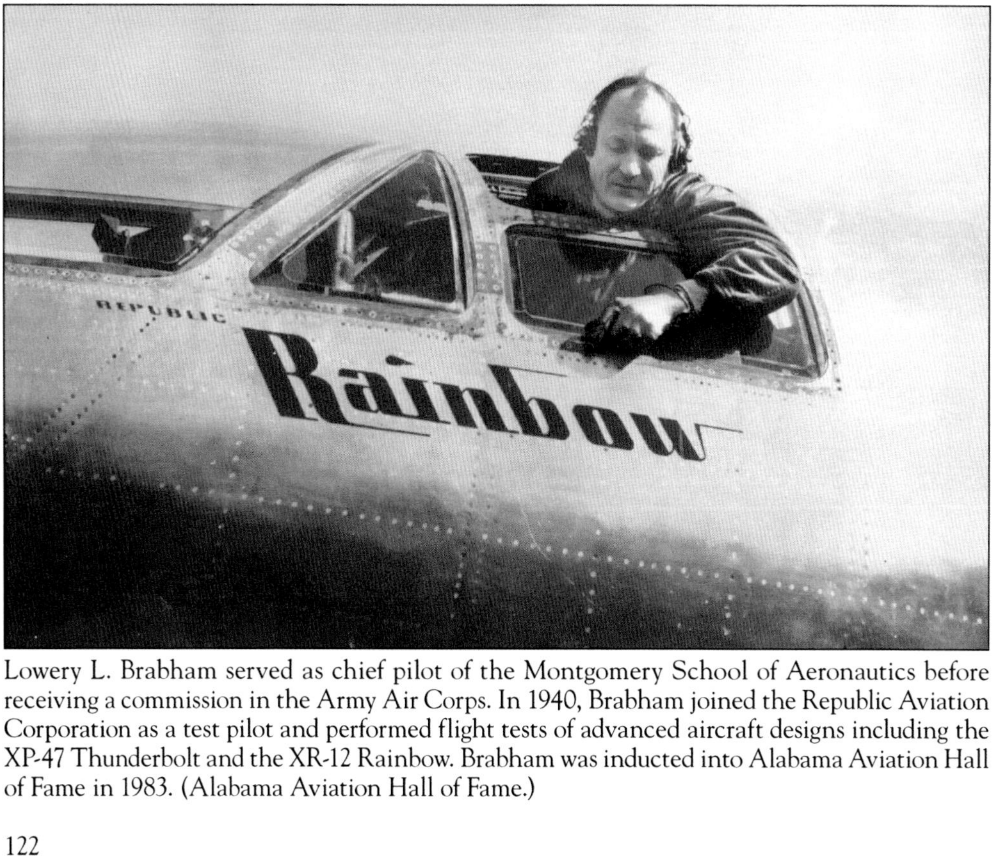

Lowery L. Brabham served as chief pilot of the Montgomery School of Aeronautics before receiving a commission in the Army Air Corps. In 1940, Brabham joined the Republic Aviation Corporation as a test pilot and performed flight tests of advanced aircraft designs including the XP-47 Thunderbolt and the XR-12 Rainbow. Brabham was inducted into Alabama Aviation Hall of Fame in 1983. (Alabama Aviation Hall of Fame.)

Sebie B. Smith began his career in the Army Air Corps in July 1931 at Maxwell Field. In July 1936, Smith was among a group of advisers and instructors selected by Claire Chennault to travel to China to assist in rebuilding the Chinese air force. Smith (left), Claire Chennault (center), and William McDonald (right) with officers of the Chinese air force. (Amelia Lucas.)

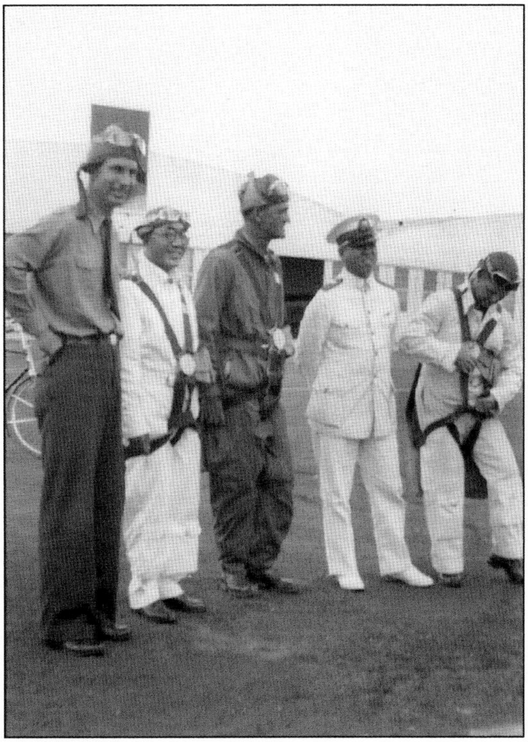

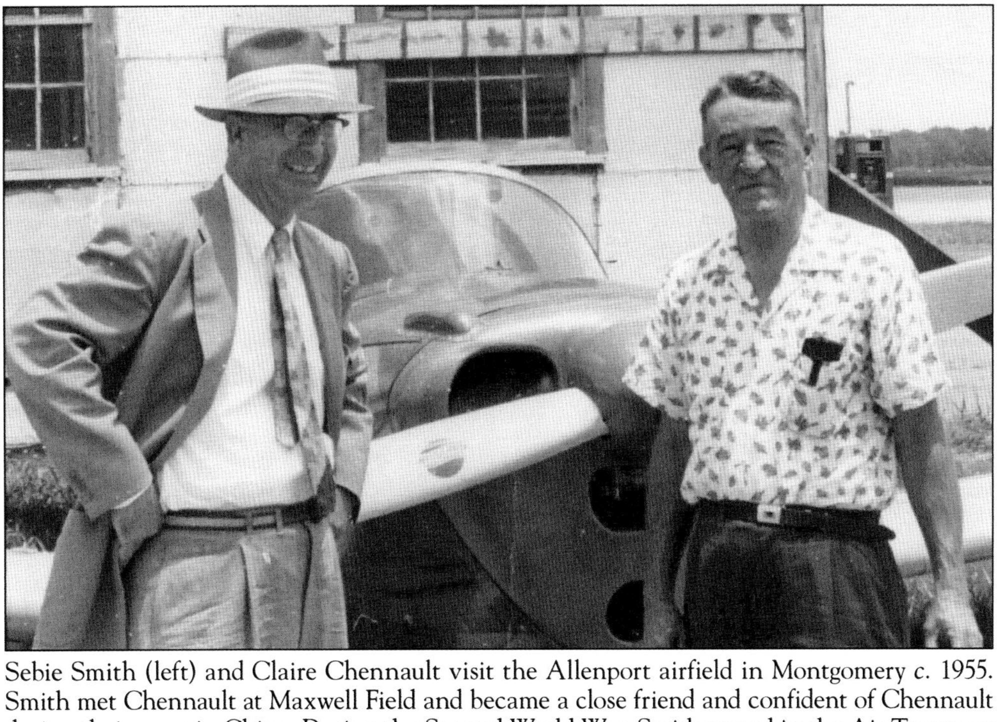

Sebie Smith (left) and Claire Chennault visit the Allenport airfield in Montgomery c. 1955. Smith met Chennault at Maxwell Field and became a close friend and confident of Chennault during their years in China. During the Second World War, Smith served in the Air Transport Command as a pilot and maintenance officer. Smith and Chennault are members of the Alabama Aviation Hall of Fame. (Amelia Lucas.)

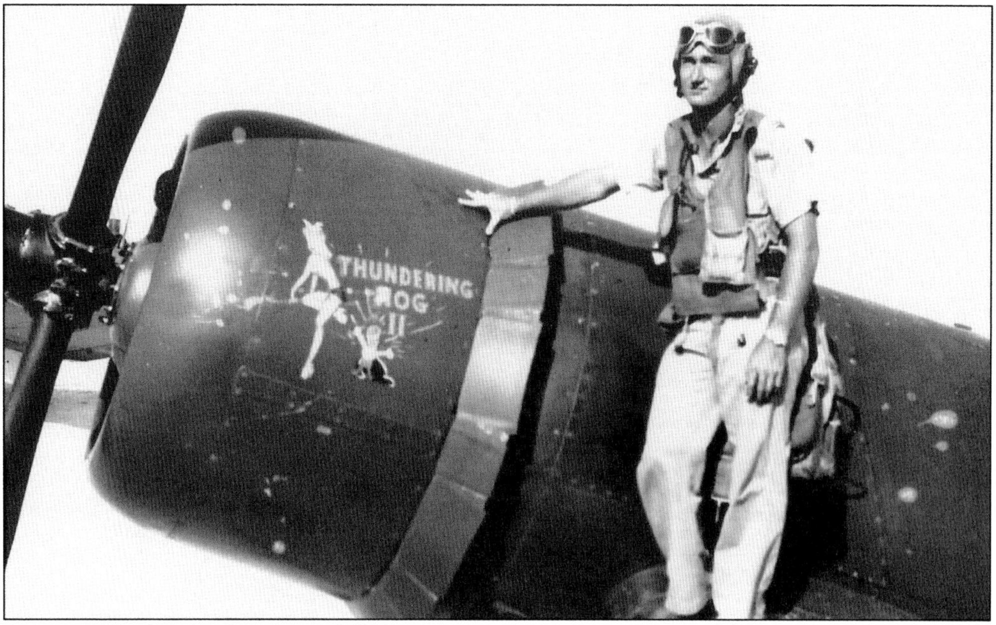

Jesse G. Folmar completed naval flight training in 1942. He served as a marine fighter pilot in the Pacific theater during the Second World War and completed a second tour of duty as a pilot of the Vought F4U-4B Corsair during the Korean War. On September 10, 1952, Folmar became the only American pilot to be credited with shooting down a Russian MiG-15 jet fighter with a piston-powered aircraft. (Gregory Folmar.)

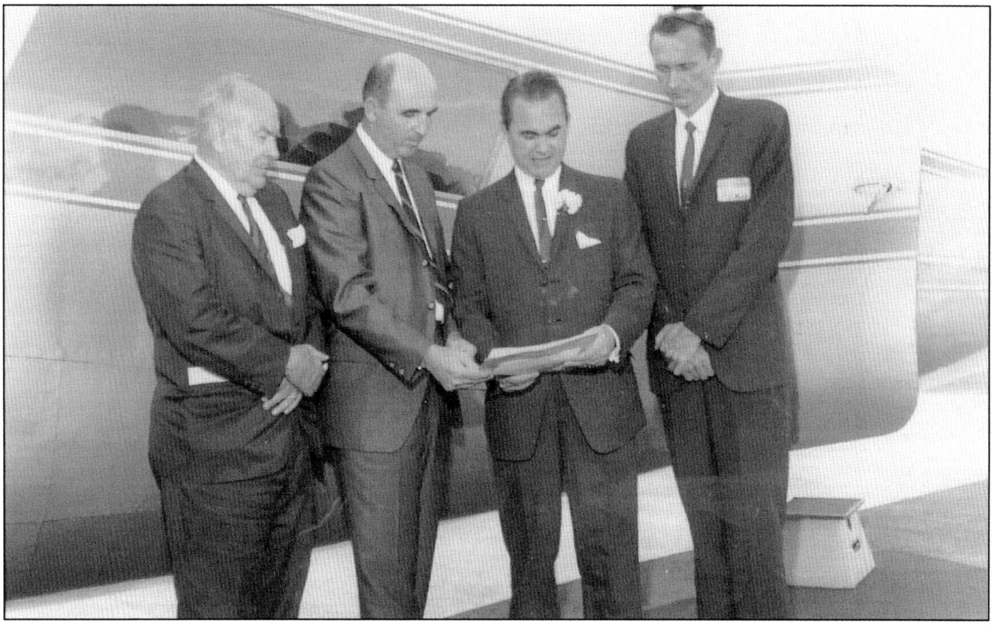

John Asa Rountree Jr. (far left) was trained as a pilot during the First World War. He joined the Alabama Airport Commission soon after it was established and was appointed director in March 1936, a position he held for more than 30 years. Rountree was inducted into the Alabama Aviation Hall of Fame in 1983. Rountree Field in Hartselle is named in his honor. (Alabama Department of Archives and History, Montgomery, Alabama.)

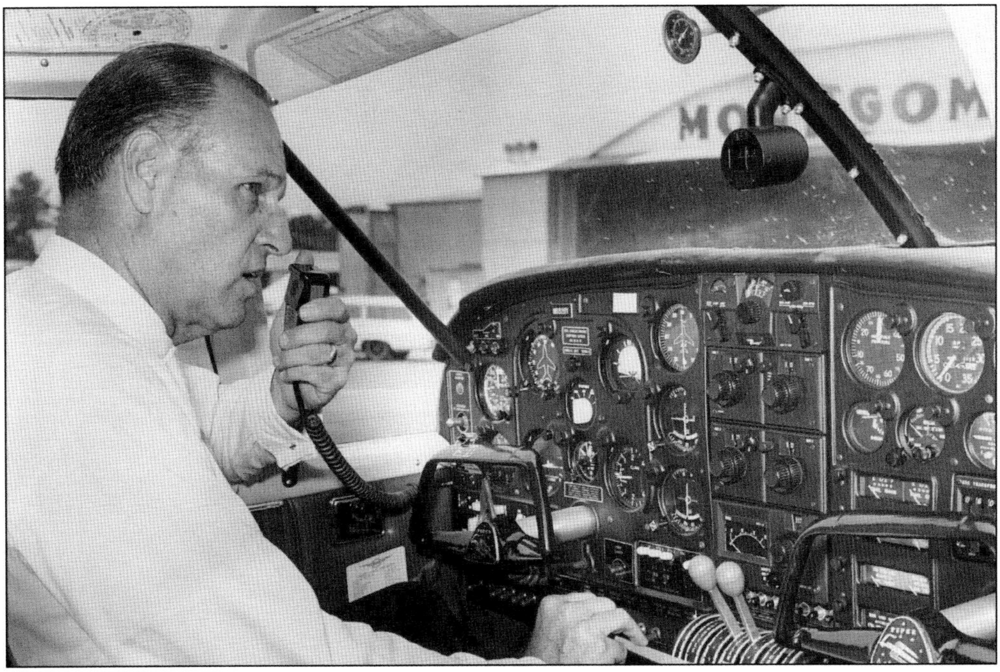

Robert P. Hudgens learned to fly in 1941 through the Civilian Pilot Training Program at Alabama Polytechnic Institute. During the Second World War, Hudgens served as an instructor at civilian contract schools before training in assault gliders. For more than 50 years, Hudgens built the Montgomery Aviation Corporation into a nationally recognized leader in aircraft sales and service. Hudgens was inducted into Alabama Aviation Hall of Fame in 1986. (Hudgens family.)

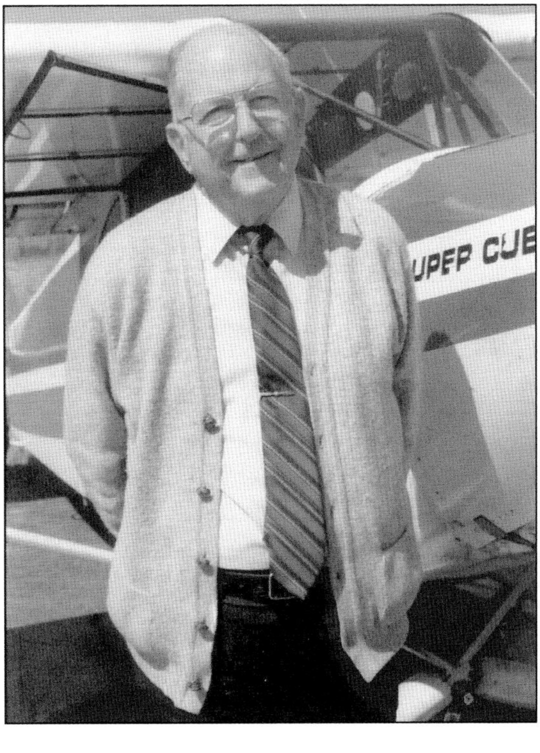

John Edward Long Jr. achieved the unique status as the most experienced pilot in the history of aviation. During his 65-year career, Long accumulated more than 64,000 hours in the air, a feat recognized by the book of *Guinness World Records*. Best remembered for his years as the power line patrol pilot for Montgomery Aviation, Long was inducted into Alabama Aviation Hall of Fame in 1989. (Paul Robertson via Montgomery Aviation.)

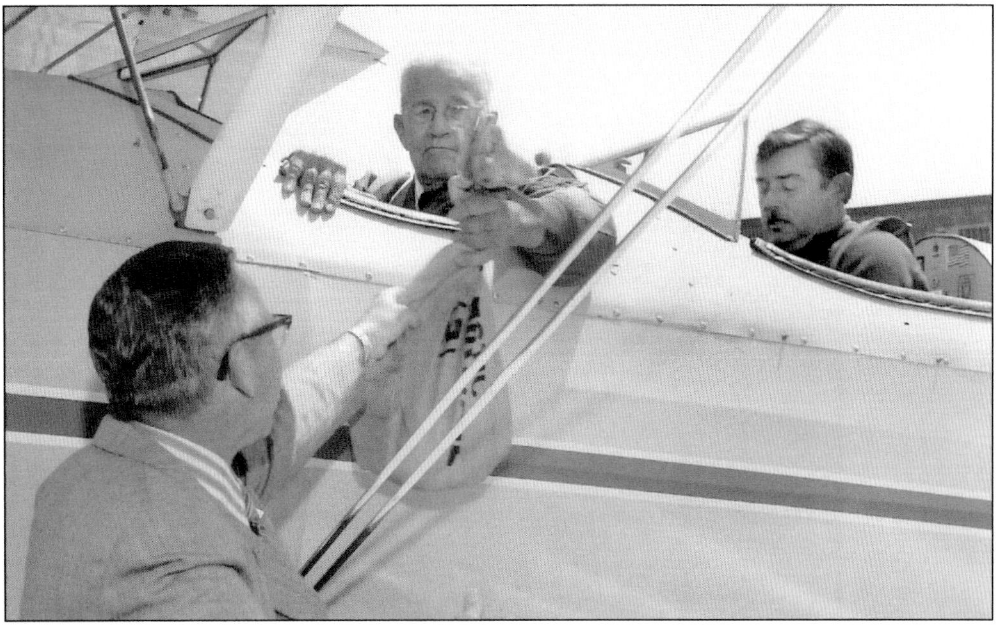

In an aviation career that spanned more than 50 years, Norman F. McGowin Jr. has devoted his efforts to the preservation of aviation history and the restoration of vintage aircraft. In April 1975, McGowin (rear cockpit) and Gen. Robert Knapp commemorated the 50th anniversary of Montgomery's first airmail flight at Maxwell Field. McGowin and Knapp are members of the Alabama Aviation Hall of Fame. (Air University Office of History.)

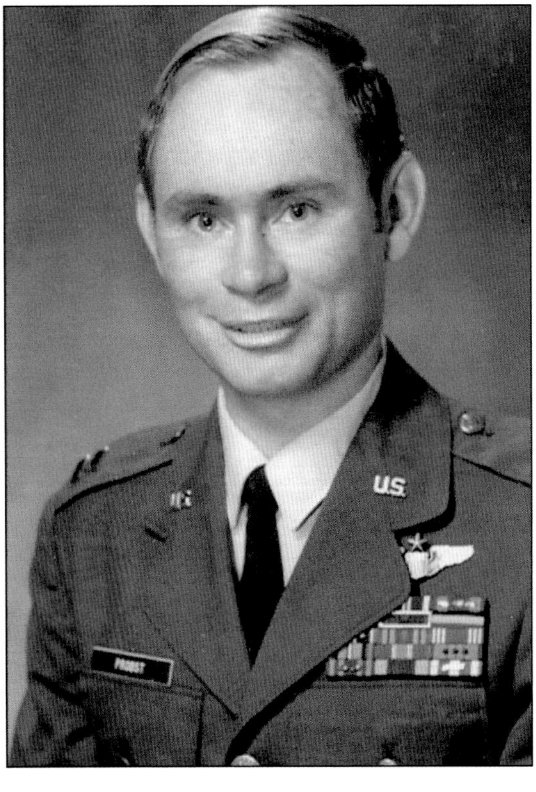

A graduate of the U.S. Air Force Academy, Lloyd J. Probst completed 1,248 combat missions during the Vietnam War. He received the Distinguished Flying Cross and eight Air Medals. For more than 20 years, Probst served as a Federal Aviation Administration pilot examiner and aviation safety counselor. Selected National Flight Instructor of the Year in 1991, Probst was inducted into the Alabama Aviation Hall of Fame in 2005. (Lloyd Probst.)

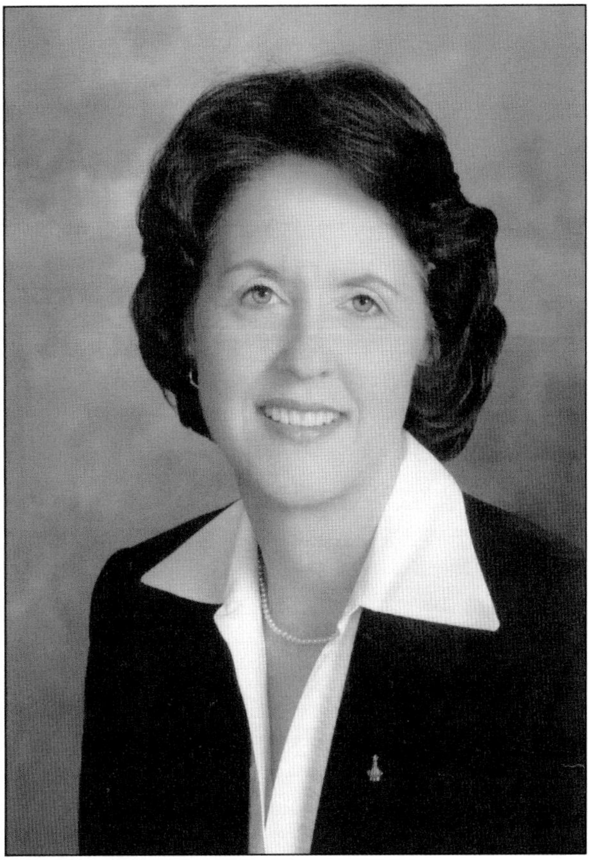

In 1984, Sidney Lanier High School graduate Dr. Kathryn Thornton was selected for training as an astronaut by NASA. During her career at NASA, Dr. Thornton served as a crew member on four space shuttle flights: STS-33, STS-49, STS-61, and STS-73. Thornton spent more than 40 days in space, including 21 hours of extravehicular activity. Until 2007, she held the record for number of space walks and the total time spent on space-walks by a female astronaut. (Dr. Kathryn Thornton.)

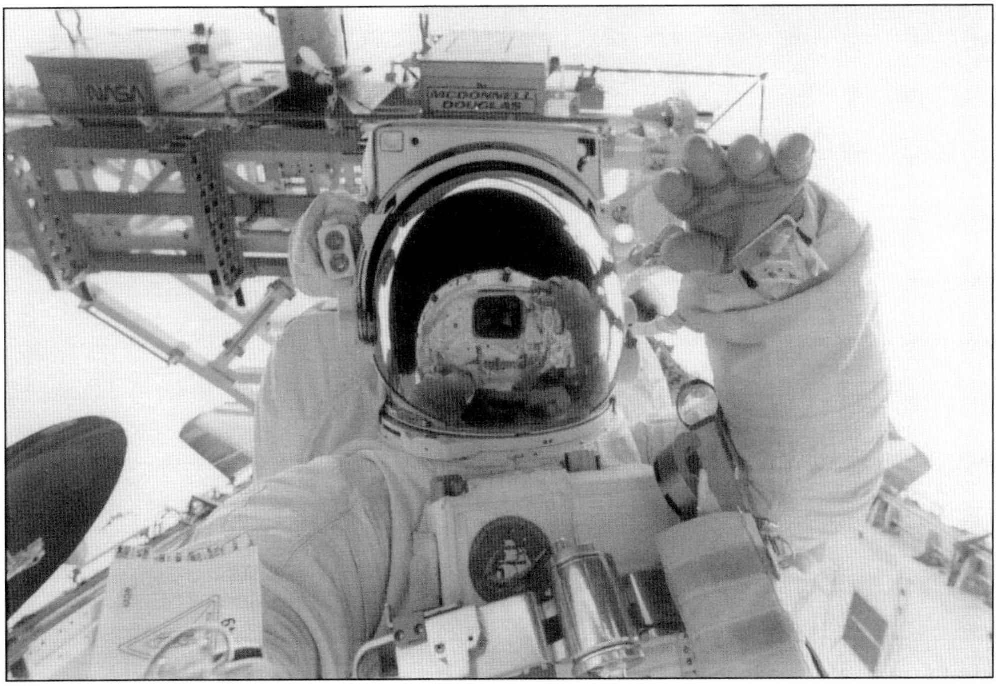